Toward a Global Civil Society

INTERNATIONAL POLITICAL CURRENTS
A Friedrich-Ebert-Stiftung Series

General Editor: Dieter Dettke

Vol. 1: Toward a Global Civil Society
   Edited by Michael Walzer

Vol. 2: Universities in the Twenty-first Century
   Edited by Steven Muller

Toward a Global Civil Society

Edited by
Michael Walzer

Berghahn Books
NEW YORK • OXFORD

First published in 1995
Reprinted in 1998 and 2002
Berghahn Books

© Michael Walzer and Berghahn Books, Inc. 1995, 1998, 2002
All rights reserved.
No part of this publication may be reproduced
in any form or by any means without the permission
of Berghahn Books.

Library of Congress Cataloging-in-Publication Data
Toward a global civil society / edited by Michael Walzer.
    p.   cm. — (The Friedrich Ebert Stiftung series on
international political currents)
    Includes bibliographical references and index.
    ISBN 1-57181-054-4
    1. Civil society — United States. 2. Civil society — Europe.
3. Social justice. 4. Public welfare. 5. Socialism. 6. Post-
communism. I. Walzer, Michael. II. Series.
JC599.U5T68   1994   94-33656
301'.09'049—dc20   CIP

ISBN: 1-57181-054-4 hb
ISBN: 1-57181-138-9 pb

British Library Cataloguing in Publication Data
A CIP catalog record for this book is available from
the British Library.

Printed in the United States on acid free paper.

Contents

V   European Socialism and American Social Reform

Foreword

Dieter Dettke

Toward a Global Civil Society is the first volume of a new series entitled *International Political Currents*, published by the Washington Office of the Friedrich Ebert Foundation. The series will address major international economic, political, and cultural issues. Publications in this series will try to contribute to a discourse on public policy issues with international dimensions. Based in Germany, the Friedrich Ebert Foundation, Germany's oldest political foundation, is involved in programs in 89 countries in Asia, Africa, Latin America, Central America and the Caribbean, the U.S., and Europe. Our activities are increasingly global and international in character.

The essays in this volume, *Toward a Global Civil Society*, address both European and American perspectives, covering a wide range of topics—communitarian approaches, economic policy, social justice, and the internationalization of politics and economics. The idea and the concept of a civil society is a particularly germane subject with which to inaugurate this series, as it embodies the very core of democratic principles. Interdependence, integration, and an increasing globalization of the economy are serious challenges for the civil society. Originally conceived in a national framework and for more or less homogeneous societies, the concept must now meet the test of enlargement and prove its usefulness in a multicultural environment.

It is no coincidence that when Eastern Europe, following the revolutions of 1989, opened up its economies and societies to democratic principles and market forces, the most important concept the West could offer the emerging democracies was the concept of a civil society. As a counter-concept to totalitarianism and all forms of authoritarian government, the idea of a civil society stands out as the key to democratic stability. It is possible to have a market economy without democracy, but it is inconceivable to have a democracy without the institutions of a civil society—unions, religious institutions, parties, political and social movements, pressure groups, the press, and independent judicial institutions.

The future challenge is to establish where the public and the private spheres of civil society should intersect and where they should be kept apart. Precisely because we live in an information society, the critical issue is how to enlarge the private sphere while maintaining public values and standards. The social contract upon which the civil society depends needs constant renewal and, consequently, vitality and adaptability in the institutions of civil society are essential. Finally, because of the need to create and maintain a culture of solidarity in a market environment, balancing the role of the state and that of the market will require new and innovative concepts.

As Michael Walzer points out, "Only a democratic state can create a democratic civil society; only a democratic civil society can sustain a democratic state." Perhaps this period of change for both East and West will result in a convergence of goals and the endeavor for common solutions based on the rich and diverse historical experiences of Europe and the United States.

Introduction

Michael Walzer

There are many definitions of "civil society," and there is considerable disagreement at the margins about what the concept includes and excludes. I won't add to that disagreement here (I offer my own, fairly imprecise definition in the first of the papers in this collection). It is enough to say that civil society incorporates many of the associations and identities that we value outside of, prior to, or in the shadow of state and citizenship. The subject is of great interest just now because of the argument that democracy requires a strong and lively civil society—if not for the sake of its initial formation then for the sake of its coherence and stability over time. The citizens of a democratic state are not, on this view, self-sufficient creatures. They must be members elsewhere, in smaller, more accessible, less demanding, less dangerous places than the modern state. For only in such places can they acquire political competence, learn to win and lose, learn to compromise, make friends and allies, explore oppositionist ideas. It is very risky for a democratic government when the state takes up all the available room and there are no alternative associations, no protected social space, where people can seek relief from politics, nurse wounds, find comfort, build strength for future encounters.

Civil society is not a new place, either practically or conceptually. It was first named and discussed in the Scottish Enlightenment of the eighteenth century; Adam Ferguson undertook the earliest theoretical explorations. The idea was centrally important for

Hegel, in whose work civil society is described as a realm of conflict and fragmentation: here economic interests, religious views, and perhaps also ethnic solidarities are organized, expressed, and confronted. The Hegelian state then creates a superior unity. But this is a unity, we may add today, always qualified by difference, and it is the experience of difference, where difference is given free rein, that underpins and makes possible a democratic union.

The idea of civil society reentered political debate in the course of the struggle against totalitarianism in Central and Eastern Europe. In practice, civil society was the site of the struggle; in theory, its goal. But the status of the idea today is determined also by two other features of contemporary political life. First, the new (or renewed) importance of national, ethnic, racial, and religious identities: these appear initially in civil society, though some of their protagonists have statist ambitions. Second, the extraordinary energy and commitment represented by the "new social movements," most importantly feminist and environmentalist, but including also a wide variety of single issue groups with strong positions on (these are American examples) abortion, gun control, school prayer, capital punishment, and so on: here large numbers of previously passive men and women have refashioned themselves as social activists. All these identities and movements cut across the old class lines, so it is important to stress the continued if also (in the United States again) declining vitality of older interest-based groupings like labor unions, professional associations, and political parties. Class remains a major determinant of social organization and activity, even when its effects are masked by race and ethnicity.

So many strongly focused concerns and self-identifications intensify the old sense of civil society as a source of tension and tumult; the realm of fragmentation has never seemed so fragmented. The contemporary state is hard-pressed to assert its "superiority," hard-pressed sometimes just to keep the peace. Now the democratic tendency of associational pluralism seems (to some social critics) less certain than it once did. Communitarianism is one response—or, better, since communitarians do not agree among themselves, a series of responses—to the spectacle of individual men and women choosing their causes and identities, engaging themselves in ever-new ways (and in more than one way at a time), dividing and re-dividing the larger society. While not explicitly statist in character, its defenders are (mostly) committed to celebrating those common convictions and commitments that make us citizens of the state and lead us to accept responsibility for its well-being. The relevant community is the political community, which gives to its members the sense of a shared destiny and a common good, alongside if not specifically transcending all the particular goods of civil society. Those particular goods and the associational life organized around them are the subject of section one of this volume, and we then turn in section two to a consideration of the communitarian approach to the difficulties generated by civil (and uncivil) particularity.

But there is no community and no common good without social justice. Political societies cannot survive on evocations of citizenly virtue, responsibility, and fellow feeling. There must also be a commitment in practice to the weaker members. This is a commitment that only the state can make in a universalizing way. The stronger civil society is, the more the state can act indirectly to fulfill its commitment, seconding the direct activity of its citizens in their voluntary associations. But given the divisions of civil society, and the inequalities that appear naturally within it (of resources, numbers, competence, and so on), the state can never cease entirely to act in its own name, addressing the needs of all its citizens. A democratic state, rooted in the associational life of civil society, will also be continually active in fostering, subsidizing, and regulating the associations—so as to maintain a fair distribution of welfare and opportunity. We consider the possible patterns of state engagement in the third section of this volume.

Civil society is usually thought to be contained within the framework of the state: it has the same boundaries as the political community. In fact, both the older and the newer associations reach for connections across those boundaries. The labor movement, the historic churches, contemporary environmentalists and feminists— all these have comrades, friends, and fellow workers in faraway places. There is today an international civil society, the very existence of which raises questions about the usefulness of the state. Marxist revolutionaries once looked to overthrow political regimes one by one, eventually creating a new (though never specified) trans-state authority. The new social movements look right now for trans-state agencies: Helsinki Watch, Amnesty International, the different organizations spun off by the United Nations, the World Court. And yet, again, the state has not been superseded. Identity politics, particularly in its nationalist version, is still focused on the achievement of sovereignty. And the dilemmas of immigration policy can be dealt with, so far, only by the state, which retains the power of closure. Civil society is infinitely open; whatever the membership requirements of particular associations, it is always possible to form a new group. Citizenship has a different profile from civility: it can only be shared as the result of a political decision. The conditions under which such decisions must be made today, and the difficulties of actually making them, are taken up in section four.

All these questions—domestic solidarity, social justice, state action, international connection—were once addressed more or less coherently by the socialist movement. Today, after the definitive collapse of the statist and authoritarian versions of socialism, all coherence is gone. The possibility of a defense and renewal of democratic socialism (as well as its American cousin, a kind of left liberalism) is taken up in section five. There is a close conceptual tie between social democracy and civil society, for the first of these calls for the self-direction of society by its members and the second represents the best possible site for the practice of self-direction—in detail, every day, by ordinary men and women. No doubt, the site must be framed and sustained by the democratic state, but it must also be *another place*, to whose independence the authors of this book are, whatever their other differences, strongly committed.

Michael Walzer
May, 1994

Part I

THE CONCEPT OF
CIVIL SOCIETY

1. The Concept of Civil Society*

Michael Walzer

My aim in this essay is to defend a complex, imprecise, and, at crucial points, uncertain account of society and politics. I have no hope of theoretical simplicity, not at this historical moment when so many stable oppositions of political and intellectual life have collapsed; but I also have no desire for simplicity, since a world that theory could fully grasp and neatly explain would not, I suspect, be a pleasant place. In the nature of things, then, my argument won't be elegant, and though I believe that arguments should march, the sentences following one another like soldiers on parade, the route of my march herein will be twisting and roundabout. I shall begin with the idea of civil society, recently revived by Central and East European intellectuals, and go on to talk about the state, the economy, and the nation, and then about civil society and the state again. These are the crucial social formations that we inhabit, but we don't at this moment live comfortably in any of them. Nor is it possible to imagine, in accordance with one or another of the great simplifying theories, a way to choose among them—as if we were destined to find, one day, the best social formation. I mean to argue against choosing, but I shall also claim that it is from within civil society that this argument is best understood.

The words "civil society" name the space of uncoerced human association and also the set of relational networks—formed for the sake of family, faith, interest, and ideology—that fill this space. Central and East European dissidence flourished within a highly restricted version of civil society, and the first task of the new democracies created by the dissidents, so we are told, is to rebuild the networks: unions, churches, political par-

---

* This essay was given as the Gunner Myrdal lecture at the University of Stockholm, Sweden, October 1990 and appeared in the Spring 1991 issue of *Dissent*.

ties and movements, cooperatives, neighborhoods, schools of thought, societies for promoting or preventing this and that. In the West, by contrast, we have lived in civil society for many years without knowing it. Or, better, since the Scottish Enlightenment, or since Hegel, the words have been known to the knowers of such things but they have rarely served to focus anyone else's attention. Now writers in Hungary, the former Czechoslovakia, and Poland invite us to think about how this social formation is secured and invigorated.

We have reasons of our own for accepting the invitation. Increasingly, associational life in the "advanced" capitalist and social democratic countries seems at risk. Publicists and preachers warn us of a steady attenuation of everyday cooperation and civic friendship. And this time it's possible that they are not, as they usually are, foolishly alarmist. Our cities really are noisier and nastier than they once were. Familial solidarity, mutual assistance, political likemindedness—all these are less certain and less substantial than they once were. Other people, strangers on the street, seem less trustworthy than they once did. The Hobbesian account of society is more persuasive than it once was.

Perhaps this worrisome picture follows—in part, no more, but what else can a political theorist say?—from the fact that we have not thought enough about solidarity and trust or planned for their future. We have been thinking too much about social formations different from, in competition with, civil society. And so we have neglected the networks through which civility is produced and reproduced. Imagine that the following questions were posed one or two centuries ago to political theorists and moral philosophers: what is the preferred setting, the most supportive environment, for the good life? What sorts of institutions should we work for? Nineteenth- and twentieth-century social thought provides four different, by now familiar, answers to these questions. Think of them as four rival ideologies, each with its own claim to completeness and correctness. Each is importantly wrong. Each neglects the necessary pluralism of any civil society. Each is predicated on an assumption I mean to attack: that such questions must receive a singular answer.

Definitions from the Left

I shall begin, since this is for me the best-known ground, with two leftist answers. The first of the two holds that the preferred setting for the good life is the political community, the democratic state, within which we can be citizens: freely engaged, fully committed, decision-making members. And a citizen, on this view, is much the best thing to be. To live well is to be politically active, working with our fellow citizens, collectively determining our common destiny— not for the sake of this or that determination but for the work itself, in which our highest capacities as rational and moral agents find expression. We know ourselves best as persons who propose, debate, and decide.

This argument goes back to the Greeks, but we are most likely to recognize its neoclassical versions. It is Rousseau's argument or the standard leftist interpretation of Rousseau's argument. His understanding of citizenship as moral agency is one of the key sources of democratic idealism. We can see it at work in a liberal such as John Stuart Mill, in whose writings it produced an unexpected defense of syndicalism (what is today called "workers control") and, more generally, of social democracy. It appeared among nineteenth- and twentieth-century democratic radicals, often with a hard populist edge. It played a part in the reiterated demand for social inclusion by women, workers, blacks, and new immigrants, all of whom based their claims on their capacity as agents. And this same neoclassical idea of citizenship resurfaced in the 1960s in New Left theories of participation, where it was, however, like latter-day revivals of many ideas, highly theoretical and without much local resonance.

Today, perhaps in response to the political disasters of the late 1960s, "communitarians" in the United States struggle to give Rousseauian idealism a historical reference, looking back to the early American republic and calling for a renewal of civic virtue. They prescribe citizenship as an antidote to the fragmentation of contemporary society—for these theorists, like Rousseau, are disinclined to value the fragments. In their hands, republicanism is still a simplifying creed. If politics is our highest calling, then we are called away from every other activity (or, every other activity is redefined in political terms); our energies are directed toward policy formation and decision making in the democratic state.

I don't doubt that the active and engaged citizen is an attractive figure—even if some of the activists that we actually meet carrying placards and shouting slogans aren't all that attractive. The most penetrating criticism of this first answer to the question about the good life is not that the life isn't good but that it isn't the "real life" of very many people in the modern world. This is so in two senses. First, though the power of the democratic state has grown enormously, partly (and rightly) in response to the demands of engaged citizens, it can't be said that the state is fully in the hands of its citizens. And the larger it gets, the more it takes over those smaller associations still subject to hands-on control. The rule of the demos is in significant ways illusory; the participation of ordinary men and women in the activities of the state (unless they are state employees) is largely vicarious; even party militants are more likely to argue and complain than actually to decide.

Second, despite the singlemindedness of republican ideology, politics rarely engages the full attention of the citizens who are supposed to be its chief protagonists. They have too many other things to worry about. Above all, they have to earn a living. They are more deeply engaged in the economy than in the political community. Republican theorists (like Hannah Arendt) recognize this engagement only as a threat to civic virtue. Economic activity belongs to the realm of necessity, they argue, politics to the realm of freedom. Ideally, citizens should not have to work; they should be served by machines, if not by slaves, so that they can flock to the assemblies and argue with their fellows about affairs of state. In practice, however, work, though it begins in necessity, takes on a value of its own—expressed in commitment to a career, pride in a job well done, a sense of camaraderie in the workplace. All of these are competitive with the values of citizenship.

The second leftist position on the preferred setting for the good life involves a turning away from republican politics and a focus instead on economic activity. We can think of this as the socialist answer to the questions I began with; it can be found in Marx and also, though the arguments are somewhat different, among the utopians he hoped to supersede. For Marx, the preferred setting is the cooperative economy, where we can all be producers, artists (Marx was a romantic), inventors, and artisans.

(Assembly-line workers don't quite seem to fit.) This again is much the best thing to be. The picture Marx paints is of creative men and women making useful and beautiful objects, not for the sake of this or that object but for the sake of creativity itself, the highest expression of our "species-being" as homo faber, man-the-maker.

The state, in this view, ought to be managed in such a way as to set productivity free. It doesn't matter who the managers are so long as they are committed to this goal and rational in its pursuit. Their work is technically important but not substantively interesting. Once productivity is free, politics simply ceases to engage anyone's attention. Before that time, in the Marxist here and now, political conflict is taken to be the superstructural enactment of economic conflict, and democracy is valued mainly because it enables socialist movements and parties to organize for victory. The value is instrumental and historically specific. A democratic state is the preferred setting not for the good life but for the class struggle; the purpose of the struggle is to win, and victory brings an end to democratic instrumentality. There is no intrinsic value in democracy, no reason to think that politics has, for creatures like us, a permanent attractiveness. When we are all engaged in productive activity, social division and the conflicts it engenders will disappear, and the state, in the once-famous phrase, will "wither away."

In fact, if this vision were ever realized, it is politics that would wither away. Some kind of administrative agency would still be necessary for economic coordination, and it is only a Marxist conceit to refuse to call this agency a state. "Society regulates the general production," Marx wrote in *The German Ideology*, "and thus makes it possible for me to do one thing today and another tomorrow ... just as I have a mind." Because this regulation is nonpolitical, the individual producers are freed from the burdens of citizenship. They attend instead to the things they make and to the cooperative relationships they establish. Exactly how one can work with other people and still do whatever one pleases is unclear to me and probably to most other readers of Marx. The texts suggest an extraordinary faith in the virtuosity of the regulators. No one, I think, quite shares this faith today, but something like it helps to explain the tendency of some leftists to see even the liberal and democratic state as an obstacle that has to be, in the worst of recent jargons, "smashed."

The seriousness of Marxist antipolitics is nicely illustrated by Marx's own dislike of syndicalism. What the syndicalists proposed was a neat amalgam of the first and second answers to the question about the good life: for them, the preferred setting was the worker-controlled factory, where men and women were simultaneously citizens and producers, making decisions and making things. Marx seems to have regarded the combination as impossible; factories could not be both democratic and productive. This is the point of Engels's little essay on authority, which I take to express Marx's view also. More generally, self-government on the job called into question the legitimacy of "social regulation" or state planning, which alone, Marx thought, could enable individual workers to devote themselves, without distraction, to their work.

But this vision of the cooperative economy is set against an unbelievable background—a nonpolitical state, regulation without conflict, "the administration of things." In every actual experience of socialist politics, the state has moved rapidly into the foreground, and most socialists, in the West at least, have been driven to make their own amalgam of the first and second answers. They call themselves democratic socialists, focusing on the state as well as (in fact, much more than) on the economy and doubling the preferred settings for the good life. Because I believe that two are better than one, I take this to be progress. But before I try to suggest what further progress might look like, I need to describe two more ideological answers to the question about the good life, one of them capitalist, the other nationalist. For there is no reason to think that only leftists love singularity.

A Capitalist Definition

The third answer holds that the preferred setting for the good life is the marketplace, where individual men and women, consumers rather than producers, choose among a maximum number of options. The autonomous individual confronting his, and now her, possibilities—this is much the best thing to be. To live well is not to make political decisions or beautiful objects; it is to make personal choices. Not any particular choices, for no choice is substantively the best; it is the activity of choosing that makes for autonomy. And the market within which choices are made, like the socialist economy, largely dispenses with politics; it requires at most a minimal state—not "social regulation," only the police.

Production, too, is free even if it isn't, as in the Marxist vision, freely creative. More important than the producers, however, are the entrepreneurs— heroes of autonomy, consumers of opportunity—who compete to supply whatever all the other consumers want or might be persuaded to want. Entrepreneurial activity tracks consumer preference. Though not without its own excitements, it is mostly instrumental: the aim of all entrepreneurs (and all producers) is to increase their market power, maximize their options. Competing with one another, they maximize everyone else's options too, filling the marketplace with desirable objects. The market is preferred (over the political community and the cooperative economy) because of its fullness. Freedom, in the capitalist view, is a function of plenitude. We can only choose when we have many choices.

It is also true, unhappily, that we can only make effective (rather than merely speculative or wistful) choices when we have resources to dispose of. But people come to the marketplace with radically unequal resources—some with virtually nothing at all. Not everyone can compete successfully in commodity production, and therefore not everyone has access to commodities. Autonomy turns out to be a high-risk value, which many men and women can only realize with help from their friends. The market, however, is not a good setting for mutual assistance, for I cannot help someone else without reducing (for the short term, at least) my own options. And I have no reason, as an autonomous individual, to accept any reductions of any sort for someone else's sake. My argument here is not that autonomy collapses into egotism, only that autonomy in the marketplace provides no support for social solidarity. Despite the successes of capitalist production, the good life of consumer choice is not universally available. Large numbers of people drop out of the market economy or live precariously on its margins.

Partly for this reason, capitalism, like socialism, is highly dependent on state action—not only to prevent theft and enforce contracts but also to regulate the economy and guarantee the minimal welfare of its participants. But these participants, insofar as they are market activists, are not active in the state: capitalism in its ideal form, like socialism again, does not make for citizenship. Or, its protagonists conceive of citizenship in economic terms, so that citizens are transformed into autonomous consumers, looking for the party or program that most persuasively promises to strengthen their market positions. They need the state but have no moral relation to it, and they control its officials only as consumers control the producers of commodities, by buying or not buying what they make.

Because the market has no political boundaries, capitalist entrepreneurs also evade official control. They need the state but have no loyalty to it; the profit motive brings them into conflict with democratic regulation. So arms merchants sell the latest military technology to foreign powers, and manufacturers move their factories overseas to escape safety codes or minimum-wage laws. Multinational corporations stand outside (and to some extent against) every political community. They are known only by their brand names, which, unlike family names and country names, evoke preferences but not affections or solidarities.

A Nationalist Response

The fourth answer to the question about the good life can be read as a response to market amorality and disloyalty, though it has, historically, other sources as well. According to the fourth answer, the preferred setting is the nation, within which we are loyal members, bound to one another by ties of blood and history. And a member, secure in membership, literally part of an organic whole—this is much the best thing to be. To live well is to participate with other men and women in remembering, cultivating, and passing on a national heritage. This is so, on the nationalist view, without reference to the specific content of the heritage, so long as it is one's own, a matter of birth, not choice. Every nationalist will, of course, find value in his or her own heritage, but the highest value is not in the finding but in the willing: the firm identification of the individual with a people and a history.

Nationalism has often been a leftist ideology, historically linked to democracy and even to socialism. But it is most characteristically an ideology of the right, for its understanding of membership is ascriptive; it requires no political choices and no activity beyond ritual affirmation. When nations find themselves ruled by foreigners, however, ritual affirmation isn't enough. Then nationalism requires a more heroic loyalty: self-sacrifice in the struggle for national liberation. The capacity of the nation to elicit such sacrifices from its members is proof of the importance of this fourth answer. Individual members seek the good life by seeking autonomy not for themselves but for their people. Ideally, this attitude ought to survive the liberation struggle and provide a foundation for social solidarity and mutual assistance. Perhaps, to some extent, it does: certainly the welfare state has had its greatest successes in ethnically homogeneous countries. It is also true, however, that once liberation has been secured, nationalist men and women are commonly content with a vicarious rather than a practical participation in the community. There is nothing wrong with vicarious participation, on the nationalist view, since the good life is more a matter of identity than activity—faith, not works, so to speak, though both of these are understood in secular terms.

In the modern world, nations commonly seek statehood, for their autonomy will always be at risk if they lack sovereign power. But they don't seek states of any particular kind. No more do they seek economic arrangements of any particular kind. Unlike religious believers who are their close kin and (often) bitter rivals, nationalists are not bound by a body of authoritative law or a set of sacred texts. Beyond liberation, they have no program, only a vague commitment to continue a history, to sustain a "way of life." Their own lives, I suppose, are emotionally intense, but in relation to society and economy this is a dangerously free-floating intensity. In time of trouble, it can readily be turned against other nations, particularly against the internal others: minorities, aliens, strangers. Democratic citizenship, worker solidarity, free enterprise, and consumer autonomy—all these are less exclusive than nationalism but not always resistant to its power. The ease with which citizens, workers, and consumers become fervent nationalists is a sign of the inadequacy of the first three answers to the question about the good life. The nature of nationalist fervor signals the inadequacy of the fourth.

Can We Find a Synthesis?

All these answers are wrongheaded because of their singularity. They miss the complexity of human society, the inevitable conflicts of commitment and loyalty. Hence I am uneasy with the idea that there might be a fifth and finally correct answer to the question about the good life. Still, there is a fifth answer, the newest one (it draws upon less central themes of nineteenth- and twentieth-century social thought), which holds that the good life can only be lived in civil society, the realm of fragmentation and struggle but also of concrete and authentic solidarities, where we fulfill E. M. Forster's injunction, "only connect," and become sociable or communal men and women. And this is, of course, much the best thing to be. The picture here is of people freely associating and communicating with one another, forming and reforming groups of all sorts, not for the sake of any particular formation—family, tribe, nation, religion, commune, brotherhood or sisterhood, interest group or ideological movement—but for the sake of sociability itself. For we are by nature social, before we are political or economic beings.

I would rather say that the civil society argument is a corrective to the four ideological accounts of the good life—part denial, part incorporation—rather than a fifth to stand alongside them. It challenges their singularity but it has no singularity of its own. The phrase "social being" describes men and women who are citizens, producers, consumers, members of the nation, and much else besides—and none of these by nature or because it is the best thing to be. The associational life of civil society is the actual ground where all versions of the good are worked out and tested ... and proved to be partial, incomplete, ultimately unsatisfying. It can't be the case that living on this ground is good in itself; there isn't any other place to live. What is true is that the quality of our political and economic activity and of our national culture is intimately connected to the strength and vitality of our associations.

Ideally, civil society is a setting of settings: all are included, none is preferred. The argument is a liberal version of the four answers, accepting them all, insisting that each leave room for the others, therefore not finally accepting any of them. Liberalism appears here as an anti-ideology, and this is an attractive position in the contemporary world. I shall stress this attractiveness as I try to explain how civil society might actually incorporate and deny the four answers. Later on, however, I shall have to argue that this position too, so genial and benign, has its problems.

Let's begin with the political community and the cooperative economy, taken together. These two leftist versions of the good life systematically undervalued all associations except the demos and the working class. Their protagonists could imagine conflicts between political communities and between classes but not within either; they aimed at the abolition or transcendence of particularism and all its divisions. Theorists of civil society, by contrast, have a more realistic view of communities and economies. They are more accommodating to conflict—that is, to political opposition and economic competition. Associational freedom serves for them to legitimate a set of market relations, though not necessarily the capitalist set. The market, when it is entangled in the network of associations, when the forms of ownership are pluralized, is without doubt the economic formation most consistent with the civil society argument. This same argument also serves to legitimate a kind of state that is liberal and pluralist more than republican (not so radically dependent upon the virtue of its citizens). Indeed, a state of this sort, as we shall see, is necessary if associations are to flourish.

Once incorporated into civil society, neither citizenship nor production can ever again be all-absorbing. They will have their votaries, but these people will not be models for the rest of us—or, they will be partial models only, for some people at some time of their lives, not for other people, not at other times. This pluralist perspective follows in part, perhaps, from the lost romance of work, from our experience with the new productive technologies and the growth of the service economy. Service is more easily reconciled with a vision of human beings as social animals than with homo faber. What can a hospital attendant or a school teacher or a marriage counselor or a social worker or a television repairperson or a government official be said to make? The contemporary economy does not offer many people a chance for creativity in the Marxist sense. Nor does Marx (or any socialist thinker of the central tradition) have much to say about those men and women whose economic activity consists entirely in helping other people. The helpmate, like the housewife, was never assimilated to the class of workers.

In similar fashion, politics in the contemporary democratic state does not offer many people a chance for Rousseauian self-determination. Citizenship, taken by itself, is today mostly a passive role: citizens are spectators who vote. Between elections they are served, well or badly, by the civil service. They are not at all like those heroes of republican mythology, the citizens of ancient Athens meeting in assembly and (foolishly, as it turned out) deciding to invade Sicily. But in the associational networks of civil society—in unions, parties, movements, interest groups, and so on—these same people make many smaller decisions and shape to some degree the more distant determinations of state and economy. And in a more densely organized, more egalitarian civil society, they might do both these things to greater effect.

These socially engaged men and women—part-time union officers, movement activists, party regulars, consumer advocates, welfare volunteers, church members, family heads—stand outside the republic of citizens as it is commonly conceived. They are only intermittently virtuous; they are too caught up in particularity. They look, most of them, for many partial fulfillments, no longer for the one clinching fulfillment. On the ground of actuality (unless the state usurps the ground), citizenship shades off into a great diversity of (sometimes divisive) decision-making roles; and, similarly, production shades off into a multitude of (sometimes competitive) socially useful activities. It is, then, a mistake to set politics and work in opposition to one another. There is no ideal fulfillment and no essential human capacity. We require many settings so that we can live different kinds of good lives.

All this is not to say, however, that we need to accept the capitalist version of competition and division. Theorists who regard the market as the preferred setting for the good life aim to make it the actual setting for as many aspects of life as possible. Their single-mindedness takes the form of market imperialism; confronting the democratic state, they are advocates of privatization and laissez-faire. Their ideal is a society in which all goods and services are provided by entrepreneurs to consumers. That some entrepreneurs would fail and many consumers find themselves helpless in the marketplace—this is the price of individual autonomy. It is, obviously, a price we already pay: in all capitalist societies, the market makes for inequality. The more successful its imperialism, the greater the inequality. But were the market to be set firmly within civil society, politically constrained, open to communal as well as private initiatives, limits might be fixed on its unequal outcomes. The exact nature of the limits would depend on the strength and density of the associational networks (including, now, the political community).

The problem with inequality is not merely that some individuals are more capable, others less capable, of making their consumer preferences effective. It's not that some individuals live in fancier apartments than others, or drive better-made cars, or take vacations in more exotic places. These are conceivably the just rewards of market success. The problem is that inequality commonly translates into domination and radical deprivation. But the verb "translates" here describes a socially mediated process, which is fostered or inhibited by the structure of its mediations. Dominated and deprived individuals are likely to be disorganized as well as impoverished, whereas poor people with strong families, churches, unions, political parties, and ethnic alliances are not likely to be dominated or deprived for long. Nor need these people stand alone even in the marketplace. The capitalist answer assumes that the good life of entrepreneurial initiative and consumer choice is a life led most importantly by individuals. But civil society encompasses or can encompass a variety of market agents: family businesses, publicly owned or municipal companies, worker communes, consumer cooperatives, nonprofit organizations of many different sorts. All these function in the market even though they have their origins outside. And just as the experience of democracy is expanded and enhanced by groups that are in but not of the state, so consumer choice is expanded and enhanced by groups that are in but not of the market.

It is only necessary to add that among the groups in but not of the state are market organizations, and among the groups in but not of the market are state organizations. All social forms are relativized by the civil society argument—and on the actual ground too. This also means that all social forms are contestable; moreover, contests can't be won by invoking one or another account of the preferred setting—as if it were enough to say that market organizations, insofar as they are efficient, don't have to be democratic or that state firms, insofar as they are democratically controlled, don't have to operate within the constraints of the market. The exact character of our associational life is something that has to be argued about, and it is in the course of these arguments that we also decide about the forms of democracy, the nature of work, the extent and effects of market inequalities, and much else.

The quality of nationalism is also determined within civil society, where national groups coexist and overlap with families and religious communities (two social formations largely neglected in modernist answers to the question about the good life) and where nationalism is expressed in schools and movements, organizations for mutual aid, cultural and historical societies. It is because groups like these are entangled with other groups, similar in kind but different in aim, that civil society holds out the hope of a domesticated nationalism. In states dominated by a single nation, the multiplicity of the groups pluralizes nationalist politics and culture; in states with more than one nation, the density of the networks prevents radical polarization.

Civil society as we know it has its origin in the struggle for religious freedom. Though often violent, the struggle held open the possibility of peace. "The establishment of this one thing," John Locke wrote about toleration, "would take away all ground of complaints and tumults upon account of conscience." One can easily imagine groundless complaints and tumults, but Locke believed (and he was largely right) that tolerance would dull the edge of religious conflict. People would be less ready to take risks once the stakes were lowered. Civil society simply is that place where the stakes are lower, where, in principle at least, coercion is used only to keep the peace and all associations are equal under the law. In the market, this formal equality often has no substance, but in the world of faith and identity, it is real enough. Though nations don't compete for members in the same way as religions (sometimes) do, the argument for granting them the associational freedom of civil society is similar. When they are free to celebrate their histories, remember their dead, and shape (in part) the education of their children, they are more likely to be harmless than when they are unfree. Locke may have put the claim too strongly when he wrote, "There is only one thing which gathers people into seditious commotions, and that is oppression," but he was close enough to the truth to warrant the experiment of radical tolerance.

But if oppression is the cause of seditious commotion, what is the cause of oppression? l don't doubt that there is a materialist story to tell here, but I want to stress the central role played by ideological singlemindedness: the intolerant universalism of (most) religions, the exclusivity of (most) nations. The actual experience of civil society, when it can be had, seems to work against these two; indeed, it works so well, some observers think, that neither religious faith nor national identity is likely to survive for long in the network of free associations. But we really don't know to what extent faith and identity depend upon coercion or whether they can reproduce themselves under conditions of freedom. I suspect that they both respond to such deep human needs that they will outlast their current organizational forms. It seems, in any case, worthwhile to wait and see.

Still a Need for State Power

But there is no escape from power and coercion, no possibility of choosing, like the old anarchists, civil society alone. A few years ago, in a book called *Anti-Politics*, the Hungarian dissident George Konrad described a way of living alongside the totalitarian state but, so to speak, with one's back turned toward it. He urged his fellow dissidents to reject the very idea of seizing or sharing power and to devote their energies to religious, cultural, economic, and professional associations. Civil society appears in his book as an alternative to the state, which he assumes to be unchangeable and irredeemably hostile. His argument seemed right to me when I first read his book. Looking back, after the collapse of the communist regimes in Hungary and elsewhere, I can easily see how much it was a product of its time—and how short that time was! No state can survive for long if it is wholly alienated from civil society. It cannot outlast its own coercive machinery; it is lost, literally, without its firepower. The production and reproduction of loyalty, civility, political competence, and trust in authority are never the work of the state alone, and the effort to go it alone—one meaning of totalitarianism—is doomed to failure.

The failure, however, has carried with it terrible costs, and so one can understand the appeal of contemporary antipolitics. Even as Central and East European dissidents take power, they remain, and should remain, cautious and apprehensive about its uses. The totalitarian project has left behind an abiding sense of bureaucratic brutality. Here was the ultimate form of political singlemindedness, and though the "democratic" (and, for that matter, the "communist") ideology that they appropriated was false, the intrusions even of a more genuine democracy are rendered suspect by the memory. Post-totalitarian politicians and writers have, in addition, learned the older antipolitics of free enterprise—so that the laissez-faire market is defended in the East today as one of the necessary institutions of civil society, or, more strongly, as the dominant social formation. This second view takes on plausibility from the extraordinary havoc wrought by totalitarian economic "planning." But it rests, exactly like political singlemindedness, on a failure to recognize the pluralism of associational life. The first view leads, often, to a more interesting and a genuinely liberal mistake: it suggests that pluralism is self-sufficient and self-sustaining.

This is, indeed, the experience of the dissidents: the state could not destroy their unions, churches, free universities, illegal markets, *samizdat* publications. Nonetheless, I want to warn against the antipolitical tendencies that commonly accompany the celebration of civil society. The network of association incorporates, but it cannot dispense with, the agencies of state power: neither can socialist cooperation or capitalist competition dispense with the state. That's why so many dissidents are ministers now. It is indeed true that the new social movements in the East and the West—concerned with ecology, feminism, the rights of immigrants and national minorities, workplace and product safety, and so on—do not aim, as the democratic and labor movements once aimed, at taking power. This represents an important change, in sensibility as much as in ideology, reflecting a new valuation of parts over wholes and a new willingness to settle for something less than total victory. But there can be no victory at all that doesn't involve some control over, or use of, the state apparatus. The collapse of totalitarianism is empowering for the members of civil society previously because it renders the state accessible.

Here, then, is the paradox of the civil society argument. Citizenship is one of many roles that members play, but the state itself is unlike all the other associations. It both frames civil society and occupies space within it. It fixes the boundary conditions and the basic rules of all associational activity (including political activity). It compels association members to think about a common good, beyond their own conceptions of the good life. Even the failed totalitarianism of, say, the Polish communist state had this much impact upon the Solidarity union: it determined that Solidarity was a Polish union, focused on economic arrangements and labor policy within the borders of Poland. A democratic state, which is continuous with the other associations, has at the same time a greater say about their quality and vitality. It serves, or it doesn't serve, the needs of the associational networks as these are worked out by men and women who are simultaneously members and citizens. I shall give only a few obvious examples, drawn from American experience.

Families with working parents need state help in the form of publicly funded day care and effective public schools. National minorities need help in organizing and sustaining their own educational programs. Worker-owned companies and consumer cooperatives need state loans or loan guarantees; so do (even more often) capitalist entrepreneurs and firms. Philanthropy and mutual aid, churches and private universities, depend upon tax exemptions. Labor unions need legal recognition and guarantees against "unfair labor practices," and professional associations need state support for their licensing procedures. And across the entire range of association, individual men and women need to be protected against the power of officials, employers, experts, party bosses, factory foremen, directors, priests, parents, patrons; and small and weak groups need to be protected against large and powerful ones. For civil society, left to itself, generates radically unequal power relationships, which only state power can challenge.

Civil society also challenges state power, most importantly when associations have resources or supporters abroad: world religions, pan-national movements, the new environmental groups, multinational corporations. We are likely to feel differently about these challenges, especially after we recognize the real but relative importance of the state. Multinational corporations, for example, need to be constrained, much like states with imperial ambitions; and the best constraint probably lies in collective security, that is, in alliances with other states that give economic regulation some international effect. The same mechanism may turn out to be useful to the new environmental groups. In the first case, the state pressures the corporation; in the second it responds to environmentalist pressure. The two cases suggest, again, that civil society requires political agency. And the state is an indispensable agent— even if the associational networks also, always, resist the organizing impulses of state bureaucrats.

Only a democratic state can create a democratic civil society; only a democratic civil society can sustain a democratic state. The civility that makes democratic politics possible can only be learned in the associational networks; the roughly equal and widely dispersed capabilities that sustain the networks have to be fostered by the democratic state. Confronted with an overbearing state, citizens, who are also members, will struggle to make room for autonomous associations and market relationships (and also for local governments and decentralized bureaucracies). But the state can never be what it appears to be in liberal theory, a mere framework for civil society. It is also the instrument of the struggle, used to give a particular shape to the common life. Hence citizenship has a certain practical preeminence among all our actual and possible memberships. That's not to say that we must be citizens all the time, finding in politics, as Rousseau urged, the greater part of our happiness. Most of us will be happier elsewhere, involved only sometimes in affairs of state. But we must leave the state open to our sometime involvement.

Nor need we be involved all the time in our associations. A democratic civil society is one controlled by its members, not through a single process of self-determination but through a large number of different and uncoordinated processes. These needn't all be democratic, for we are likely to be members of many associations, and we will want some of them to be managed in our interests, but also in our absence. Civil society is sufficiently democratic when in at least some of its parts we are able to recognize ourselves as authoritative and responsible participants. States are tested by their capacity to sustain this kind of participation—which is very different from the heroic intensity of Rousseauian citizenship. And civil society is tested by its capacity to produce citizens whose interests, at least sometimes, reach farther than themselves and their comrades, who look after the political community that fosters and protects the associational networks.

In Favor of Inclusiveness

I mean to defend a perspective that might be called, awkwardly, "critical associationalism." I want to join, but I am somewhat uneasy with, the civil society argument. It can't be said that nothing is lost when we give up the singlemindedness of democratic citizenship or socialist cooperation or individual autonomy or national identity. There was a kind of heroism in those projects—a concentration of energy, a clear sense of direction, an unblinking recognition of friends and enemies. To make one of these one's own was a serious commitment. The defense of civil society doesn't seem quite comparable. Associational engagement is conceivably as important a project as any of the others, but its greatest virtue lies in its inclusiveness, and inclusiveness does not make for heroism. "Join the associations of your choice" is not a slogan to rally political militants. And yet that is what civil society requires: men and women actively engaged—in state, economy, and nation, and also in churches, neighborhoods, and families, and in many other settings too. To reach this goal is not as easy as it sounds; many people, perhaps most people, live very loosely within the networks, and a growing number of people seem to be radically disengaged—passive clients of the state, market dropouts, resentful and posturing nationalists. And the civil society project doesn't confront an energizing hostility, as all the others do; its protagonists are more likely to meet sullen indifference, fear, despair, apathy, and withdrawal.

In Central and Eastern Europe, civil society is still a battle cry, for it requires a dismantling of the totalitarian state and it brings with it the exhilarating experience of associational independence. Among ourselves what is required is nothing so grand; nor does it lend itself to a singular description (but this is what lies ahead in the East too). The civil society project can only be described in terms of all the other projects, against their singularity. Hence my account in these pages, which suggests the need (1) to decentralize the state so that there are more opportunities for citizens to take responsibility for (some of) its activities; (2) to socialize the economy so that there is a greater diversity of market agents, communal as well as private; and (3) to pluralize and domesticate nationalism, on the religious model, so that there are different ways to realize and sustain historical identities.

None of this can be accomplished without using political power to redistribute resources and to underwrite and subsidize the most desirable associational activities. But political power alone cannot accomplish any of it. The kinds of "action" discussed by theorists of the state need to be supplemented (not, however, replaced) by something radically different: more like union organizing than political mobilization, more like teaching in a school than arguing in the assembly, more like volunteering in a hospital than joining a political party, more like working in an ethnic alliance or a feminist support group than canvassing in an election, more like shaping a co-op budget than deciding on national fiscal policy. But can any of these local and small-scale activities ever carry with them the honor of citizenship? Sometimes, certainly, they are narrowly conceived, partial and particularist; they need political correction. The greater problem, however, is that they seem so ordinary. Living in civil society, one might think, is like speaking in prose.

But just as speaking in prose implies an understanding of syntax, so these forms of action (when they are pluralized) imply an understanding of civility. And that is not an understanding about which we can be entirely confident these days. There is something to be said for the neoconservative argument that in the modern world we need to recapture the density of associational life and relearn the activities and understandings that go with it. And if this is the case, then a more strenuous argument is called for from the left: we have to reconstruct that same density under new conditions of freedom and equality. It would appear to be an elementary requirement of social democracy that there exist a society of lively, engaged, and effective men and women—where the honor of "action" belongs to the many and not to the few.

Against a background of growing disorganization—violence, homelessness, divorce, abandonment, alienation, and addiction—a society of this sort looks more like a necessary achievement than a comfortable reality. In truth, however, it was never a comfortable reality, except for the few. Most men and women have been trapped in one or another subordinate relationship, where the "civility" they learned was deferential rather than independent and active. That is why democratic citizenship, socialist production, free enterprise, and nationalism were all liberating projects. But none of them has yet produced a general, coherent, or sustainable liberation. And their more single-minded adherents, who have exaggerated the effectiveness of the state or the market or the nation and neglected the networks, have probably contributed to the disorder of contemporary life. The projects have to be relativized and brought together, and the place to do that is in civil society, the setting of settings, where each can find the partial fulfillment that is all it deserves.

Civil society itself is sustained by groups much smaller than the demos or the working class or the mass of consumers or the nation. All these are necessarily fragmented and localized as they are incorporated. They become part of the world of family, friends, comrades, and colleagues, where people are connected to one another and made responsible for one another. I have no magic formula for making connections or strengthening the sense of responsibility. These aren't aims that can be underwritten with historical guarantees or achieved through a single unified struggle. Civil society is a project of projects; it requires many organizing strategies and new forms of state action. It requires a new sensitivity for what is local, specific, contingent—and, above all, a new recognition (to paraphrase a famous sentence) that the good life is in the details.

2. Private and Public Roles in Civil Society

Terry Nardin

There is an ambiguity in the idea of "civil society" as the arena of private economic and social relations, rather than of government. First, there is the idea that these relations are freely chosen. Civil society, as Michael Walzer puts it, is "the space of uncoerced human association." But second, there is the idea that these relations depend upon shared values. Civil society is therefore also "the set of relational networks—formed for the sake of family, faith, interest, and ideology—that fill this space." ... The idea of civil society, then, can receive both liberal and communitarian interpretation, depending on whether one emphasizes individual liberty or associational solidarity.

How are these two interpretations of civil society related? Walzer suggests that in a liberal polity, when ties of family, religion, and nationality dissolve, there is really not much left beyond the marketplace, with its conception of the good life as a life of consumption. But the market alone has little incentive to provide the "social minimum" required to give everyone a piece of the good life so conceived.

Against this market liberalism Walzer argues for an actively political conception of civil society, one that recognizes the need to use state power to make redistributive adjustments. "Civil society requires political agency. And the state is an indispensable agent." It follows that "the state can never be what it appears to be in liberal theory, a mere framework for civil society. It is also the instrument of the struggle, used to give a particular shape to the common life."

Commitment to an unregulated market and the minimal state is not a necessary part of the liberal argument, however. I think F.A. Hayek correctly articulates the central idea of liberalism by defining the social order—civil society—as a system without ultimate ends. It is, however, more than just a market. It is a complex of relationships, practices, and associations that gives shape to human activity. Civil society needs to be governed, but it can't be governed by invoking universally shared values (there are none) but only through relatively abstract formal rules and procedures. On the liberal model, then, the state is what the late Michael Oakeshott called "civil association," a framework of rules that is formally indifferent to particular interests, though it may affect the success with which particular interests are pursued. Once the state takes sides in the play of substantive interests in civil society, it becomes a source of disorder. It becomes a player in civil society rather than an umpire, the custodian of its rules.

Walzer explicitly rejects this liberal model, as the "civil society project"—the effort to strengthen both individual liberty and associational solidarity—cannot "be accomplished without using political power to redistribute resources and to underwrite and subsidize the most desirable associational activities." This is putting it very strongly, needlessly strongly. All Walzer really has to claim is that if the state remains no more than a framework, an umpire, then the solidarity on which civil society rests can never be realized, at least for a substantial portion of the community. The question, then, is how, in a market-dominated society, pressure for a social minimum can be applied by the state. We need not become embroiled in the question of whether there are other values and activities that state power should be used to encourage.

Walzer is concerned with what he calls the paradox of the civil society argument: that "civil society, left to itself, generates radically unequal power relationships, which only state power can challenge." But there is a second paradox of civil society which he does not sufficiently consider: that the state, by intervening to correct the inequalities generated by civil society, becomes a participant civil society in ways that threaten to undermine its essential role as a constitutive framework for civil society. If civil society is constituted by the state, by the framework of law, then the state as agent must use its power in ways that do not contradict or undermine that constitution. The test of proper state action should therefore probably be stricter than the one Walzer proposes—not "to redistribute resources and to underwrite and subsidize the most desirable associational activities," but to pursue only those redistributions that are required to sustain the kind of civil society that is compatible with a liberal order—a civil association, based on the rule of law, whose members are really members and have the all the rights and dignity of membership.

Of course this conception needs interpretation—political and judicial, more than philosophical, interpretation—but it rules out action to promote substantive ends that are desirable according to this or that conception of the good life but which cannot be justified in terms of the narrower goal of extending the benefits of civil society to all its members.

These are the familiar issues of political controversy in the West, and it is therefore a bit puzzling to see them surface again in the debate over "civil society." One wonders about the audience for Walzer's paper. It makes most sense as a reminder to East Europeans who think that civil society can stand on its own, without political support. In Eastern Europe before 1989 the civil society concept was needed to identify the underground life and politics of totalitarian society, and it may still have some purchase in describing the current politics of societies learning how to live without totalitarianism. The question is whether the concept adds much that is new to debates in the West.

By arguing that civil society needs state power, Walzer seems to dismiss the experience of those East Europeans who nurtured civil society as an alternative to the state. In the shadow of the communist state, civil society was about choices, often dangerous ones, to write, publish, or join prohibited associations. From the perspective of the dissident, Walzer's concern with using state power to "underwrite the most desirable associational activities" might even seem a bit ominous. Who decides what is desirable? Wasn't this instrumental conception of the state part of the communist problem? East European social critics such as Michnik and Havel, like critical theorists in the West, have tried to articulate alternatives to the instrumentalism of the technocratic order under both communism and capitalism. In this strand of the civil society argument, a decent society is created not by relying on political power as an instrument for producing a just future, but by acting decently here and now while letting the future take care of itself. One creates good not as a result of action but in acting. While in the ethic of instrumentalism means and ends are distinct things, connected causally, in the dissidents' ethic of "living in truth" they are related conceptually and immanently.

By insisting that we must rely on the state as the agent for promoting good ends, we risk courting the very dangers Michnik and Havel warn against. Doubtless Walzer would reply that I am being anti-political, and in a sense he would be right. But there are different understandings of politics, and we need to worry about what the state might do as an agent as well as what it may fail to do as a framework. Which is the more reasonable worry depends on circumstances. Walzer's discussion assumes a substantially just society, one already enjoying the rule of law but in which the benefits of justice need to be shared more widely. But we must not minimize social conflict, nor take for granted the benefits of formal equality and political order. It would indeed be better to make liberal regimes more inclusive by creating the kind of solidarity that would broaden political participation, do away with the underclass, and distribute the benefits of membership more evenly. But these are not the problems that the civil society project was designed to solve.

Now not all understandings of associational solidarity raise the kinds of difficulties I have been discussing. The idea of communitarianism as a commitment to a common set of associational principles is a profoundly ambiguous one. Most often, the focus is on shared conceptions, shared values, shared traditions. But these can be either (1) some specific set of conceptions and values—a plea for these values, for example, for a particular nationalism—or, alternatively, (2) a meta-claim: that there must be some set of shared values (it doesn't matter which). But this claim can be grounded in two quite different ways either because this is what the good society is—agreement, consensus, solidarity, *Gemeinschaft*, community—or because shared values are contingently required for a society to be viable.

Each of these conceptions leads to its own kind of politics. The first two—the plea for particular values, or the claim that agreement is intrinsically valuable—are monistic and potentially totalitarian. Only the third is consistent with pluralism and democracy—with *Gesellschaft*, the "watery fidelity" of civil association, which is an association of common practices, rules, and procedures, but not shared values.

To sum up: Walzer's conception of civil society, with its communitarian as well as liberal dimension and its emphasis on active government, raises many questions, most quite familiar in political theory and practice.

First, what kind of civil society do we want, and how much? There are different kinds and degrees of liberty, and also of solidarity. The existence of great inequalities of wealth and power may be unjust, they may unbalance civil society, but they do not necessarily destroy it. We must be careful not to confuse the concept of civil society itself with various idealizations of it, various understandings of what a "just" civil society might look like.

Second, to what extent does civil society need political agency (as opposed to other kinds of agents)? Walzer speaks of the need for state action but doesn't develop the argument. Specifically, what kinds of state action are required? What alternatives to state action might be preferable? And what limits to state action need to be respected?

All these questions lead to another, more basic, question: What are the criteria for choosing and judging state action to strengthen civil society? It's not enough to say that it is a matter of judgment, of prudence, or of democratic politics. Judgment presupposes criteria, prudence a context of criteria from which it departs and which it modifies. And politics, even democratic politics, must respect limits.

My suggestion is merely that a partial answer may already be implicit in the idea of civil society itself. The state may, or must, intervene to strengthen civil society—to strengthen both individual liberty and associational solidarity—but only within the limits of civility; that is, within the limits of public morality, the rule of law. Developing these criteria—the constitutional principles of public policy—may help to counter the play of existing powers. For it is a big practical problem to get government to act in ways that are not just a mirror image of what already exists, merely replicating existing inequalities and power distributions.

3. Interpreting the Notion of Civil Society

Jean Cohen

I will address three questions disturbing to those who make use of the concept of civil society.

1. Is the term "civil society" really a code word for the market, private property, capitalism?

2. If not, is the discourse of civil society necessarily traditionalistic—does it ignore hierarchies and forms of domination on the terrain of the social?

3. Is the politics of civil society necessarily a- or anti-political? What is the relation between a politics of civil society and the state or the economy?

The concept of civil society has recently become fashionable thanks to struggles against communist and military dictatorships, first in Eastern Europe and the Soviet Union, and second in Latin America. Accordingly, to some, it seems to indicate what the West has already achieved, and thus the concept appears to be without any critical potential vis-a-vis the disfunctions and injustices in our type of society. I believe this mistaken view relies on a two-part model that opposes civil society to the state. And I want to argue that no version of the two-part model, whether liberal and/or Marxian, whereby civil society includes everything outside of the state sector, is helpful today. The stark polemical opposition between civil society and the state can only be a slogan, a starting point for analysis or for mobilization against statist regimes, but it is certainly not adequate for serious analysis or politics within civil societies.

Nevertheless, I do believe that the discourse of civil society involves a politics, a democratic politics potentially more engaging and mobilizing than the slogan "join the association of your choice" (Michael Walzer).

I begin from a three-part model which differentiates between civil society, the state, and the economy. Its roots lie in Hegel, but theorists as different as Gramsci, Parsons and Habermas also make use of it. The three-part model has two advantages. First, it avoids an unpleasant ambiguity in the program of the defense of civil society against the state, for it allows one to distinguish between the "civil" and the "bourgeois." On a three-part model, the autonomy of civil society is not the same as the autonomy of the market. To put it another way, a bourgeois society that places the market and property rights at its center is only one version of this, and a problematic one at that. The advantage of a three-part model is that it allows us to differentiate between the task of establishing or maintaining viable market economies (whatever the forms of property) and the project of strengthening civil society vis-a-vis the state and the liberated market forces. As we know from the West, economic power can represent as great a danger to social solidarity, social justice, and autonomy as the power of the modern state. So only a concept of civil society differentiated from the economy could become the center of a critical theory in societies where the market economy has already developed its own autonomous logic or is in the process of doing so.

Second, the three-part model also helps us to counter conservative conceptions of the social life. It allows us to see that the defense of civil society does not have to entail a traditionalistic hierarchy as opposed to a modern (egalitarian) life world. If civil society can take many forms, then it can also be a target of democratization. The politics of civil society can try to change the institutions of civil society in a direction away from hierarchical, inegalitarian, patriarchal, nationalist, racist versions toward egalitarian, horizontal, non-sexist, open versions based on the principles of individual rights and democratic participation in associations, and public. No one can argue convincingly that such a movement is realized anywhere in the West. However, with the demise of Marxism and the revolutionary rhetoric of communism, the question confronting political theorists everywhere is whether utopian thought and meaningful political projects are conceivable at all. Or are the great mobilizing ideals embedded in the earlier utopias consigned to the dustbin of the history of ideas?

The ideals generated in the age of democratic revolutions—liberty, political equality, solidarity, justice—were each embedded in totalistic utopias: anarchism, libertarianism, radical democracy, Marxism. Sober reflection on the history of the past century and a half should dissuade responsible persons from trying to revive any of these utopias in their original form. Yet a society without action-orienting ideals, without political projects, is equally undesirable, for the civil privatism or "realism" that would result would involve a political culture unable to generate enough motivation to even maintain, much less expand, existing rights, democratic institutions, social solidarity, or justice.

I believe that the discourse of civil society helps here. For this discourse reveals that collective actors and sympathetic theorists are still oriented by the utopian ideals of modernity, even if the fundamentalist revolutionary rhetoric within which they once were articulated is on the wane. Indeed, the movement of civil society is itself a new kind of utopia: the normative principles underlying it, plurality, publicity, legality, equality, justice, voluntary association, and individual autonomy, constitute a self-limiting utopia that calls for a plurality of democratic form, a complex set of social, civil, and political rights compatible with a highly differentiated society. It also calls for what I label a self-limiting, radical politics.

Let me briefly redefine more clearly my conception of civil society and point to the possible politics this entails. I understand civil society as a sphere of social interaction distinct from economy and state, composed above all of associations (including the family) and publics. Modern civil society is created and reproduced through forms of collective action, and it is institutionalized through laws, especially subjective rights that stabilize social differentiation. While the active and institutionalized dimensions can exist separately, in the long run both independent action and institutionalization are necessary for the reproduction of civil society.

I do not, however, identify civil society with all of social life outside the state and economic spheres. First, one must distinguish civil society both from what I call a "political society" of parties, political organizations, and political public spheres (parliaments) and from an "economic society" composed of the organizations of production, distribution, and associated publics, usually firms, cooperatives, institutions of collective bargaining, unions, councils, etc. The actors and institutions of political and economic society are directly involved with state power and economic production. They cannot afford to subordinate strategic and instrumental criteria to the patterns of normative integration and open-ended communication characteristic of civil society. While the associations of civil society are communicatively coordinated, modern political and economic institutions must be coordinated through the media of power and money, however much communicative interaction can be found there. Even the public spheres of political society involve important formal and temporal constraints in processes of communication. In turn, the political role of civil society is not directly related to the conquest of power, but to the generation of influence, through the life of democratic associations and unconstrained discussion in a variety of cultural and informal public spheres. Thus, the mediating role of political society between civil society and the state (political society sets up receptors for the influence of civil society) is indispensable, but so is the rootedness of political society in civil society. In principle, similar considerations pertain to the relationship of civil and economic society, even if historically, under capitalism, economic society has been more successfully insulated from the influence of civil society than political society, despite the claims of elite theories of democracy. Of course, I have now apparently replaced a three-part with a five-part model, but it should be obvious that the concepts of political and economic society are mediating categories between the three core terms of my framework.

Indeed, I want to stress that under liberal democracies it would be a mistake to see civil society in opposition to economy and state by definition. My notion of economic and political society refers to mediating institutions through which civil society can gain influence over political/administrative and economic processes. An antagonistic relation of civil society or its actors to economy and state arises when these mediations fail, or when economic or political institutions insulate decision making and decision makers from the communication with and influence of social organizations, initiatives, and discussions.

This conceptual framework obviously translates categories of general social theory into political sociology. The point of this translation is to get beyond a strictly dichotomous framework and the one-sided models of politics that flow from it. On the dichotomous model we are left with a rather varied set of theoretical choices: the defense of civil society against the state, participation in the political system on strictly strategic terms, or attempts to dispense with the opposition altogether in the name of a republican model of participatory democracy. The first position is typical of the antipolitics of some components of the new social movements, the second of elite theorists of democracy. What both have in common is a view that severs the link between civil and political society. The third model is based on a republican conception of political society, which tends to denigrate civil society as individualistic, apolitical, and privatistic. The politics of civil society looks far more promising on the three-part model. As I said at the beginning, civil society is a project, a terrain and target of democratic politics. The institutions of civil society can and ought to be the target of democratization, of egalitarian projects aimed at expanding rights and solidarities, and the institutions of political and economic society can and ought to be the targets of actors in civil society seeking to render them more receptive to their influence. In short, I can identify, on my conception, four types of politics which I call the politics of identity, influence, inclusion, and reform, which address civil, political and/or economic society, the economy, and state, respectively. All of these comprise the policies of civil society.

Contemporary collective actors consciously struggle over the power to construct new identities, and to reshape institutions, cultural and normative expectations accordingly. Civil society proper is the terrain and target of this politics of identity. It is here that collective actors defend spaces for the creation of the new identities and seek to render more egalitarian and democratic the institutions and social relations in which identities are generated. It is through such action that traditions are reassessed, renewed, or revised, and inegalitarian social relations or forms of domination within civil society properly challenged.

The target of the politics of influence is public opinion in civil and political society. Or rather, the politics of influence aims at making the actors in political society (or in economic society) responsive and receptive to those in civil society. In short, the politics of influence seeks to alter the universe of political discourse such that it keeps up with the basic principles and cultural changes articulated in civil society. The politics of influence indicates how actors of civil society can accomplish something on the level of the political or economic system without losing their identity as civil actors or social movements.

In political society, actors get to participate through political inclusion in the form of parties, lobbies, and recognized partners in bargaining forums. A similar point can be made for economic society. Collective action aimed at the expansion of political or economic society to include new actors, in order to gain access to power or benefits, is what I call the politics of inclusion. Finally, recognized actors seek to accomplish some of their goals through strategic action in order to make policy: this is the politics of reform, at least in the case of actors arising from social movements.

I believe that all of the important contemporary movements can be analyzed in these terms. I also believe that construed in this way, the concept and politics of civil society take us beyond the unattractive alternatives of soulless reformism and revolutionary fundamentalism. Utopian ideals are not on the wane, political projects are still possible, we need not indulge in resignation, for a democratic and egalitarian civil society is still a project worth fighting for.

4. Reconceptualizing Civil Society for Now: Some Somewhat Gramscian Turnings[1]

Kai Nielsen

I.

"Civil society," much more than "state," "government," "power," or even "democracy," is a term of art in political theory. There is no discovering what the concept means, let alone what it "really means." What instead is to be done is to see if we can forge some conceptualization or reconceptualization of civil society which would be useful, given, on the one hand, some important political or ethical purposes or, on the other, some theoretical purposes.

In ancient usage, *civilis societas* (in Cicero, for example) referred to the condition of living in a civilized political community: a community with a legal code, cities, commercial arts, and the refinements of living. For there to be a civil society, according to the ancient conception, is for there to be this kind of political community. Skipping a few centuries, by the time we get to contractarian thought, there is a considerable change. In John Locke, for example, political and civil society were taken to be the same thing (whether it was a society of refinement or not) and this contrasted with paternal authority and the state of nature. But still there remained the identification of political society and civil society.

1. Portions of this article have previously appeared in print in *Arena Journal*, No. 2 (1993/94), 159-174.

With Hegel and Marx, the conception of civil society (*bürgerliche Gesellschaft*) underwent a much greater change. For them, civil society was contrasted with political society. Civil society referred to a social order, and most fundamentally, an economic order operating according to its own principles, independent of the ethical requirements of law and political association. It was, for both Hegel and the early Marx, part of social life where avariciousness and egoism, sometimes accompanied by economic rationality, were the order of the day.[2] This part of social life lacked all the qualities of warmth, solidarity and moral cohesion at least supposedly characteristic of the *Gemeinschaften* of simpler societies.

Today many political theorists of rather different theoretical orientations and political commitments rather uncontroversially think of civil society as the nonpolitical and non-private aspects of society. It is located in a conceptual space distinct from, and between, the state and the at least supposedly private sphere of the family and spousal arrangements and the like. As opposed to ancient usage, where "civil society" was synonymous with a certain sort of "political society," the contemporary use of "civil society" generally refers to economic and other social arrangements whether they be practices, codes, institutions, or organizations, as long as they are apart from the state and also apart from the private sphere of the family. Still, economic institutions remain the central element in civil society so conceived. Thus I do not think much, if any, exception would be taken to Michael Walzer's remarks that "the line between political community and civil society was meant to mark off coercive decision-making from free exchange,"[3] and that "the separation of civil society and political community creates the sphere of economic competition and free enterprise, the market in commodities, labor, and capital."[4] This, of course, as Walzer is perfectly aware, is only the civil society of our bourgeois societies. Civil society here is quite literally just a *bürgerliche Gesellschaft*. But the point is, that it is in such societies that these forms of life have

---

2. In Marx's mature thought the term disappears. It is a moot point how much of the concept remains.

3. Michael Walzer, "Liberalism and the Art of Separation," *Political Theory* 12, no. 3 (August 1984), 321.

4. Ibid., 316.

gained prominence. Moreover, there are analogies in earlier pre-capitalist societies and in what once were State Socialist societies.

However, this by now rather orthodox conception of civil society is not the only way civil society has been conceptualized. Antonio Gramsci, from an historicist but still thoroughly Marxian perspective, reconceptualized civil society into a tripartite conception in which civil society is juxtaposed not only against the state, taken as a coercive governmental apparatus, but, strikingly, against the economy and the private sphere of the family as well.[5] Although he was thoroughly Marxist, he is not to be understood here (Noberto Bobbio, to the contrary, notwithstanding), as having abandoned historical materialism for a kind of Crocean historical idealism.[6] He did take the state, civil society, and the economy to be distinct elements in the social fabric, but he also stressed that they were methodological (analytical) distinctions used for purposes of perspicuous representation, analysis and critical praxis. In the real world their boundaries are blurred, indeed they even flow into each other, and are not separable. He might have even taken a page from that great "atomist," David Hume, and have reminded us that everything that is distinguishable is not separable: being physical and being extended or being an equiangular triangle and being an equilateral triangle, for example. They are not like a chair with its various parts or a human body with its various parts. In societies complex enough to have a state there can be no state without civil society and no economic relations without both and no private sphere without all of these elements. They are analytically separable (distinguishable) but not separable in reality. They are not like the parts that make up an automobile. Still, there are important systematic connections between these elements of society. In reality

---

5. Jean Cohen and Andrew Arato, "Politics and Reconstruction of the Concepts of Civil Society," in Axel Honneth, et al., eds., *Zwischenbetrachtungen: Im Prozess der Aufklärung* (Frankfurt am Main: Suhrkamp Verlag, 1989).

6. Noberto Bobbio, "Gramsci and the Conception of Civil Society," in Chantal Mouffe, ed., *Gramsci and Marxist Theory* (London: Routledge & Kegan Paul, 1979), 21-47. For a well-reasoned rescuing of Gramsci from the charge of being an historical idealist, see Jacques Texier, "Gramsci, Theoretician of the Superstructures: On the Concept of Civil Society," 48-79, in the same volume. For a clear articulation of the difference between historical materialism and historical idealism, see Allen W. Wood, *Karl Marx* (London: Routledge & Kegan Paul, 1982).

they form a continuous whole. But it is often useful to make these analytical distinctions.

It is not only Gramsci that has in general terms such a conception but also ex-Marxists such as Leszek Kolakowski, neo-Marxists such as Jürgen Habermas, and social theorists influenced by Habermas such as Andrew Arato, Jean Cohen, and Claus Offe.[7] It is my hunch—a hunch I will pursue to see if it is anything more than a hunch—that a clarified form of this conception of civil society is both politically and theoretically more useful than the more standard conceptions. It helps us to understand what makes societies tick. I shall turn to that after I have characterized rather more fully what this Gramscian conception of civil society comes to.

II.

Walter Adamson aptly defines this Gramscian conception of civil society as follows: "By civil society ... I mean the public space between large-scale bureaucratic structures of state and economy on the one hand, and the private sphere of family, friendships, personality, and intimacy on the other."[8]

We need an adequate conception of civil society. In addition, we need to understand the politics of civil society in order to provide a corrective for a characteristic failure of liberalism, namely, that of operating with a simplistic conception of the distinction between public/private, state/society, and social/individual. Liberalism lacks, or at least seems to lack, the conceptual resources to make clear how there is a nongovernmental public sphere, a civil

---

7. Jürgen Habermas, *The Structural Transformation of the Public Sphere: An Inquiry into a Category of Bourgeois Society*, trans. Thomas Berger (Cambridge, MA: MIT Press, 1989) (This book was originally published in German in 1962.); Arato and Cohen, "Politics and Reconstruction of the Concepts of Civil Society"; Jean Cohen, *Class and Civil Society* (Amherst, MA: The University of Massachusetts Press, 1982); and Claus Offe, *Disorganized Capitalism*, (Cambridge, MA: MIT Press, 1985). I should add that Arato and Cohen do not, I think rightly, follow Gramsci in taking the family to be part of the private sphere.

8. Walter Adamson, "Gramsci and the Politics of Civil Society," *Praxis International* 7, nos. 3/4 (October 1987 and January 1988), 320. See also his *Hegemony and Revolution: Antonio Gramsci's Political and Cultural Theory*, (Berkeley: University of California Press, 1980).

society, which, though closely related to the state, is still not a part of the state apparatus. But this nongovernmental public sphere is nonetheless a vital force in forming public opinion, constructing consent and generating a *de facto* legitimation.[9] Here we need to think of organizations such as schools, churches, labor unions, businessmen's clubs, ethnic associations, the media, various professions like medicine with its institutional setting, the legal profession with its institutional setting, and the like. Just what role—to take the most obvious example—do the media and the schools play in the forming of individuals (that is, in the forming of them as persons) or in the stabilizing or destabilizing of the state or the economy, and how does the economy interact with these institutions? Would a newspaper of any extensive circulation or a television network last long, indeed any time at all, if it took a persistently oppositional stance to the economic order of the time? Indeed it is very unlikely it would even come into being. Do we tend, when there is little conflict between the forces of production and relations of production, to have a nice functional meshing between the economic structure of society and the way its schools or media operate, or do we not? And if there is a meshing, just how does it work? Our political thinking tends to be so individualistic, with (as Ronald Dworkin puts it) individual rights taking center stage, that these problems tend not even to surface, to say nothing of being carefully and clearly examined in a way that might be helpful in the creation of a good or at least a just society.[10]

In locating civil society we must look for those organizations or practices that are not directly governmental or economic but which generate opinions and goals, in accordance with which people who partake in these practices and are a part of these organizations seek not only to influence wider opinion and policies within existing structures and rules, but sometimes also to alter the structures and

---

9. For the distinction between *de facto* and *de jure* authority and legitimation see Robert Paul Wolff, "Violence and the Law," in Robert Paul Wolff, ed., *The Rule of Law* (New York: Simon and Schuster, 1971), 54-72, and Kai Nielsen, "Legitimation in Complex Societies: Some Habermasian Themes," *Annals of Scholarship* 7, no. 1 (1990), 51-89.

10. Ronald Dworkin, *Taking Rights Seriously* (Cambridge, MA: Harvard University Press, 1977), 171-77.

rules themselves.[11] Such a conception of civil society is valuable in coming to understand how the dominant classes often, indeed typically, rule by something other than force, how they achieve and sustain hegemony—that is, cultural leadership — across the society in which they are dominant, and how subaltern classes constitute themselves politically and mount challenges to the dominant political and economic order.

For Hegel, and for Marx as well, civil society was most centrally the sphere where the economic struggles of public life were played out. For Gramsci, by contrast, "the conflicts of civil society are centrally political ... their point is not merely the making of economic contracts and dividing of the existing labor product"—something which Gramsci took to be both economic and political—but in civil society, what is both more characteristic and more central is the formation of and the giving expression to political points of view by parties, religious groups, organs of information, and so forth deployed to "influence the political identification of the masses and the institutional nature and boundaries of civil society itself."[12]

III.

At this juncture, a brief digression is in order on historical materialism, on how Gramsci's historical materialism is to be understood, and on its relation to how he conceptualized and on how we should conceptualize civil society. Gramsci was not an historical idealist, but what G.A. Cohen and Andrew Levine have aptly characterized as someone reasoning in accordance with a weak and restricted form of historical materialism.[13] Historical materialism, let us remind our-

---

11. Adamson, "Gramsci and the Politics of Civil Society," 321.

12. Ibid., 322.

13. G.A. Cohen: *Karl Marx's Theory of History: A Defense* (Princeton: Princeton University Press, 1979); *History, Labour, and Freedom: Themes from Marx* (Oxford: Oxford University Press, 1988), "Reply to Four Critics," *Analyse & Kritik* 5 (1983), 195-222. Andrew Levine: *Arguing for Socialism: Theoretical Considerations* (London: Routledge & Kegan Paul, 1984); *The End of the State* (London: Verso, 1987), "Review of Jon Elster's *Making Sense of Marx*," *Journal of Philosophy* LXXXIII, no. 12 (Dec 1986), 721-25; and "Review of G.A. Cohen's *History, Labour, and Freedom*," *Journal of Philosophy* (1990), 267-75. Joshua Cohen: "Minimalist Historical Materialism" in Rodger Beehler, et al, eds., *On the Track of Reason: Essays in Honor of Kai Nielsen* (Boulder: Westview Press, 1992), 155-174.

selves, is a theory of epochal social change. From epoch to epoch, human history has a determinate structure and a direction resulting from an endogenous dynamic process in which social relations of production rise and fall in order to maintain functional compatibility with developing material forces of production. During a given epoch the relations of production exist as they are because they facilitate and do not fetter the development of the forces of production. Similarly, the political, legal, moral, and religious institutions exist as they are because they sustain the relations of production (the economic structures) that occur during that period. Restricted historical materialism restricts the explanatory scope of historical materialism. On the standard unrestricted account, economic structures (relations of production) explain all superstructural phenomena; on the restricted account, historical materialism only seeks to explain the superstructural facts which, via their effect on the relations of production, are required to explain how the distinctive dynamic forces of production remain in place, which in turn cause the rise and fall of economic structures. Restricted historical materialism seeks to be a general theory of history by explaining general trends, namely, epochal social change, but it is not a theory of general history; it does not try to explain all historical phenomena. However, it is still a strongly foundational theory for it explains how it is, from epoch to epoch, that there are major structural changes in our social life. Though Gramsci did not put things in this way, he was (and I think to his credit) a restricted historical materialist.

Gramsci also operated with what I shall characterize (following Levine) as a weak historical materialism. Traditional historical materialism (strong historical materialism, if you will) purports to give an account of the necessary and sufficient conditions for epochal social transformation. Traditional historical materialism purports to explain how we go from one set of relations of production, from one economic structure to another. It holds that certain levels of development of productive forces are both necessary and sufficient for the inception and reproduction of particular and distinctive economic structures or sets of production relations and that "continuous development ... generates structural instabilities between forces and already existing relations of production."[14]

---

14. Levine, "Review of *History, Labour and Freedom*," 273.

Traditional historical materialism holds that the development of the productive forces is sufficient, as well as necessary, to explain the movement from one set of production relations to another; weak historical materialism, by contrast, only claims that the development is necessary for such a movement. "Weak historical materialism," as Levine well puts it, "does not advance sufficient conditions for epochal historical change but only necessary material conditions. It does not purport to explain what actually happens, other things being equal (or nonexistent), but only what is (materially) possible."[15] But it still yields a determinate historical agenda, something that is essential for Marxian praxis, by giving us a characterization of (a) historically possible epochal economic structures (a typology if you will) and (b) a characterization of the possibilities of moving from one epochal structure to another. The rest, on a Marxian account, is a matter of political action in class struggle. And it is here, of course, that a good account of civil society, and most particularly of civil society in industrialized societies, is of crucial importance.

If historical materialism is to stand much chance of being a true account of epochal or social change, it should be a restricted weak historical materialism. It is that form that fits very well with Gramsci's historicism, his activism, and his account of civil society.

Marxist fundamentalists (if there still are any) believe in the inevitability of socialism and that, in some sense of "inevitability," fits well with traditional historical materialism. Where these beliefs—historical materialism and historical inevitability—are well-entrenched, there is a tendency for Marxists to move toward economism or, pessimistically, to self-consciously abandon class struggle and to content themselves with social democracy, while patiently waiting for the forces of production to develop. There are, however, as has been evident for a long time, good reasons, both political and theoretical, for not endorsing socialism's inevitability. But a Marxian revolutionary, which was what Gramsci was, need not and indeed should not believe in socialism's inevitability, but only that it is a feasible historical possibility, and

---

15. Ibid., 277.

thus on the historical agenda—and so, given that it is also desirable, something to strategically plan for and to struggle for.

IV.

With this construing, or perhaps in effect rational reconstructing, of Gramsci as an historical materialist in the weak and restricted sense, let us return to his account of civil society. Walter Adamson, one of Gramsci's most astute interpreters, remarks:

> Gramsci wanted to preserve both the Marxian insight that the forces of production (not the state) are the primary determinant of modern social evolution, and the Crocean insight that civil society is primarily a sphere of "ethical-political" contestation among rival social groups. The first point implies that the widening contradiction between the forces and relations of production remains the most basic precondition for the historical realization of a new socialist mode of production. But the second point implies that the fundamental political contest is unlikely to be a direct confrontation between capital and labor for control of the state and, thus, the means of production, at least not in the near term. Rather, the contest is likely to be a "positional" one for civil society conceived essentially as a cultural-political domain, indeed the sole public domain where mass consent is at issue.[16]

This whole passage fits very well with restricted weak historical materialism. The first point in the passage, with its talk of basic preconditions, brings out the necessary conditions side; the second point provides a plausible and politically fruitful way to proceed for someone who was such an historical materialist. In the situation we are now in, the political context would be that of the class politics of civil society. What specific struggles and what kind of politics— that is, concrete political strategies—would obtain will be strongly conditioned by what is possible at a given time and place. And intelligent moral agents should keep that firmly in mind. But that leaves plenty of *Lebensraum* for particular political strategies, for contestations of how civil society is to be forged. It provides conceptual space for what a Marxian politics or any other politics should be. So it is sensible enough to call Gramsci (as he has been called) a Marxist of the superstructures without at all suggesting (as has also been

---

16. Adamson, "Gramsci and the Politics of Civil Society," 325.

suggested) that he has set aside the bedrock of historical material-ism for a Crocean historical idealist framework.[17] Keeping this in mind will help us to understand better the importance of his account of civil society.

Much of Gramsci's discussion of civil society, understandably enough, was focused on the Italian society of his time. A critical question we need to consider is how much of his analysis can more generally be extended to our present *bürgerliche Gesellschaften*. In Italy, since its unification, no group, not even the Catholic Church, had gained cultural leadership—what Gramsci called hegemony. The principal players here were Fascism, traditional Catholicism, laical liberalism led by Croce as a kind of "lay Pope," and Marxism. In the struggle to gain hegemony in civil society and to extend this to the state and to the economy, Croce understood (and Gramsci took keen note of this) that "the great problem of the modern age was to learn to live without religion, that is, without traditional con-fessional religion."[18] Croce thought that traditional religion was, as such a social force, dead, but he also believed that the liberal tradi-tion could be revived and refurbished and made to serve as a secu-lar "religion of liberty": an ersatz religion, if you will. He thought his *History of Europe in Nineteenth Century* (1932) provided the kind of narrative that would advance that.

Gramsci thought that Croce had posed the problem in the right way. Some form of secular religion was a key element in achieving a hegemonic culture in Italy—though, of course, he dif-fered with Croce about what the content of this new secular equiv-alent of a religion should be. But he believed as firmly as Croce that Italy needed one, and that more generally modern societies need one. Gramsci wrote that Italy needed a "coherent, unitary, nation-

---

17. This is done very well by Jacques Texier, "Gramsci, Theoretician of Superstruc-tures: On the Concept of Civil Society," in Chantal Mouffe, ed., *Gramsci and Marxist Theory* (London: Routledge & Kegan Paul, 1979), 48-74. See also Anne Sasson, "Civil Society," in Tom Bottomore, ed., *A Dictionary of Marxist Thought* (Cambridge, MA: Harvard University Press, 1983), 72-74.

18. Benedetto Croce's views, taken up by Gramsci, were most succinctly stated in his "Religione e serenita," *La Critica* 23, (March 20, 1915), 153-55. Gramsci repub-lished it in his own journal, *La Citta Futura* (Feb. 11, 1917). Croce's article is available in English translation in Croce's *Ethics and Politics*. See Adamson, "Gramsci and the Politics of Civil Society," 326.

ally diffused 'conception of life and man,' a 'lay religion,' a philosophy that has become precisely a 'culture,' that has generated an ethic, a way of life, a civil and individual form of conduct."[19] He agreed with Croce that there was then in Italy a crisis in authority, what we would now call a crisis in legitimation. The Church and the ruling classes had lost their firm hold on the populace. These authorities could no longer rely on a consensus in society in which the allegiances and behavior of the masses were predictably stable. He further agreed with Croce that as a consequence the Italian state was forced into operating more and more by something approximating pure force. The masses had become "detached from their traditional ideologies" such that they "no longer believe what they used to believe, etc."[20]

In formal terms, then, Gramsci agreed with Croce about the need for a secularized religion as the functional replacement of traditional religion, which in Italy was Catholicism, and, if he had known of his work, he would have agreed with Emile Durkheim as well about the role of religion in our social life. About such matters Durkheim more than anyone else in the twentieth century probed very deeply. He saw how very much modern society was in need of a secularized religion, in a world, as Durkheim put it, in which "the old gods are growing old or already dead, and the others are not yet born."[21] But in content, as I have noted, Gramsci differed from both of them. What was needed, he believed, was not liberalism's religion of liberty, which Gramsci thought was little more than an "atheism for aristocrats." It neither could nor should succeed as a secular religion; what was needed instead was Marxism, what Gramsci, under the eye of the censors, called "the philosophy of praxis." It, he said, was an "absolute secularization and earthiness of thought, an absolute humanism of history."[22] What Marxism

---

19. Antonio Gramsci, *Quaderni del Carcere*, 4 volumes, V. Gerrantana, ed. (Turin: Einaudi, 1975), 2185-86. See Adamson, "Gramsci and the Politics of Civil Society," 327.

20. Gramsci, *Quaderni del Carcere*, 311. See Adamson, "Gramsci and the Politics of Civil Society," 327.

21. Emile Durkheim, *Elementary Forms of the Religious Life*, trans. J.W. Swain (New York: Free Press, 1965), 475-76.

22. Gramsci, *Quaderni del Carcere*, 1854-64. See Adamson, "Gramsci and the Politics of Civil Society," 328.

needed to do was to form its own intellectual body to "combat modern ideologies in their most refined forms." This he thought would take time and strategic and organizational skill. Moreover, the central struggle in civil society was not with liberalism, which he saw as having no mass backing, but with the Catholic Church with its long tradition and complex entrenched organization. But, historical materialist that he was, he thought a nontranscendental conception of religion, an utterly secularized religion, was on the historical agenda and that, as the struggle in civil society played itself out for our time, it would become gradually apparent that Marxism was the "only religious faith that is adequate to the contemporary world and can produce a real hegemony."[23]

This is surely a remark that would startle analytical Marxists and scientific socialists, but I think Adamson rightly remarks that for Gramsci "Marxism is less a philosophy, political strategy, or understanding of history than a new religion which integrates its world view and practical ethic into a distinctive culture."[24] So viewed, it could facilitate the acquisition of class consciousness in ways similar to the way any religion socializes its members. And what we get, when a population achieves class consciousness, is not just a knowledge of what a class is and what our particular class position is (though we do get that) but also, by what Gramsci regarded as a catharsis, a vivid feeling of group solidarity with a keen sense of "them" and "us," a feeling for and a sense of "the collective power of a mutually shared vision of what the future can be and a mutually shared faith in the group's ability to arrive at that destination."[25] Marxism's power, Gramsci believed, derives not from science or from its having a set of firmly warranted beliefs, but from culture, from a collectively shared faith.

Gramsci saw Marxism, in the political struggle for hegemony, as "containing in itself all the fundamental elements needed to construct a total and integral conception of the world," but, even more importantly, he saw Marxism as having the cultural and intellectual

23. Gramsci, *Quaderni del Carcere*, 1295, 1319-20, and 1380-81. Adamson, "Gramsci and the Politics of Civil Society," 328.

24. Ibid., 328-29.

25. Gramsci, *Quaderni del Carcere*, 1505, 1682-83, and 1860. Adamson, "Gramsci and the Politics of Civil Society," 329.

resources needed "to give life to an integral practical organization of society, that is to become a total integral civilization."[26] In short, he saw Marxism, far in advance of Fascism, Catholicism, and liberalism, as offering a new and higher principle of civilization.[27]

V.

How much (if any) of this Gramscian conception of the politics of civil society makes sense for us standing where we stand? How much of this, if much of anything, answers to our needs both purely intellectual and political? Adamson, a knowledgeable and sympathetic interpreter of Gramsci, writing in 1987, remarks, "In today's world, of course, the possibility that Marxism represents history's anointed successor to Calvinist Christianity appears extremely unlikely. That such a world-historical vision was still plausible in the 1930s dramatizes the very great political and cultural distance we have travelled in the last half century."[28] As a cultural force communism, and probably socialism too, is, for the present at least, a spent force.[29] Great masses of people may well never again march under red banners or sing *The*

26. Gramsci, *Quaderni del Carcere,* 1434-35 and Adamson, "Gramsci and the Politics of Civil Society," 329.

27. Gramsci, *Quaderni del Carcere,* 1434 and Adamson, "Gramsci and the Politics of Civil Society," 329.

28. Adamson, "Gramsci and the Politics of Civil Society," 331.

29. About communism as a viable intellectual conception what needs to be said is much more complex. See Andrew Levine, "Communism after Communism" (unpublished manuscript). The conception of communism in Marx, Luxemburg, and even Lenin may very well have been more confirmed than refuted by recent events. Russian and similar communisms are so different from the communism envisioned by Marx that the collapse of the terrible authoritarian statism of Russian communism may have, theoretically speaking, made no difference at all to Marx's communism, to genuine communism. Russian communism, to say nothing of what went on in Romania, was at best a grotesque caricature of communism. But, as Levine well realizes, things are not that simple. As a political-cultural phenomena, these regimes represented themselves, and were in some sense accepted as, the embodiment of Marxism. But it is these "embodiments" that have been so thoroughly rejected by their own populations, including their own working class. Given such considerations, where will the political clout come from to move societies along to a genuine socialism? What, practically speaking, will take the place of a class-conscious proletariat? What will fuel the drive for proletarian emancipation through revolution? Given that there is a proletariat (even though it does not see itself as such) how is that proletariat,

Internationale. Gramsci's "new religion" seems not to have stuck—I say this with what for me is a deep sadness. I have very little hope that the world we can reasonably expect to obtain during our lives will resemble even a minimally decent world. It will not be just and it certainly will not be humane and probably not even be very intelligently ordered. But, aside from fears—I think not unfounded—about the uncontrolled and now hardly effectively opposable, American domination of the world—or (alternatively) trilateralism (the joint American-cum-European-cum-Japanese domination of the world)—I have no sorrow at all for the passing of the Russian Thermidor, along with its client communist (pseudo-communist is more accurate) regimes. But I had hoped—a hope that proved illusory—that something would be salvaged of a genuine socialist tradition from the ashes and that there would not be in those countries a capitalist restoration. But the capitalist countries won the Cold War and a capitalist restoration is well in progress, though not without opposition, along with an American or at least a trilateral world domination. Communism and socialism appear at least to be conceptualizations, culturally speaking, of times past. (Still, this may be too hasty a judgement. In many ways, things look uncertain.)

There is an irony in this for Marxian theoreticians. Marxism as a social force is dead, for the present at least, just as we are gaining from the work of such analytical Marxists as G.A. Cohen, Andrew Levine, Erik Olin Wright, and John Roemer a sophisticated and appropriately rigorous Marxian social theory that is arguably the best holistic social theory in or out of town.[30] Marxism has always

---

given the turning of the world, going to come to see itself as a proletariat and take matters into its own hands and thereby emancipate itself, or more accurately begin the process of emancipation? Have we the slightest reason to think that anything like that will happen in the foreseeable future? Things look very bleak, but there are some hopeful signs as well. Things are working badly in capitalist societies and alienation is extensive. And so far at least, the turn to capitalism in the formerly state socialist societies has in most respects made matters even worse in those societies. Circumstances could arise in which that alienation would be transformed into opposition to the capitalist order. See here Russell Hardin, "Efficiency vs. Equality and the Demise of Socialism," *Canadian Journal of Philosophy,* Vol. 22, no. 2 (June 1992), 149-161. See also the references in footnotes 30 and 48.

30. See references in note 12 and Erik Olin Wright, "What is Analytical Marxism?" *Socialist Review* 19, no. 4 (Oct.-Dec. 1989); Erik Olin Wright, *Class* (London: New

been something more (indeed very much more) than a theory, even a good theory, and now it will have no basis for its praxis. It will, whatever its intentions, not be a theory in the service of a revolutionary movement. But this is to take away its very underlying rationale.

So the wheel of the world having turned, our analysis of the politics of civil society will have to be somewhat different from Gramsci's. Still, deploying the notion of civil society may continue to be useful, perhaps even more useful than before, for analyzing and critiquing the contemporary world.

For the institutions of civil society to be in place and properly functioning, two essential preconditions must be met: (a) the society must be a complex society with many different social functions and roles into which people are slotted and (b) the state and economic organizations cannot incorporate or even completely control the various practices, organizations, and institutions of the society that are non-economic and non-governmental. Vulgar Marxism with its economic determinism and reductionism sees the state and other non-economic institutions as utterly in control of the ruling class that goes with the economic structure. But Gramsci plainly was not such a Marxist and, even if he were, such a Marxism is plainly false.[31] In our societies these two essential preconditions for the possible viability of civil society are met, albeit perhaps insecurely. The key critical question for us should be: how should the politics of civil society appear, given present-day social realities? Put differently: what practices, organizations, and institutions should the particular civil society that is ours have and what kind of life together for ourselves should we seek to achieve? We, of course, cannot sensibly answer the latter question without a good understanding of what is feasibly possible: of what is on the historical agenda.

The preconditions for civil society are met in our world, but it is also true that the strength, and so far the growing strength, of economic-corporate and political-bureaucratic organizations

---

Left Books, 1985); and John Roemer, *Free to Lose* (Cambridge, MA: Harvard University Press, 1988), and Kai Nielsen, "Analytical Marxism: A Form of Critical Theory," *Erkenntnis*, Vol. 39 (1993), 1-21.

31. It should be added that Marx was not such a Marxist. See Cohen, *Karl Marx's Theory of History: A Defense.*

threatens to undermine the institutions of civil society. There is, as Habermas puts it, a colonization of the life-world. Adamson is only being slightly hyperbolic when he remarks that "we face a social world in which the power of corporate-bureaucratic structures is so great as to threaten the very existence of civil society and even the private sphere as we know them."[32]

A viable civil society as a kind of third force between the state and economy, on the one hand, and the private sphere, on the other, seems to require some effective sense of community and of there actually being a community to which people are committed. That was plainly Gramsci's hope and indeed he thought that it would come about with the establishment of communism. In the long war of position for the challenging class—the working class—it can, in that struggle, forge partial structures of community within civil society, though this will not be achieved without class struggle. But an overarching sense of community is what he thought, with the entrenchment of socialism, the new religion of Marxism would articulate and enhance for us. Remember that this community would be a total integral civilization rooted in a total and integral conception of the world, with a unitary conception of the common good supported by an integral practical organization of society, yielding, when fully developed, a regulated society but a society that is regulated for the common good—a common good that would be so comprehensive that it would articulate justified norms for what Gramsci called a total integral civilization. It is understandable that this, given our past history, would give some people the jitters. For others it will just seem thoroughly unrealistic given the diversity of present day complex societies.

Hitler made the word *'Gemeinschaft'* a dirty word and Stalinist and neo-Stalinist realities in what once were the actually existing socialisms have stamped that feeling in. We have a well-warranted aversion for total ideologies, grand meta-narratives, or comprehensive totalizing theories. Yet what are the goals of our civil society, if indeed there is any consensus about this at all, in the really existing capitalist world? What conception of a truly human community can we plausibly come up with that we could aim to have instanti-

---

32. Adamson, "Gramsci and the Politics of Civil Society," 335-36.

ated and that could gain our reflective allegiance? Such a conception, if we can forge one, must not only be normatively warranted, it must as well be something that is feasible: that there could actually be such institutions, organizations, and practices in our world as distinct from their simply being something of which we dream—create in our philosophers' closets—for an ideal but unachievable world. When we are talking about such an unachievable world, the fact that we do this with elegance, rigor and adroit conceptualization matters very little. We are—if this is how we proceed—just playing little games. (Doing that is an old philosophical pastime.) The norms of a viable civil society must be justified and the conceptualized civil society must really be a civil society that could come to be in our world or at least in a near possible world that could actually come to be our own. But there is the rub, for I do not believe that a humanly viable civil society is on the historical agenda for at least the foreseeable future. Our societies are pretty rotten, to put it crudely and bluntly, but I think correctly, and I do not see much prospect for them being changed for the better.[33] I think Michel Foucault and Noam Chomsky, in their different ways, are nearer to the mark about the prospects for a just and humane world order than social democratic communitarians such as Charles Taylor and Michael Walzer or Habermasian neo-Marxists. I would, of course, very much like to be mistaken and perhaps I am too pessimistic, too derailed by the death of anything like

---

33. Indeed in many respects things seem to be getting worse. In the United States between 1977 and 1987 the real income of the poorest 20 percent of the population fell by 9 percent, while for the richest 5 percent the real income went up nearly 53 percent. Homelessness and child poverty increased. Among homeless children, once declining diseases like whooping cough and tuberculosis are becoming common again. The United States is strikingly bad in these respects but similar phenomena occur in the other rich capitalist countries. When we turn to the Third World, things get dramatically worse. Given the productive wealth of the world, these things are not necessary, but these things go right along without much in the way of an outcry. People seem, for the most part, to accept them like they accept the onset of winter. William Plowden, "Welfare in America," *London Review of Books* 13, no. 13 (July 11, 1991), 8. See Howard Karger and David Stoesz, *American Social Welfare Policy: A Structural Approach* (London: Longman, 1990) and Theodore Marmor, et al., *America's Misunderstood Welfare State* (New York: Basic Books, 1990). The best that we can hope for, is that because things are so rotten, so irrationally structured, that the capitalist societies will begin, with their citizens becoming increasingly disenchanted and disgusted, to collapse from within.

a Marxian utopian vision for a future society. I will close by giving some reasons for my pessimism while quite sincerely wishing to be shown that things are not as bleak as I am about to portray them.

VI.

There are a number of not so pessimistic, roughly social democratic moves that could be made here, including Habermasian ones and Rawlsian ones. I shall not consider the Habermasian and Rawlsian ones here. I shall, rather, consider only one such attempt to defend a conception of civil society for our time and a social democratic political culture: namely, the communitarian attempt. Sometimes, such an orientation, taking as it does some clues from Machiavelli, Montesquieu, and Tocqueville, has been called (more ambiguously I believe) the civic humanist tradition, defending in its contemporary forms republicanism, industrial democracy, and with the latter a kind of democratic socialism.

Such communitarian accounts, and Habermas's as well, seek to reinvigorate the public sphere, to make us conscious again of how politicized civil society is, to make it self-consciously and overtly politicized, and to render it a viable mediator between the private sphere and the corporate-bureaucratic state apparatus with its linked capitalist economic order (by now a world order). I choose to examine communitarian defenses of social democracy because they are more directly normative and political than the more procedurally based accounts we have in Habermas and Rawls. But any detailed examination of the rationale for social democracy and the role civil society plays in that would have to include them too. I leave that for another day.

What centrally sets communitarian social democrats apart from social democratic liberals such as Ronald Dworkin and John Rawls is that the latter pair believes that the state should be neutral between different conceptions of the good life espoused by individuals, while the former group believes that a good society, including a genuinely constitutional democracy, needs some commonly recognized, socially sanctioned, conception of the good life.[34] The

---

34. Ronald Dworkin: *A Matter of Principle* (Cambridge, MA: Harvard University Press, 1985), 181-233, and "Liberal Community," *California Law Review* 77, no. 3 (1989), 479-507. John Rawls: "Justice as Fairness: Political not Metaphysical," *Philosophy*

communitarians believe that without that there will be no viable community, including a political culture. Without such an authoritative conception of the good life there will not be the social cement to make us an *us* (a distinct people) and without such an *us* there will be no viable civil society.

What is needed in a good society (including, of course, a just society), communitarians argue, is an identification with others, in particular others in a determinate society or a cluster of closely related societies. The attachment needs to be to some particular community or cluster of communities (say, for a Dane the Scandinavian communities) and only secondarily, if at all, to some universal moral principle or set of moral principles, e.g., Stoic, Kantian or utilitarian principles. "Functioning republics are like families," Taylor remarks, "in this crucial respect, that part of what binds people together is their common history."[35] "Only when this obtains can there be a viable community, including a viable civil society. To have this is to have a common identification with an historical community founded on certain values."[36]

In the individualistic tradition—what Taylor misleadingly calls the atomistic tradition—of Hobbes, Locke, and Bentham, common institutional structures are conceived of as collective instruments: as things that have instrumental value only. The only good reason for having them is that we, as collections of individuals thrown together as we are, can attain benefits and avoid distresses that we

and Public Affairs 14, no. 3 (1983), 223-51; "The Idea of an Overlapping Consensus," *Oxford Journal of Legal Studies* 7, no. 1 (1987), 1-25; and "The Domain of the Political and Overlapping Consensus," *New York University Law Review* 64, no. 2 (1989), 233-55. For communitarians see Charles Taylor, "Cross-Purposes: The Liberal-Communitarian Debate," in N. Rosenblum, ed., *Liberalism and the Moral Life* (Cambridge, MA: Harvard University Press, 1989), 159-82; Charles Taylor, "The Nature and Scope of Distributive Justice," in Frank Lucash, ed., *Justice and Equality Here and Now* (Ithaca: Cornell University Press, 1986), 34-67; Michael Walzer, "The Communitarian Critique of Liberalism," *Political Theory* 18, no. 1 (1990), 6-23; Michael Walzer, "Justice Here and Now," in Frank Lucash, ed., *Justice and Equality Here and Now* (Ithaca: Cornell University Press, 1986), 135-50; and Michael Walzer, *Spheres of Justice* (Oxford: Basil Blackwell, 1983).

35. Taylor, "Cross-Purposes: The Liberal Communitarian Debate," 166. Taylor has a very naive and unrealistic picture of families as havens of trust and love.

36. Ibid., 178.

could not secure or escape individually. "The action," as Taylor puts it, "is collective but the point of it remains individual. The common good is constituted out of individual goods, without remainder."[37] This is the only kind of common good that such individualists acknowledge or in some instances can even make sense of. Indeed it is the only kind that their methodologies allow them to recognize. Taylor thinks these methodologies are fetters and that they are arbitrary and confused. He also believes, though he thinks the methodological fetters keep many from being self-conscious about this, that in reality (though sometimes unwittingly) people in such societies as ours (as in all societies) do have, at least in practice, a richer conception of the common good than that purely instrumental one, though admittedly some kinds of common good are just instrumental goods. But there are other kinds that are not. This richer conception of the good shows itself in the very way we talk and act and in some quite mundane and unproblematic practices. What should be obvious is obscured from us by the atomistic individualistic theories that are pervasive in our societies: theories that in reality are little better than distorting ideologies.

That we have a conception of the common good that is not just constituted out of our individual goods can be shown in the following way. We need to distinguish between I-identities and we-identities and "between matters which are for me and for you, on the one hand, and those which are for us, on the other."[38] Suppose one member of an academic department, namely myself, notes that it is raining and observes as well that a colleague is looking out the window and sees that it is raining. I see him, as he is about to go to the Faculty Club, go to his office and get his umbrella. I then say to him, "Lousy weather we are having. It's raining again," and he acknowledges that it is and we go on for a bit about how this year has been very unusual. Prior to that remark, I was attending to the weather and so was he, and I was also aware that he was attending to the weather. It was a matter for him and a matter for me but they were distinct matters. What, as Taylor puts it, "the conversation opener does is make it now a matter of us: we are now attending to it together". It is important to see that this "attending-together is

37. Ibid., 166.

38. Ibid., 167.

not reducible to an aggregation of attending separately."[39] Plainly, it involves something more than each of us noting the bad weather alone and just silently noting that the other notes it.

Now consider matters of genuine importance. When I talk about things that matter to me, those to whom I talk are my intimates. But it is important to note that intimacy "is essentially a dialogic phenomena: it is a matter of what we share, of what's for us."[40] The "move from the for-me-for-you to the for-us, the move into public space, is one of the important things we bring about in language and any theory of language has to take account of this."[41]

The same thing holds for goods. Some things, like health, have value to me and to you as well and to everyone individually. We can have health and value it individually but it is not essentially linked to an us. But there are some things that essentially have value for us. We cannot have them individually. Their being for us, and not just for you and just for me, enters into and constitutes their value for us. Friendship is a good example, as is intimacy. What "centrally matters for us is just that there are common actions and meanings."[42] The good in such contexts is what we share. We cannot have it alone. There is nothing there, as there is for goods like health or pleasure, which we could just have and of which our individual having would, just for us, quite alone as individuals, constitute a good. With friendship and intimacy we have a kind of good that is a common good, that is not just an instrumental good to individual havings. It is something we essentially have to have together if we are going to have it at all.

Taylor transfers this talk of such a common good to what he takes to be a similar political common good. In a good republic, a good polity, its citizens are animated by such a shared common good. Where there is a friendship between Jane and Janet, there is a shared common good. Similarly "the identification of a citizen with the republic, as a shared common enterprise, is essentially the recognition of a common good."[43] Compatriots in a functioning

---

39. Ibid.
40. Ibid., 168.
41. Ibid.
42. Ibid.
43. Ibid., 170.

republic have a bond of solidarity that "is based on a sense of shared fate, where the sharing itself is of value."[44] What the civic humanist tradition or communitarian social democracy seeks is a government and civil society that would instantiate that tradition: that would nurture and sustain or, if necessary, bring into being a political culture where the citizens of that community had that kind of solidarity, and where such common goods were acknowledged and prized. The political culture of such a republic would be one in which there would be a socially sanctioned conception of the common good and, as well, political liberty, namely, its being the case that all citizens will have a say in the decisions made in the political domain and in the sphere of civil society. And, with these democratic collective decisions, things they do as a people, they will shape their lives together. Everyone, where political liberty obtains, would have an equal say in how their common life together is to be ordered. There would, with such political liberty, be a sense that the political institutions and the institutions of civil society were expressions of themselves as citizens, as a people, and there would, as well, be an identification with the political community.[45] In sustaining political liberty, there would have to be a well-functioning public sphere where there would be debate and discussion, where the interchange would not principally, or perhaps even at all, be a matter of bargaining and compromise, but would be a genuine matter of citizens deliberating together, as we might as individuals deliberate with ourselves over what to do or seek or, with the same ends in view, deliberate in the private sphere with people with whom we are intimate. There would crucially in this public sphere be genuine citizen deliberation over the refinement, reconceptualization, the applications and implications of their shared conception of the common good. They would not bargain but instead morally deliberate together about it. There would, linked with that, be a participating in self-government and in such a situation the common actions of a free citizenry would be animated by common identifications.

Every political society, despotic or democratic, requires some sacrifices and restraints and demands some discipline from its citi-

---

44. Ibid.

45. Ibid., 165, 170.

zens. Citizens have to pay taxes, serve in the armed forces, do jury duty, pick up after their dogs, and the like. In a despotic society these sacrifices, restraints, and disciplines are obtained by coercion or the threat of coercion. In a free society, where there is citizen dignity, these disciplines are willingly accepted as the doing of one's share in maintaining the commonwealth. It isn't that we like doing them—most of us do not—but that we realize we have a duty to shoulder our fair share of the burdens, where what is to count as a fair share has in turn been subject to democratic discussion and decision in a genuine public sphere. Where, that is, there is dispute about what these sacrifices and restraints should be, and how we should respond to them, this will be deliberated over and decided on by a free citizenry reasoning and deciding together. What is done, what is mandated, is what is freely consented to after free and fair deliberation, approximating, as much as possible, conditions of undistorted discourse and carried out in a public sphere.

Such a democratic regime calls on its members to do things that mere subjects would avoid and, in that way, by requiring service in public life, it is more onerous and demanding than in despotic or managed regimes whose citizens are treated as mere subjects; but, though it is more onerous, citizens in a genuine republic will have control over their own lives, have reasons for being loyal and not merely obedient to the regime and will have reasons, as well, for identifying with their state. In being such (if indeed it could be that) the state would be an ethical state. Hegel's conception is not conceptually incoherent.

This civic humanism is indeed an attractive *picture*, but it seems to me to be in fact only that. It is as unrealistic and unworldly as the classical normative theories of democracy. Just think how far we are from having anything like this public sphere and of what it would be like to achieve it in mass societies such as our own. The very idea of getting from here to there is staggering. We haven't any good sense of what would be an effective means here. Whether this civic humanism takes the communitarian form described above or a more Habermasian form, it is unrealistic, given contemporary, large-scale, bureaucratically organized and inegalitarian societies— inegalitarian in almost all spheres—but particularly deeply inegalitarian and hurtful about the distribution of power; power being in the hands of a few.[46] But this is the reality of our societies.

Such civic humanism is in a bad sense utopian, taking us away from the grim realities of political life, realities it is urgent to attend to if we are ever to have decent societies. What might have worked in a small scale, face-to-face, society is utterly unworkable in large-scale societies such as our own. Perhaps it would work in Iceland but never in Germany, the United States, or Canada. It is unworkable not because we are ideologically blinded by ontological theses about atomistic individualism but because of (a) the inescapability of powerful and dominating bureaucracies (both state and capitalist) and (b) the plain and inescapable fact—a fact stressed by John Rawls—of the extensive and entrenched *de facto* pluralism of our societies.[47] Our societies have a rich variety, and not always a har-

---

46. See Kai Nielson, *Equality and Liberty: A Defense of Radical Egalitarianism* (Totowa, NJ: Rowman and Allanheld, 1985), and Richard Norman, *Free and Equal* (Oxford: Oxford University Press, 1986). Michael Walzer perhaps does not stress this as much as he might. Commonly liberals ignore it or downplay it. However, Walzer does rightly remark: ". . . it is a false view of civil society, a bad sociology, to claim that all that goes on in the marketplace is free exchange and that coercion is never an issue here. Market success overrides the limits of the (free) market in three closely related ways. First of all, radical inequalities of wealth generate their own coerciveness, so that many exchanges are only formally free. Second, certain sorts of market power, organized, say, in corporate structures, generate patterns of command and obedience in which the formalities of exchange give way to something that looks very much like government. And third, vast wealth and ownership or control of productive forces convert readily into government in the strict sense: capital regularly and successfully calls upon the coercive power of the state." Walzer, "Liberalism and the Art of Separation," 321-22. But Milton Friedman's dreams to the contrary notwithstanding, this is the name of the game for really existing capitalisms, even capitalisms with a human face such as Sweden's. What the liberal needs to tell us is how capitalist societies of any complexity can be reformed so that that will no longer be the case. It seems to me that a necessary condition for that ceasing to be the case is the public ownership and control of the means of production. But that is socialism. It baffles me why committed socialists such as Jürgen Habermas no longer see things in these terms.

47. John Rawls, "Justice as Fairness: Political not Metaphysical," 223-52. See also Kai Nielson, "Rawls and the Socratic Ideal," *Analyse & Kritik* (Fall 1991) and Kai Nielson, "Philosophy within the Limits of Wide Reflective Equilibrium Alone," *Iyyun, The Jerusalem Philosophical Quarterly*, Vol. 43 (Juli/Vol. 13, 67-93, 1994) 3-41. For some cautionary notes, not as distant from Rawls as he seems to believe,

monious variety, of people with different ethnic backgrounds, religious identifications, moral outlooks, political orientations, class positions, and the like. There is not much reality to the melting pot or the vertical mosaic metaphors of the United States and Canada respectively. There is no chance at all that in such societies—that is, in our societies—that there will be anything like a consensus about a conception of a common good. One could perhaps, just perhaps, be imposed by a despotic or authoritarian state (though even that is rather doubtful), but one would not be accepted as part of what constitutes the citizens' moral point of view, even by an active citizenry—even if, counterfactually, we could galvanize citizens of such societies into participation. (Günther Grass was appropriately and effectively ironical about such participation.) Furthermore, when we consider citizens' feelings about their society, what we need to note is that very widely there is no such sense of loyalty, there is no such identification with contemporary governments even in the constitutional democracies, there is no such actual public sphere in which to exercise such republican virtues and there is little likelihood that such institutions are coming into being. Philosophers can deliberate about what the common good of their society is or over whether there is such a good or should be. With some groups of philosophers, it just might be possible to secure, after much deliberation, a conception that was recognized for a short period of time by these philosophers to be nearer to the mark than others, but even if, as is very unlikely, there could be a kind of local philosophical consensus here there still would be no chance at all of there being a general consensus across the society of the various people that inhabit those societies. Pluralism, for the foreseeable future, is just an inescapable social fact in societies such as ours. Whether it is or isn't a desirable thing is quite another matter; desirable or undesirable, we will have to live with it.

That, in the United States, some citizens responded with outrage to the Vietnam War, to Watergate, to the Iran-Contra affair, perhaps shows there are some residues among some citizens of a concern about republican virtues, some rather attenuated sense of citizen dignity, of what it is for a country to behave honorably, but

about the power of philosophy, see Michael Walzer, "Flight from Philosophy," *The New York Review of Books* (Feb 2, 1989), 42-43.

the evidence that there is a commitment to anything like civic humanism is rather slim, given the quiescence over the Persian Gulf affair and over the not infrequent American military interventions in the world, over the racism of American society coupled with the indifference to widespread poverty and in other ways extensive inequalities in the society. That the sight of the homeless evokes anger directed at the homeless and not at the society that allows this is symptomatic of the sickness of our societies. There is very little civic humanism in our societies and there is nothing to be patriotic about.

If to such considerations we add facts about voter turnouts and additional facts about the number of corrupt or incompetent politicians that get elected and re-elected, we seem at least to have rather strong disconfirming evidence concerning the existence of anything like the polity that Taylor and other social democratic communitarians regard as existent. The ship of state isn't what the communitarians take it to be. It is a nice ideal but ideals need to be tied to the real world. We need something more than pretty dreams. Moreover, to put the point directly normatively, why should one have any loyalty, patriotic commitment, or identification with such regimes? Obedience can be, and is, achieved out of fear, prudence, a recognition that there are no better alternatives around, and from a bitter recognition that the Marxian utopian visions of society are just that: at least supposedly unfeasible utopian visions that show no prospect of being realized or even approximated in a form that would yield human emancipation.[48] But the tradition of civic

---

48. I do not mean to give to understand that I think there is anything drastically wrong or in a bad sense utopian about sophisticated forms of Marxian theory either in their weak historical materialism, class analysis, more generally in their political sociology, or (in some cases) in their understanding of the role of moral notions in social life. On the contrary, these accounts seem to me realistic and reasonable. Indeed, seeing Marxian theory, principally through the work of analytical Marxians, as a developing theory being repeatedly refined, it seems to me that that account, though of course flawed (what account isn't?), is the best account we have to date of large-scale social phenomena. My point is rather that, given the political realities of the past few years, there will be no audience, at least for a time, for the case for socialism, no matter how well it is articulated and defended. That is unfortunate, but that is the way it is. The world has turned, but it can turn again in ways that are not so uncongenial to the possiblity of worker self-emancipation. Tough-minded idealists can hardly fail to be pessimistic, the way things stand. But that need not be crippling either for thought or struggle. See here G.A. Cohen, "The

humanism is every bit as much an unfeasible utopian vision. It is a conception of a political culture that could have no instantiation in our complex societies, and it does not bring with it a civil society that is much of a bulwark against the economic order or a state that is anything but the realization of an ethical ideal.

Future of a Disillusion, " in Jim Hopkins and Anthony Savile: *Psychoanalysis, Mind and Art: Perspectives on Richard Wollheim*, (Oxford: Blackwell's, 1992), 147-160.

5. Civil Society, Hard Cases and the End of the Cold War

Tracy B. Strong

The passage that Michael Walzer quoted from *The German Ideology* continues on from "doing just as one wishes to, hunting in the morning, fishing in the afternoon, and criticizing after dinner" by indicating that one will be able to undertake these activities "without ever thereby becoming a hunter, a fisherman, or a critical critic." I mention this not to critique Walzer but to extend what I take to be one possible thrust of his comments. I take Marx's continuation in this passage to be an expression of anxiety on Marx's part. The danger with what one might call civil society, for Marx, is that one might become something fixed, a hunter, a critic and so forth. So the question latent in this passage is what one loses when one becomes a social category. I suppose that the answer to that, and a potential threat of a focus on civil society, is that one might stop being a human being. (Here we might hear echoes of Aristotle in Marx: if politics is the realm of the human for Aristotle, then civil society is lacking something of that quality. Perhaps this is not too high a price to pay).

I take the interest in civil society, therefore, to be an interest in a form of life in which one constantly has to keep refusing or pushing back or resisting the temptation it offers to become an "X," to fix one's identity.

Let me express this a different way. An attraction of civil society is that it is the realm in which the first person singular ("I am ..." statements) tend to correspond to and to evoke at least a limited version of first person plural statements ("We are …"). One of the attractions of civil society is that it naturally overcomes the anomie latent in liberalism.

What one must do is to keep the two from fusing, keep the "I" from being identical with the "we."

From this it seems to me that the question of the relation between communitarianism and liberalism is best formulated not as oppositions to each other (in the way that Michael Sandel wants to), but as the existence of various lines of tension that come down to us from the multiplicity that we have called "the enlightenment project." Whether or not the "enlightenment project" has or is coming to an end, like Nietzsche's dead God, its shadows will be with us for some while to come, and we had better deal with it.

I take the enlightenment project to rest on two intuitive premises. The first of these is that of the separateness and distinctness of individuals, one from another. This does not have to imply that I am completely other than you, only that I am I and you are you. One of the consequences of this premise, incidentally, is the ultimate insufficiency of utilitarianism as a moral doctrine. Utilitarianism assumes that in the end my difference from you is not fundamental: my pains and pleasures and yours can be added together—they are of the same nature.

The second intuitive premise of the enlightenment project I take to be the notion that these differences are, in and of themselves, never morally adequate reasons for the domination of one person over another. That has to be worked out in a particular given historical community.

Let us call the first of these the "separateness principle" and the second the "togetherness principle." Now these two premises, both of which I think true, are in a certain kind of tension with each other. Libertarians such as Robert Nozick suggest that we deserve our particular qualities, the accidents that make us up and make us separate, and that we are entitled to them. And he builds an impressive theory on that.

Communitarians, such as Michael Sandel, Charles Taylor, and some of these present in this collection, suggest that the particular qualities that we have are, in fact, the sign of our embeddedness in a particular historical social group and that we are, therefore, also entitled to them.

Notice that both of these positions derive from emphasizing one part of what I have understood the enlightenment project to be. I would like to suggest now that the maintenance of the enlightenment project, as we turn to civil society, requires that we maintain a tension between these two intuitive premises. This tension will keep people from completely identifying their person with either their separateness or their togetherness. To give up the tension for one or the other pole is to yield to totality. It is the resistance to totalization that seems to me the necessary precondition for the existence of civil society.

How might we then maintain this tension? One answer that has been given to this, the liberal answer, is to suggest that there exists or can exist a realm of political discourse in which only certain limited types of behavior and types of language and discourse are appropriate. One could pursue this most fully, I suppose, in the work of Rawls.

Another answer is to suggest in fact that the political realm, which is different from the realm of public discourse (though not unrelated to it, at least in democratic states) can be the regulator of the tension and can ensure that one never succumbs to the temptation to merge the "I" and the "we" in one or another of the ways—economics, nationalism, and so forth—that we are constantly tempted with.

Now, both of those answers, the liberal public discourse realm and the Walzerian vision of a democratic political realm, seem to me to have very strong claims on us. In the name of perhaps extending our notion of civil society, I want to try to add here a third way of looking at this.

How can we maintain this tension of difference and togetherness, a tension that I have suggested is necessary to the notion of civil society and the preservation of which is necessary if we want to retain any idea or viable idea of society? How do we retain both the "I" and the "we" in the tension? I would suggest the answer is clearly not by invoking one form or another of tradition. For one thing,

there is no such thing as "the tradition." I can think of at least four
or five things that would count as traditions in this society. And
somehow the answer can't be to reassert traditional values of one
kind or another. The question then becomes which traditions one
makes viable or available to oneself.

A different, and I think more interesting way to approach this,
is to suggest that we should look for the politics that might maintain
and make possible a civil society precisely in the areas that do *not*
permit resolution or consensus. A number of the chapters herein
are about integrating fragmented societies, about integrating the
various portions of our increasingly disjointed life. While this cor-
responds to desires that one understands, it seems to me that this
focus is a mistake. It is precisely in the realms that are essentially
contestable, that is, in the realms where there is no final correct
answer, that we will find the kinds of politics that will make possible
the maintenance of this ambiguity or tension that I am suggesting
is the basis of any viable understanding of civil society.

To overdramatize this a bit, we should seek out the hard cases,
cases for which there is no consensual public discourse. Where or
what would be the dramas that would afford us this kind of arena?

I might say: where do we find our Antigones? Such drama was
after all the stuff of political and civic education in classical Greece.
And I might start out, to continue that thought for a minute, by
rejecting the claim of many liberals—including Isaiah Berlin, who
has been invoked here several times—to the effect that the fundamental characteristic of our life is that we live in a world of irre-
solvable moral claims, that we're all constantly facing incompatible
claims. That may be true, but most of us ignore most of them most
of the time. Liberals make this claim most often not to confront it,
but to pass it by.

When I say seek out hard cases, when I seek out problems that
do not have answers, it strikes me that it is in realms like abortion
in this country, like ecology in Germany, where we will find the
kind of political dynamics that might eventually produce the kind
of persons who are capable of living in the kind of civil society that
I or Michael Walzer would want.

There appears to be no single good resolution of the abortion question.* And it seems to me that the beginning of wisdom in the pursuit of civil society is to recognize that it is those areas in which we cannot resolve disputes, where anything we want to conclude, at least in a final manner, will be wrong, that we find the best opportunity for seeking out some kind of new beginning.

I have looked to the domestic political scene for immediate examples of these hard cases or realms of essential contestability. Additional interesting questions for our purpose would be found in the realm of international politics. I am astonished, for instance, that the question has not been raised as to whether or not there is a difference in the import of the end of the Cold War for the United States as opposed to Europe. Does the end of what we call the Cold War, or what we call the end of what we call the Cold War, make a different difference for the United States than it does for Europe? My intuition is that it does. But what that difference is, I'm not entirely clear. And it seems to me an object that we need to pursue.

About seven or eight years ago, Georgi Arbatov made a speech in this country in which he announced to an American audience, "We are going to do a terrible thing to you. We are going to take away your enemy." If it is true that the quality of the resolutions offered to the problems of American civil society has for forty years depended upon the existence of an enemy, with all that that has entailed, what are the consequences of taking this away? What difference is it going to make for our economic life, for our trade meetings, for our industry, for our religions, and so forth?

I know a little of what we lost when the Cold War started. Immediately after World War II, for instance, the United Automobile Workers began a series of negotiations with General Motors and the automobile industry in which they, at that point, refused to rule anything out of the sphere of collective bargaining, including what products should be made, what profit ratio there should be, who

---

* The most interesting thing about the women's movement in relation to abortion is the way in which it has slowly resolved itself into the question of whether women have the right to make up their own moral minds about what they're going to do. And if that is the way the whole argument comes out, then another group of people will have been collectively recognized as participants in forms that have taken a great deal of struggle to achieve.

should make decisions about production, who should make decisions about profits, and so forth. Not just wages and working conditions were up for discussion, but everything. Within two years, whatever had impelled the UAW and other unions I might mention to make those kinds of claims had completely disappeared from the American political scene.

I don't know whether such political dynamics are recoverable. I don't know whether they are still part of our tradition. But it certainly was part of whatever the traditions there were in American life by the end of the Second World War.

This leads me paradoxically to say, or to hope, that the possibilities for the left are actually greater now, or at least more open now, in the United States than they may be in Europe precisely because, in some sense, our stage, our arena has been opened so much more widely by the end of the Cold War than has, I suspect, the European.

Part II

THE COMMUNITARIAN APPROACH

6. In Common Together: Unity, Diversity, and Civic Virtue

Jean Bethke Elshtain

The question of the one and the many, of unity and diversity, has been posed since the beginning of political thought in the West. The American Founders were well aware of the vexations attendant upon the creation of a new political body. They worked with, and against, a stock of metaphors that had previously served as the symbolic vehicles of political incorporation. As men of the Enlightenment, they rejected the images of the body politic that had dominated medieval and early modern political thinking. For a Jefferson or a Madison such tropes as "the King's two bodies" or John of Salisbury's twelfth century rendering, in his *Policraticus*, of a body politic with the Prince as the head and animating force of other members, were too literalist, too strongly corporatist, and too specifically Christian, to serve the novus ordo saeclorum. But they were nonetheless haunted by Hebrew and Christian metaphors of a covenanted polity: the body is one but has many members. There is, there can be, unity with diversity.

Indeed, one could even go so far as to insist that it is incorporation, enfolding, within a single body that makes meaningful diversity possible. Our differences must be recognized if they are to exist substantively at all. We cannot be "different" all by ourselves. A political body that simultaneously brings persons together, creating a "we," but enables these same persons to separate themselves and to recognize one another in and through their differences as well as in what they share in common—that was the great challenge. If debates in recent years between the individualist and communitarian positions, as these have been tagged, are any indication, the problems generated by the need for unity that goes beyond mere "law and order," as well as the quest for diversity that goes beyond mere "tolerance," has become ever more acute. There is, then, an unresolved tension embedded in our history and our primary documents between individual rights and immunities and the vision of "we the people."

This ambiguity is inherent in American political culture and has persisted since the time of the founding. It is an ambiguity encoded in the Constitution and the Bill of Rights, in a simultaneous commitment to a "we" and to protection of the "one," and it is at one and the same time a source of strength and a cause for concern. Current individualist and communitarian debates are not, therefore, engagements between traditionalists and anti-traditionalists, or liberals and restorationists. Rather, the intensity of, and interest in, this discussion is best understood as a contestation over the appropriation of tradition itself.[1] The Founders were Enlightenment figures who rejected traditions embodied in monarchical absolutism, but they also thought in some very traditional ways: natural law and natural right were not their invention. Preoccupied from time to time with classical republican precedents, the Federalists and anti-Federalists struggled with a general fund of ideas, a repertoire of stock concerns and understandings, much as contemporary interlocutors do.

Modern American political culture is neither an a la carte menu nor a fixed dinner. No one among us could participate in all the possibilities contemporary culture spreads before each human subject. Neither is it really workable to be so totally immersed in one fixed mode that no alternative to this conception, this belief, this way of doing things ever presents itself. Traditions exist; they are never created de novo. To "think" a tradition is to bring matters to the surface, to engage in debate with interlocutors long dead or protagonists who never lived save on the page and, through that engagement, to elaborate alternative conceptions through which to

---

1. See, for example, Stephen Holmes' ill-tempered attack, "The Community Trap," *The New Republic*, (Nov. 28, 1988, 24-29). Holmes charges the communitarians with reviling the tradition of freedom.

apprehend one's political culture and the way that culture represents itself or is represented. The meaning and rationale of the most basic things about us—we the people—as well as each one of us taken singly is at stake.

Thus Robert Bellah argues for a vision of community that opposes both radical individualism, on the one hand, and a flattened-out, homogenous union that obliterates differences, on the other. Michael Walzer reminds us that much of the strength of our tradition is its protesting, separating, even privatizing tendency, with the Bill of Rights the touchstone of this robust individuating dynamic. We look to a second prong, our "federal" or constitutional tradition, to help to create and to revitalize associative life, a process subject to a number of pitfalls. Specifically, according to Walzer, despite "its anticipation of collective action, the Constitution has turned out to favor something else, nicely summed up in the twentieth-century maxim about doing your own thing.[2] In this essay I begin by building on Bellah's and Walzer's insights, but from a somewhat different angle of vision. I go on to offer reflections on an epoch in our history, the Progressive Era, which was the point at which a rather loose, federated union moved in the direction of building and justifying the need for a powerful, centralized, bureaucratic order. That, in turn, helps to set the stage for my turn to two evolving traditions—Catholic social thought and the democratic theorizing of civil society emerging from Central Eastern Europe—as sources of insight and strength for American political thinkers who, with me, have grown weary of the stark alternatives, individualism versus collectivism, or choice versus constraint, choices all too often presented to us when the philosophic debate over tradition takes actual shape in our political rhetoric and public policy alternatives.

A preliminary discussion is needed to frame the horizon for my consideration of the ways in which the quest for national unity under the auspices of the state has, over time, exercised a corrosive effect on America's regional and localist images of community and, as well, on a once deeply and widely shared, religiously grounded concept of the human person, the "exalted individual," in the

---

2. See Michael Walzer's analysis in this volume. Please note that a version of my own essay appeared originally in Robert Calvert, ed., *The Constitution of the People* (Lawrence, Ks.: University of Kansas Press, 1993.)

words of political theorist Glenn Tinder. Tinder has argued that the idea of an individual whose ontological dignity is such that he or she deserves "attention" and is not to be "grossly violated" is fundamental to the Christian standpoint, which is constitutive of our political institutions and culture at its best. Were the horizons of our political life to cease being framed in this way, that is, through an insistence that the destiny of each and every individual matters, that life would become what it now is only in part, "an affair of expediency and self interest."[3] Communitarians focus on civil society, "the many forms of community and association that are not political in form: families, neighborhoods, voluntary associations of innumerable kinds, labor unions, small businesses, giant corporations, and religious communities."[4] Some may cavil at the notion that such associations are not "political," but theorists of civil society would insist, in response, that this network and the many ways we are nested within it lie outside the formal structure of state power. Walzer claims that the Bill of Rights aimed specifically to promote and to protect such associative group rights, not merely or solely individual immunities or entitlements. There is no sharp dichotomy between state and society in this understanding; rather, a complex dialectic pertains, or ideally ought to pertain, between the two. State and society are intimately intertwined—at least this is the assumption that guides the most thoughtful constructions of that relationship.

By contrast, the statist, one whose thoughts and hope culminate in and are designated by a powerful centralizing apparatus, wants to thin out the ties of civil society and the plural loyalties and diverse imperatives they give rise to and sustain. State-dominated ieology identifies us primarily as beings available for mobilization by a powerful centralized mechanism, rather than as friends, families, neighbors, members of the social club or a feminist health cooperative, activists trying to save the African elephant from extinction, participants in a reading group, Baptists, and so on. Statist politicians and

---

3. Glenn Tinder, "Can We Be Good Without God?," *The Atlantic Monthly*, (December, 1989, 69-85), 76.

4. David Hollenbach, S.J., "Liberalism, Communitarianism, and the Bishops' Pastoral Letter on the Economy," *The Annual of the Society of Christian Ethics*, ed. D.M. Yeager (1987, 19-53,) 18.

philosophies often design programs and policies aimed at destroying alternative loyalties and the many identities they provide.

Civil society, by contrast, is a realm that is neither relentlessly individualist nor collectivist. It is a movement to construct a good in common that we cannot know alone, a possibility that our associative relationships as well as our identity as citizens makes possible. It is a world evoked, at points, by the anti-Federalists in debates over the ratification of the United States Constitution. From time to time, anti-Federalists no doubt pushed an idealized image of a self-contained and self-reliant republic that shunned imperial power and worked, instead, to create a polity modeled, in part, on classical principles of civic virtue and a common good. Writes a historian of this argument: "Anti-federalists saw mild, grass-roots, small-scale governments in sharp contrast to the splendid edifice and ambition implicit in the new Constitution—and, indeed, heralded by Publius and its other proponents. The first left citizens free to live their own lives and to cultivate the virtue (private and public) vital to republicanism, while the second soon entailed taxes and drafts and offices and wars damaging to human dignity and thus fatal to self government."[5] Despite the often roseate hue with which anti-Federalists surrounded their arguments, they were onto something, as we like to say. They hoped to avoid, even to break, a cycle later elaborated by Alexis de Tocqueville in which highly self-interested individualists, disarticulated from the constraints and nurture of overlapping associations of social life, require more and more checks, balances and controls from above in order that the disintegrative effects of untrammeled individualism be at least somewhat muted in practice.

To this end, the peripheries must remain vital; political spaces other than or beneath (it is almost impossible not to deploy spatial metaphors as a kind of lexicon of power-talk) those of the state need to be cherished, nourished, kept vibrant. They had in mind local councils and committees and they had in mind to avoid concentrations of power at the core or "on the top." Too much centralized power was as bad as no power at all. Only small-scale civitates would enable individuals, as citizens, to cultivate authentic

---

5. See Ralph Ketcham, ed., *The Anti-Federalist Papers and the Constitutional Convention Debates* (New York: 1986) 18.

civic virtue. For such virtue turns on meaningful participation in a powerful ideal of community. Too much power exercised at a level beyond that which permits, indeed demands, active citizen participation is destructive of civic dignity and, finally, fatal to any authentic understanding of democratic self-government. Anti-Federalist fears of centralized and over-nationalized power presaged Tocqueville's later worry that imperial greatness bought through force of arms is "pleasing to the imagination of a democratic people" because it sends out lightning bolts of "vivid and sudden luster, obtained without toil, by nothing but the risk of life."[6]

Communitarians think about a dilemma articulated by Tocqueville in his classic work, *Democracy in America.* Tocqueville worried that even as the reality of American democracy freed individuals from the constraints of older, undemocratic structures and obligations, individualism and privatization were also unleashed. Tocqueville's fear was not that this invites anarchy; rather, he believed that the individualism of an acquisitive commercial republic, especially one bent on a course of empire, would engender new forms of social and political domination. All social webs having disintegrated, the individual would find himself or herself isolated, exposed and unprotected. Into this power vacuum would move the organized force of a top-heavy, centralized state. This Tocquevillian anxiety has spurred thinkers in the communitarian tradition to score American individualism and to urge upon us a more communal ethic. My worry is that critics of excessive, atomistic and acquisitive individualism often do not distinguish carefully enough between the phenomenon grasped in the 1980s slogan, "greed is good," and the strengths of our tradition of individuality, of respect for the human person, taken as single, unique, an irreplaceable self.

I ask the reader to return with me, for just a moment, to the Greeks, to that classical world dominated by the ideal of the city-state, the polis. One sees a world in which war is construed as the natural state of mankind and an imperious source of communal loyalty and purpose. The Greek city-state was a community of warriors whose political rights were determined by the fundamental privilege of the soldier to decide his own fate, to choose death

---

6. Alexis de Tocqueville, *Democracy in America*, Vol. 2 (New York: 1945), 293.

nobly. There was a direct line of descent from the Homeric warrior assemblies to Athenian naval democracy. The franchise was restricted to those who bore arms—hence the exclusion of women. One reigning definition of justice, repeated by Thrasymachus in his sparring with Socrates in the first book of Plato's Republic, was "the interest of the stronger." The Greek citizen army was an expression of the Greek polis, its creation one of the chief concerns and consequences of the formation of the city-state. In Sparta, the army organized into mess groups was substituted for the family as the basic element of the state. Another custom of the male group, homosexuality, was developed and institutionalized, most systematically at Thebes in the fourth century, to create a aacred band of fraternal lovers fighting side by side. Such institutions served to insure that fellowship was deemed a prerequisite of disciplined courage in war, of the willingness to risk death together.

The human body in Greek, then Roman, antiquity was wholly conscripted into society, an insight I owe to the great historian of late antiquity, Peter Brown. His is an important point. His argument in many books, including *The Body and Society*, is as follows:[7] The pre-Christianized individual was not free to withhold his or her body from conscription into the extant social order. One could with Socrates endorse withdrawal of the soul from the body but one could not take oneself out of the group—one could not constitute one's body as a protest against its conscription into the social body in the form of warrior, slave, or householder. The classical view is that the city-state should have complete control of human bodies for the purposes of labor, procreation, and war.

The body, hence the self, existed at the behest of the wider social order. St. Augustine argues that Rome perfected the regime of *cupiditas* run rampant, the triumph of the lust to dominate. The distinctive mark of Roman life as a *civitas terrena*, a city of man, was greed and lust for possession, which presumed a right of exploitation. This became a foundation for human relationships, warping and perverting personality, marriage, the family, all things. Augustine writes: "For he who desires the glory of possession would feel that

---

7. Peter Brown, *The Body and Society: Men, Women and Sexual Renunciation in Early Christianity* (New York: 1988).

his power were diminished, if he were obliged to share it with any living associate ... he cherishes his own manhood."[8]

The political importance of Christianity, one marked by an impressive array of analysts, critics, and political theorists (including Sheldon Wolin, Michael Walzer, Robert Bellah, Gilbert Meilaender and many others) is that Christians created a new vision of community, one that sanctioned both each life as well as everyday life, especially the lives of society's victims, and granted each member a new-found dignity. The warrior politics of the ancient world found itself put on trial. Writes Tinder: "No one, then, belongs at the bottom, enslaved, irremediably poor, consigned to silence; this is equality. This points to another standard: that no one should be left outside, an alien and a barbarian."[9]

Christianity introduced a strong principle of universalism into the ancient world even as it proclaimed a vision of the "exalted individual," brought into being by a loving creator—not, therefore, the mere creature of any government, any polis, any empire. Although early Christians saw themselves as a very particular community, theirs was a community open in principle to all. Had not St. Paul proclaimed that in Christ there is neither Jew nor Greek, free nor slave, male nor female? As early as Monica's death in 387 A.D., (Monica, of course, is St. Augustine's indefatigable mother), Christian universalism had taken strong hold. As Monica approached her death on foreign soil, far away from her city, Carthage, she renounced a "vain desire" to be buried in that soil next to her husband. She was not frightened at leaving her body so far from her own country, for "Nothing is far from God—he knows where to find me."[10] Augustine himself declares in *The City of God* that a person's body "belongs to his very nature," and is no "mere adornment, or external convenience."[11] Thus, human beings were not instruments to be put to a civic purpose over which they had no say; rather, persons qua persons "deserve attention." There is a minimum standard of care and concern for every person who "has been immeasurably

---

8. St. Augustine, *The City of God* (Baltimore: 1972).

9. Tinder, "Can We Be Good Without God?" 72.

10. St. Augustine, *The Confessions* (Baltimore: 1961), 199-200.

11. *The City of God*, Book I, 13, p. 22.

dignified." To be sure, as Tinder almost wearily suggests, this ideal is often "forgotten and betrayed" but "were it erased from our minds, our politics would probably become altogether what it is at present only in part—an affair of expediency and self-interest."[12]

The heady drama of this moral revolution in the ancient world is a story that has lost none of its excitement or importance. The legitimacy once accorded automatically to the claims of the city-state and the empire upon the human body of each and every one now had to make its case and could not be assumed unproblematically. The human body could withdraw from the demands placed upon it by society. The sexual-social contract could be broken. Freedom of the will could be brought to bear on the body itself as a tangible locus, a sign, of a newfound relation of the self to the social world. An elemental freedom was endorsed. Liberated individuals formed communities to validate their new-found individualities and to shore up the transformed, symbolically charged good represented by the new social body: the body is one but has many members.

It is important to be clear about the nature of this freedom. The body was not exempt from a self-imposed discipline. To be a member of the faithful, one embraced this discipline as one's own. The aim was to be "truly alive," to slough off the "deadness" of abuse of the body through an ontology of lust and domination. The human will—and the concept of "will" is unknown before Christianity, most importantly St. Augustine—freely imposed a discipline on itself as a visible sign, a semiotics, of freedom: freedom from the abuses of one's time; freedom for involvement in an alternative construction of self in community.[13] For Christian thinkers, as Hannah Arendt observes, "Free Choice of the Will" was a "faculty distinct from desire and reason" and Augustine is "the great and original thinker" who posited two active principles, willing and nilling, as constitutive of the "faculty of Choice, so decisive for the liberum arbitrium ... to the choice between velle and nolle, between willing and nilling."[14]

---

12. Ibid., 76.

13. See, for example, Margaret Miles, *Fullness of Life* (Philadelphia: 1981); on bodily discipline and practices of the self see Michel Foucault, *The Use of Pleasure* (New York: 1985).

14. Hannah Arendt, *The Life of the Mind*, Vol. 2. (New York: 1978), 88-89.

The Christian life was not primarily a solitary life, but a communal one. Nevertheless, the principle introduced by Christians is one in which persons are irreducibly individuals—but this individuality is exquisitely social. The person is neither absorbed totally into a communal order, having no identity outside its boundaries, nor is he or she defined wholly apart from the society of others. The Christian ideal of community not only departs radically from that of the classical city-state, it also challenges the revivification of this ideal of fraternal order in the civic republican tradition associated most importantly with Machiavelli and Rousseau. Rousseau scorns any particular interest that might block the general will. He lambastes Christianity as a notion wholly at odds with that of "republic." For the polity must be as one; the national will must not be divided; citizens must be prepared to defend civic autonomy through force of arms; whatever puts the individual at odds with himself is a threat to "la nation une et indivisible." I call this version of the republican ideal one of "armed civic virtue," for the human virtues are given a strong civic description and culminate in bearing arms for the republic. Although never embraced in any full-blown form in the United States, in part because of the breaks to its attainment encoded in the Bill of Rights, enlivened in Tocquevillian associations, and enshrined in Christian ideals of individuality and sociality, we have flirted with and even witnessed moments of "armed civic virtue" extolled as an ideal of a community coterminous with a great nation-state unified and speaking with one voice.

Now join me on the shores of the New Land. The founders have done their work. Federalist arguments have won the day though anti-Federalist fears simmer just beneath the surface of things. By the nineteenth century, the Christian ideal of the exalted self has taken on a solitary profile in the thoughts and writing of such important celebrants of individual freedom as Thoreau, Emerson, Anne Hutchinson, and others. In contrast to the strong Puritan ideal of a commonwealth, this refurbished American self stands out more and more in bold relief against a showy and less and less distinctive social background. Philip Abbott has elaborated the peculiarly American ideal of "perfect freedom," the freedom of a self apart from community rather than not-wholly-dominated-and-defined-by an overarching civic body. Americans began to revel in the celebration of an ahistorical privileging of personal experience, whether political, social, or sexual, a celebration that involved a highly evolved, romantic "reading" of both the Lockean and Christian traditions.[15]

This mirror of freedom is held up beautifully, even chillingly, in an essay by the great Elizabeth Cady Stanton called "The Solitude of Self." In common with many American thinkers and activists, Cady Stanton embraced a bewildering smorgasbord of different civic and personal philosophies—liberal, republican, utopian, scientific, and nativist—throughout her long life. As with many Americans of her epoch, she praised the free market yet longed for a community of like-minded souls. She is thus both a representative figure and, as one of the movers and shakers of early feminism and the suffrage movement, an exceptional one. As a representative, even quintessential American thinker of her time, she did not break new intellectual ground, nor did she articulate a coherent system of thought that launched new fields of inquiry or altered the way human beings see their world. She is, however, justifiably regarded as a feminist philosopher whose work embodies an eclectic synthesis and often uncritical embrace of philosophies of individualism and social harmony, laissez faire and social cooperation.

But when she got down to brass tacks philosophically, Stanton embraced an ideal of almost perfect freedom, framed from the standpoint of a self she declares sovereign. She—correctly in my view—locates this ideal in "the great doctrine of Christianity," namely, "the right of individual conscience and judgement." You will not find an ideal of the sovereign self in "the Roman idea ... that the individual was made for the State."[16] As a vision of the self alone, hers is a very selective appropriation of "the great doctrine of Christianity." One could, of course, line her up against other Christian thinkers—particularly those in the social gospel tradition—in order to chasten her robust, romantic embrace of the soul alone. But that is beside the point for my purposes. I call upon Stanton as one of the foremothers of contemporary individualism, particularly in its expressivist variation.

---

15. See Philip Abbott, *States of Perfect Freedom* (Amherst: 1987).

16. This and the previous citation are from Stanton's autobiography, *Eighty Years and More* (New York: 1971), 231.

The individual is preeminent, first and foremost, Stanton argues, deploying the Robinson Crusoe metaphor to characterize women on their solitary islands. After the sovereign self comes citizenship, then the generic woman, and last the "incidental relations of life, such as mother, wife, sister, daughter."[17] But such incidental social relations are not essentially constitutive of self. The self is prior to social arrangements. She speaks of the self-sovereignty of women and men and calls human beings solitary voyagers. We come into the world alone. We go out alone. We "walk alone." We realize "our awful solitude." Life is a "march" and a "battle" and we are all soldiers of the self who must fight for our own protection. In "the tragedies and triumphs of human experience, each mortal stands alone." Ideally, she notes almost off-handedly, this complete individual development is needed for the "general good." The exalted individual is one who exults in her own solitude, and Christianity's specifically socially and communal features recede.

Stanton's words conjure up a universe stripped of meaning save what the individual gives to it and its objects. She aims to dis-enthrall the self, to dis-encumber it in the sure and certain hope that a lofty and invigorating ideal of freedom will be the end result—and redound to the general good. But this admittedly bracing ideal of the self is too thin to sustain any notion of a social good, of a civic virtue we experience "in common together" that we cannot know alone. Because, in Wolin's words, the political is based on a possibility of commonality, on "our common capacity to share, to share memories and a common fate," a recognition of our common being is "the natural foundation of democracy" for "we have an equal claim to participate in the cooperative undertakings on which the common life depends."[18] Stanton attempts to construct commonality based upon a vision of isolated, Robinson Crusoe-like, sovereign selves. Her social project falters for this reason. She failed to see the irony embedded in proclamations of a totally individualistic ontol-

---

17. These and all later citations are drawn from her speech, "The Solitude of Self," (Kailua, Hawaii: published privately by Doris M. Ladd and Jane Wilkins Pultz, 1979).

18. Sheldon Wolin, "Hannah Arendt: Democracy and the Political," *Salmagundi* (Spring-Summer, 1983, No. 60, 3-9), 18.

ogy that would, she optimistically trusted, enter unproblematically into a politics of the common good, a politics of civic virtue.

When America entered the twentieth century, it was a society driven by dreams and fears of rapid industrialization and commercial expansion, dreams and fears of empire, dreams and fears of perfect freedom, dreams and fears of community. I will pick up the story of these tangled threads and themes in the World War I era when the siren allure of an overarching, collective civic purpose took a statist turn that seemed a cure for what ailed the republic, at least on the view of those who lamented our excessive diversity. Stanton's ideal self, together with throngs of diverse immigrants, invited a centralist response. Nationalizing progressives, disheartened at the messy sprawl that was American life, appropriately outraged at the excesses of corporate capitalism, and desirous of finding some way to forge a unified national will and civic philosophy, saw the coming of World War I, championed by President Woodrow Wilson, as a way to attain at long last a homogenous, ordered, and rational society. The central organ of progressive opinion, *The New Republic,* had long inveighed against "unassimilable communities," a fear prompted by the enormous surge in immigration during the waning decades of the nineteenth century and the early decades of the twentieth.

"To be great" wrote John R. Commons, a progressive labor economist, "a nation ... must be of one mind."[19] Walter Lippmann decried the "evils of localism" and fretted that American diversity was too great and had become a block in the way of "order, purpose, discipline."[20] Even before Wilson committed American troops to the European War, Lippmann and other progressives claimed that war would be good for the state. Writes one critic of Lippmann and progressives in general: "His conception of both [reform and civic good] presupposed a monolithic, static social structure in which a scientific elite directed a docile, relatively homogenous public."[21] A unity engineered from the top must, argued the nationalizers, triumph over pluralism, diversity, excessive and necessarily backward localisms.

19. Cited in Edward Abrahams, *The Lyrical Left* (Charlottesville, VA: 1986) 16.

20. Ibid., 17.

21. Ibid.

World War I was to be the great engine of social progress, with conscription an "effective homogenizing agent in what many regarded as a dangerously diverse society. Shared military service, one advocate colorfully argued, was the only way to yank the hyphen out of Italian-Americans or Polish-Americans or other such imperfectly assimilated immigrants."[22] President Wilson, who had already proclaimed that "any man who carries a hyphen about him carries a dagger that he is ready to plunge into the vitals of this Republic," and who championed universal service as a way to mold a new nation, now thundered in words of dangerously unifying excess: "There are citizens of the United States, I blush to admit, born under other flags but welcomed under our generous naturalization laws to the full freedom and opportunity of America, who have poured the poison of disloyalty into the very arteries of our national life.... Such creatures of passion, disloyalty, and anarchy must be crushed out.... The hand of our power should close over them at once."[23] Armed civic virtue had found a home on the shores of the new land and this mobilized and manipulated common good proved very common indeed.

A few brave, dissenting voices held out against the tide of xenophobic unity championed by academics and politicians alike. Most important among them was Randolph Bourne. Bourne bitterly attacked his old idol and master, John Dewey, for going for the war and talking blithely of its "social possibilities." His essay on "The State" retains its force nearly fifty years after he left it incomplete at his untimely death in the flu pandemic of the winter of 1918-1919:

> War—or at least modern war waged by a democratic republic against a powerful enemy—seems to achieve for a nation almost all that the most inflamed political idealist could desire. Citizens are no longer indifferent to their Government, but each cell of the body politic is brimming with life and activity.... In a nation at war, every citizen identifies himself with the whole, and feels immensely strengthened in that identification.[24]

---

22. This quote and those to follow on the World War I era are drawn from my book, *Women and War* (New York: 1987).

23. Cited in Bruce Clayton, *Forgotten Prophet. The Life of Randolph Bourne* (Baton Rouge: 1984), 189-90.

24. *Radical Will: Randolph Bourne. Selected Writings 1911-1918* (New York: 1977), 361.

Bourne championed the "trans-national" state. He yearned for a civic unity, a politics of commonalities, that cherished and celebrated the bracing tonic that perspicacious contrasts offer to the forging of individualities and communities. He called for an experimental ideal where each of us is free to explore in a world of others; where we can act in common together and act singly. Such an ideal is necessarily hostile to any overly robust proclamation of civic virtue that demands a single, overarching collective unity to attain or to sustain its purposes.

If one cherishes and champions individuality and community, diversity and commonalities, what resources are available in our contemporary civic repertoire that push in this complex direction? We—late-modern or post-modern citizens of the United States—are no longer naive. We have witnessed and are witnessing the corrosive effects of acquisitive individualism as well as those of the hypernationalistic, collective fevers that have occasionally run rampant in our history. With Bourne's saving and healing irony ready at hand, I will conclude this essay with intimations of a chastened version of civic virtue, one that embraces civility as a feature of that virtue yet also endorses, quite heartily, a fractious, even rumbustious politics.

I will draw from two perhaps unlikely sources—Catholic social thought and the theorizing of civil society that has emerged in a rapid and heartening transformation of Central Eastern Europe. This move seems to me politically and discursively justified because we are all citizens of the Occident, shaped by Catholicism, the Enlightenment, and the Reformation. One emergent feature of our current pluralism is the growth in numbers and public visibility of Catholics in a culture still riddled with anti-Catholic prejudice. Patterns of recent immigration are adding more Catholic citizens to our numbers. It behooves us to pay attention. We are dominantly a Protestant and not a Catholic nation. But mainline Protestantism has lined itself up a modernist project that tilts, finally, so far to the expressivist-individualist pole, that it is increasingly difficult for its spokesmen and spokeswomen to address questions of community and searching for common goods. Once again, what is at stake is not jettisoning a tradition—robust Protestant individualism—in favor of some other; rather, I have in mind to chasten the project of the untrammeled self with alternative reading of Christianity and civil society as traditions of discourse.

If one turns to recent Catholic social thought one finds, first, adamant criticism of "superdevelopment, which consists in an excessive availability of every kind of material good for the benefit of certain social groups." Superdevelopment "makes people slaves of possession and of immediate gratification, with no other horizon than the multiplication of continual replacement of the things already owned with others still better. This is the so-called civilization of 'consumption' or 'consumerism,' which involves so much 'throwing away' and waste."[25]

The "sad effects of this blind submission to pure consumerism," argues Pope John Paul II, is a combination of materialism and a relentless dissatisfaction, as "the more one possesses the more one wants." Aspirations that cut deeper, that speak to human dignity within a world of others, are stifled. John Paul's name for this alternative aspiration is "solidarity," not "a feeling of vague compassion or shallow distress at the misfortunes of so many people" but, instead, a determination to "commit oneself to the common good; that is to say, to the good of all and of each individual because we are really responsible for all." Through solidarity we see "the 'other' ... not just as some kind of instrument ... but as our 'neighbor,' a 'helper' (cf. Gn. 2 2:18-20), to be made a sharer on a par with ourselves in the banquet of life to which we are all equally invited by God."[26] The structures that make possible this ideal of solidarity are the many associations of civil society "below" the level of the state.

To the extent that John Paul's words strike us as forbiddingly utopian or hopelessly naive, to that extent we have lost civil society. Or so, at least, Alan Wolfe concludes in his important book, *Whose Keeper? Social Science and Moral Obligation*. Wolfe updates Tocqueville, apprising us of how far we have come, or how rapidly we have traveled, down a road to more and more individualism requiring more and more centralization of political and economic power. For all our success in modern societies, especially in the United States, there is a sense, desperate in some cases, that all is not well, that

---

25. Pope John Paul II, "Sollicitudo Rei Socialis," *Origins* (March 13, 1988, Vol. 17: No. 38, 641-660), 650.

26. Ibid., 20.

something has gone terribly awry. We citizens of liberal democratic societies understand and cherish our freedom but we are "confused when it comes to recognizing the social obligations that make ... freedom possible in the first place."[27] This confusion permeates all levels, from the marketplace, to the home, to the academy.

The political fallout of our current moral crisis is reflected in the irony of a morally exhausted left embracing rather than challenging the logic of the market by endorsing the relentless translation of wants into rights. Although the left continues to argue for taming the market in a strictly economic sense, it follows the market model where social relations are concerned, seeing in any restriction of individual "freedom" to live any sort of lifestyle an unacceptable diminution of choice. On the other hand, many conservatives love the untrammeled (or the less trammeled the better) operations of the market in economic life but call for a restoration of traditional morality, including strict sexual scripts for men and women, in social life. Both rely either on the market or the state "to organize their codes of moral obligation" when what they really need is "civil society—families, communities, friendship networks, solidaristic workplace ties, voluntarism, spontaneous groups and movements— not to reject, but to complete the project of modernity."[28]

Wolfe reminds us that early theoreticians of liberal civil society were concerned to limit the sphere of capitalist economics by either assuming or reiterating a very different logic, the moral ties that bind in the realms of family, religion, voluntary association, community. The market model, Adam Smith insisted, should not be extended as a metaphor for a process of all-encompassing exchange. Were we to organize "all our social relations by the same logic we sue in seeking a good bargain,"—and this is the direction we are pushed by the individualist project—we could not "even have friends, for everyone else interferes with our ability to calculate conditions that will maximize self-interest."[29]

Nor is the welfare state as we know it a solution to the problems thrown up by the operations of the market. The welfare state

27. Alan Wolfe, *Whose Keeper? Social Science and Moral Obligation* (Berkeley: 1989), 2.

28. Ibid., 20.

29. Ibid., 30.

emerged out of a set of ethical concerns and passions that led into the conviction that the state was the "only agent capable of serving as a surrogate for the moral ties of civil society" as these began to succumb to market pressure. But over forty years of evidence is in and it is clear that welfare statism as a totalizing logic erodes "the very social ties that make government possible in the first place." Government can strengthen moral obligations but cannot substitute for them. As our sense of particular, morally grounded responsibilities to an intergenerational "we" falters and the state moves in to treat the dislocations, it may temporarily "solve" delimited problems broadly defined, but these solutions, over time, may serve to further thin out the skein of obligation.

Wolfe today, just as Tocqueville in the nineteenth century, appreciates that a societal crisis is also an ethical crisis. Although he presents no menu of policy options, Wolfe calls for a "third perspective on moral agency different from those of the market and the state," one that "allows us to view moral obligation as a socially constructed practice negotiated between learning agents capable of growth on the one hand and change on the other."[30]

This formulation is similar to one offered by David Hollenbach, S.J., when he endorses a "pluralist-analogical understanding of the common good and human rights." Hollenbach with Wolfe, recognizes that social and institutional change is not only inevitable but needed "if all persons are to become active participants in the common good, politically, economically and culturally."[31]

At this point, Catholic social thought, here represented by Hollenbach, makes contact with American experiences and theories of community, association, and local autonomy. Latter-day Tocquevillians and Catholic social thinkers share communitarian hopes that the social practices in which individuals engage in their everyday lives in modern American democracy are richer and reflect greater sociality than atomistic visions of the acquisitive, unencumbered self allow. Perhaps, they muse, most of us usually do not govern our lives by principles of exchange, despite the totalizing logic of rational-choice contractarians and hard-core individualists. The call is

---

30. Ibid., 220.

31. Hollenbach, "The Common Good Revisited," 58.

not for some utopian vision of participatory democracy but for a more effective, more authentic form of representative democracy embodied in genuinely viable, overlapping social institutions.

As well, the notion of rights central to the American tradition becomes the counterpart of responsibilities. Rights are not "spoken of exclusively as individual claims.... Rights are intelligible only in terms of the obligations of individuals to other persons."[32] This understanding of persons steers clear of the strong antinomies of individualism versus collectivism. Catholic social thought begins from a fundamentally different ontology from that assumed and required by individualism on the one hand and statism on the other—assumptions that provide for individuality and rights as the goods of persons in community, together with the claims of social obligation. This version of individuality makes possible human unity as a cherished achievement and acts as a brake against coerced uniformity.

Or take these words from the U.S. Bishop's Pastoral Message on the economy: "The dignity of the human person, realized in community with others, is the criterion against which all aspects of economic life must be measured." All economic decisions must be judged "in light of what they do for the poor, what they do to the poor and what they enable the poor to do for themselves."[33] The Bishops draw upon the principle of subsidiarity, central to Catholic social teaching, when they speak of the "need for vital contributions from different human associations," considering it a disturbance of the "right order" of things to assign to a greater and higher association what a "lesser" association might do. In this way, institutional pluralism is guaranteed and "space for freedom, initiative and creativity on the part of many social agents" is made possible.[34] Hollenbach calls this "justice-as-participation," noting that the Bishops' contribution to the current, deadlocked "liberal/communitarian

32. Lisa Sowle Cahill, "Toward a Christian Theory of Human Rights," *Journal of Religious Ethics* (277-301), 284.

33. U.S. Catholic Bishop's Pastoral Message and Letter, "Economic Justice for All: Catholic Social Teaching and the U.S Economy," *Originss*(November 27, 1986, Vol. 16: No. 24, 409-455), 415.

34. Ibid., 422-23.

debate" lies in the way justice is conceptualized "in terms of this link between personhood and the basic prerequisites of participation.[35]

Ironically, or perhaps not so ironically, the richest theorizing of democratic civil society in the past decade or more has come from citizens of countries who were subjected for forty years or more to authoritarian, even totalitarian statist regimes.

Consider Solidarity theorist and activist Adam Michnik's characterization of democracy. In an interview, he insists that democracy "entails a vision of tolerance, and understanding of the importance of cultural traditions, and the realization that cherished human values can conflict with each other.... The essence of democracy as I understand it is freedom—the freedom which belongs to citizens endowed with a conscience. So understood, freedom implies pluralism, which is essential because conflict is a constant factor within a democratic social order." Michnik insists that the genuine democrat always struggles with and against his or her own tradition, eschewing thereby the hopelessly heroic and individualist notion of going it alone. Michnik here positions himself against our contemporary American tendency to see any defense of tradition as necessarily "conservative"; indeed, he criticizes our rigid distinctions between right and left. He proclaims: "A world devoid of tradition would be nonsensical and anarchic. The human world should be constructed from a permanent conflict between conservatism and contestation; if either is absent from a society, pluralism is destroyed." [36]

One final, vital voice, that of Vaclav Havel's. For years an oft-imprisoned champion of civic freedom and human rights, as well as Czechoslovakia's premier playwright, Havel became the President of the Czech Republic. In an essay on "Politics and Conscience," he writes: "We must not be ashamed that we are capable of love, friendship, solidarity, sympathy and tolerance, but just the opposite: we must see these fundamental dimensions of our humanity free from their 'private' exile and as the only genuine starting point of meaningful human community." Havel addresses himself to the successful liberal democracies of the West. Perhaps, he muses, we can

---

35. Hollenbach, "Liberalism, Communitarianism and the Pastoral Letter," 34.

36. From an interview in Times Literary Supplement, (Feb. 19-25, 1968, 188-198.

remind you of our common legacy, the importance of individual responsibility for the common good. He adds: "I favor 'anti-political' politics, politics not as the technology of power and manipulation, of cybernetic rule over humans or as the art of the useful, but politics as one of the ways of seeking and achieving meaningful lives, of protecting them and serving them. I favour politics as practical morality, as service to the truth, as essentially human and humanly measured care for our fellow humans. It is, I presume, an approach which, in this world, is extremely impractical and difficult to apply in daily life. Still, I know no better alternative."[37] Nor in truth, do I.

At the conclusion of *Public Man, Private Woman*, I articulated a vision of an "ethical polity." I was not thinking specifically of diversity and unity, individuality and solidarity, as I wrote, but that seems to have been what I was all along aiming for. I wrote: "Rather than an ideal of citizenship and civic virtue that features a citizenry grimly going about their collective duty, or an elite of citizens in their public space cut off from a world that includes most of us, within the ethical polity the active citizen would be one who had affirmed as part of what it meant to be human a devotion to public, moral responsibilities and ends." For the body is one but has many members.

---

37. Vaclav Havel, *Living in Truth*, ed. by Jan Vladislav (London: 1986), 152, 155.

7. Too Many Rights, Too Few Responsibilities

Amitai Etzioni

A sociological prize of sorts ought to be given to the member of the TV audience who, during a show about the savings and loan mess exclaimed, "The tax payers shouldn't pay for this, the government should!" He reflected quite well a major theme in American civic culture: a strong sense of entitlement, demanding the community to give more services, strongly upholding rights—coupled with a relatively weak sense of obligation, of serving the commons, and without a feeling of responsibility for the country. Hence: Americans recently called for more government services but showed greater opposition to new taxes; they express their willingness to show the flag anyplace from Central America to the Gulf, but a great reluctance to serve in the armed forces; and they even have a firm sense that one ought to have the right to be tried before the jury of one's peers, combined with frequent maneuvers to evade serving on such juries.

While the imbalance of rights and responsibilities may well have existed for a long time, some may argue it is a basic trait of the American character. In recent years, leadership has followed in exacerbating this tendency. Thus, while John F. Kennedy was still able to generate a tremendous response, including a stream of thousands of volunteers to serve in the Peace Corps when he stated, "Ask not what your country can do for you. Ask what you can do for you country," in recent years, Reagan and Bush preferred the less challenging course of suggesting to the citizenship that they could have their cake and eat it, gaining ever more economic growth to pay for the government services, while paying ever less for them via tax cuts. In many other areas, from public education to the war on drugs, facile non-taxing "solutions" have been offered. For example, it has been suggested that we may improve our system of education without additional expenditures by simply increasing parental choice among schools and thus, it is said, "drive the bad schools out of business." And to deal with the illicit demands for drugs we are told to "just say no." Radical individualists, from the ACLU to libertarians, have effectively blocked most steps to increase public responsibilities, from drug testing even of people who are directly involved in public safety (such as the engineers who drive trains) to measures that would enhance public health (e.g., requiring disclosure of sexual contacts by carriers of the AIDS virus). Last but not least, in both state legislatures and in Congress the role of special interests has grown so much, especially through campaign contributions, that the public interest is very often woefully neglected, and suggestions for reform have so far found only a rather small constituency.

A new communitarian movement is now taking on this set of issues, making restoration of civility and commitment to the commons its core theme. The young movement is in part social philosophy and sociology, in part a moral call, and in part a matter of taking a different slant on public policies.

Communitarians point out the ill logic of demanding the right to be tried before a jury of one's peers without agreeing to serve on it. Aside from being a selfish, indecent position (asking to be given but not willing to give) it is absurd to expect that most of us can be tried before our peers if most of us are not willing to be one of the peers. Communitarians know that in the longer run it is not possible to have ever more governmental services and at the same time pay less for them. They point out that a government that is trying to make do by serving numerous special interests neglects the other important matters for which there are no powerful pressure groups, from public education to public safety and health. And communitarians are showing that the Constitution, being a living thing rather than a dead letter the Founding Fathers left behind, can be adapted to the changing challenges of the time.

A discussion of specific measures communitarians are consider-ing follows. Before those are outlined, it is necessary to stress two points to avoid common misunderstandings. While several of these measures involve legal matters and governmental actions, that is, matters of the state, the core of the communitarian position is moral and community-based rather than statist. What is needed most is a change in the moral climate of the country, a greater willingness to shoulder communitarian responsibilities, and a greater readiness to curb one's demands. Such a change is essential because without it, the required changes in public service and the definition of rights will not be considered acceptable and, most important, the more the called-for changes are made morally acceptable and socially enforced, the less need there will be for governmental actions— from policing to courts and jails. One example will have to stand for numerous others that could be given. To enhance public safety we need fewer drunken drivers. To combat drunken driving we need, among other things, a willingness of individuals, as a moral com-mitment, to embrace the notion of a designated driver (the way Scandinavians do), that is, one person per car who will not consume alcohol during an outing, party, etc. This is best done on a moral, social base. For example, those couples who come to parties and both drink would be subject to social criticism (unless, of course, they carpool); the person who proudly states (as if saying, "look how responsible I am!") that they are not drinking tonight because they are the designated driver, would gain social approval accordingly, and so on. Similarly, we need to support sobriety checkpoints (rather than fight them as the ACLU does) to help enforce the new social, moral dictum. The changed moral orientation ensures that drunken driving will be significantly reduced without any state action and that whatever limited state action will be needed, it will merely be to round off new social pressures (e.g., in the form of des-ignated drivers rather than supporting drinking to excess) and will be supported by the electorate.

There is no simple recipe for building a new social, moral cli-mate for a more communitarian orientation. Societies change their moral orientation in complex, far from fully predictable or con-trollable manners. Among the steps that are being taken are those that historically did result in the desired change. First, just as Betty Friedan's writing helped launch the women's movement, and

Rachel Carlson's *Silent Spring* helped the environmental movement take off, so various communitarian writings call attention to the need for greater responsibility to the commons. These include Robert Bellah, R. Madsen, W. Sullivan, A. Swidler, and S. Tipton's *Habits of the Heart*, books by Michael Walzer, Michael Sandel, Charles Taylor, Alisdair MacIntyre, and dearest to the author's heart, a new quarterly, *The Responsive Community*, whose editors are James Fishkin, William Galston, Mary Ann Glendon, and Amitai Etzioni, with an editorial board that includes both conservatives and liberals, ranging from Nathan Glazer and Ilene Nagel, to Martha Nussbaum and Benjamin Barber. Second, a variety of public interest groups have made communitarianism their theme, whether or not they use the term—including Common Cause and Ralph Nader's groups, as well as numerous grass-roots organizations. There is also a strong communitarian element in many organizations whose explicit purpose is something other, especially the environmental movement. Less advanced but definitely moving in the right direction are various attempts to strengthen the teaching of civics in schools by groups such as the Thomas Jefferson Center. What is yet to come is a major social movement, a kind of neo-progressive movement that would shore up the commons, making its main agenda curbing special interests and serving the public interests.

Unfortunately, the recent public frustration with politicians has focused on attempts to "throw out the rascals," and impose term limitations, which will only lead to a new set of politicians committed to special interests replacing the other. Until elected officials' need for private money to win elections, the main mechanism by which they become obligated to special interests, is systematically curbed by various campaign reform laws and public financing of elections, part of the communitarian movement will lag. Finally, the suggestion of creating a year of national service is meant to further enhance the education for and the practice of service for and to the public.

The second misunderstanding that must be avoided is that the call for enhanced civic responsibilities and a greater measure of community service entails majoritarianism or even a measure of authoritarianism. To suggest that young Americans (or everyone) ought to volunteer more and more often to serve the commons is not to suggest that those who refuse for reason of conscience are to be disciplined. It is not to say that the civic "religion" or set of values will replace the religious or secular values people uphold. Nor does the call for more sobriety checkpoints, drug tests, and disclosure of sexual contacts by carriers of the AIDS virus legitimate the beginning of a police state. Communitarians are careful to craft suggested changes in public mores and regulation to allow for greater public safety, health, and education, without falling into the opposite trap of radical communitarianism, that of authoritarianism.

The thrust of responsive communitarianism is illustrated by the following examples: to curb drug abuse it has been suggested that the U.S. should conduct massive drug tests on all school kids, government employees, and in corporations. This would entail massive violations of privacy, both because a function traditionally surrounded by much privacy would have to be performed under controlled conditions, and because the tests would often reveal private, off the job behavior. More persuasion not to use drugs seems more appropriate and keeps the door to a police state shut. On the other hand, drug testing of select groups of people whose drug violation directly endangers the public, e.g., pilots, seems justified on communitarian grounds. This is especially the case if they are informed beforehand that their jobs will entail such tests so that those who are hired are, in effect, consigned to these tests as part of their job requirements (in contracts, if this is done for all jobs, workers no longer have an opportunity to choose whether they are willing to consent or not).

Concerning matters of the rights of criminals versus those of their victims and public order, a wholesale removal of the Miranda rights, as had been suggested by the Reagan Administration, may well return us to more authoritarian days. At the same time, it seems reasonable and prudent not to throw out evidence when the Miranda rules were violated only technically and clearly in good faith. Thus, for instance, one can fully support the court's decision, when a person confessed to a crime before his rights were read to him, after which they were read and he confessed again, that the second confession be allowed to stand.

In the same vein, sobriety checkpoints, especially when they are publicly posted so that drivers who enter public highways consent to be subject to them, should be viewed more as a way to secure the right to drive freely than as a curb on that right. Nor are airport screenings, used to deter terrorist bombs, to be viewed as an unreasonable search and seizure, as they are by the ACLU. The intrusion is minimal and the contribution to public safety, including the freedom to travel, is considerable.

The debate over the rights of students provides still another example of a reasonable communitarian position between giving students full-fledged Fourth Amendment rights, (deterring teachers and principals from suspending them) and declaring them fair game to any capricious school authority. It seems reasonable that students who are subject to expulsion and suspension should be granted due process to the extent that they are notified of the nature of their misconduct and given an opportunity to respond; both actions must occur before the expulsion takes place. Still, expulsion need not guarantee students the rights of council or call for cross examination and calling of witnesses, because this would unduly encumber the ability of schools to maintain an educational environment. It also allows schools to maintain for internal purposes additional restrictions and simplified procedures because they are meant to be small communities rather than adversarial environments. This is far from a novel approach; several state courts have already been modifying school policies in the direction we suggest.

Regarding the rights of people with AIDS, we should reduce the deleterious effects of tracing contacts to protect public health. For example, AIDS testing and contact-tracing can lead to a person losing his or her job and health insurance if confidentiality is not maintained. Hence, any introduction of such a program should be accompanied by a thorough review of access control to lists of names of those tested, procedures used in contracting sexual partners, professional education programs on the need for confidentiality, and penalties for unauthorized disclosure and especially for those who discriminate against AIDS patients or HIV carriers. All this may seem quite cumbersome, but in view of the great dangers AIDS poses for individuals and the high costs to society, these measures are clearly appropriate.

One may and ought to argue about the details involved in such policies. Indeed, the changes should be carefully crafted. We need to reset a legal thermostat to afford a climate more supportive of public concerns, without melting away any of the basic safeguards of individual liberties. Those who argue that the various present interpretations of the Bill of Rights are untouchable, that any modification will push us down the slippery slope toward authoritarianism, must come to realize that the greater danger to the Constitution arises out of a refusal to recognize that the Constitution is living thing that can and does adapt to the changing social situation. Without such adaptation, without some measure of increased communitarianism, the mounting frustrations of the American people over politics being governed by special interests, over unsafe cities and spreading epidemics of violence, will lead to much more extreme adjustment. Legitimate public needs are not attended to, in part because quite reasonable adaptations, such as selective drug testing, sobriety checkpoints, and other such measures are disallowed. Basically the issue is not one of legal measures but a change of orientation to a stronger voice for the commons and less room for me-ism and special interests. At this stage of American history, the danger of excessive communitarianism, theoretically always present, seems quite remote.

8. Progressive Politics and Communitarian Culture

William Galston

One of the hallmarks of communitarianism is its sensitivity to cultural and historical differences that may differentiate one community or subcommunity from another. And in precisely that spirit, I must introduce a question: how much can Europe learn from America, and how much can America learn from Europe, if what differentiates us is arguably as important as what unites us?

From a communitarian perspective, a fascinating problematic has been established, which is an empirical question that cannot be resolved philosophically or ideologically. But it is nevertheless a question I have reflected on through the exemplary person of Alexis de Tocqueville, who has traveled back and forth across the Atlantic bearing misunderstood messages from one culture to another.

It seems clear that while history hasn't ended, at least a phase of it has. With the events of the past few years, the French Revolution is finally over. And in the wake of the closure of the French Revolution, in spite of heroic efforts of definition and redefinition, the old French Revolutionary categories of left and right are simply not very serviceable or useful anymore. In trying to think through our situation, we need a new kind of empiricism and openmindedness, one that involves, among other things, the disaggregation of rigid, comprehensive ideological structures of every stripe. The past two centuries offer us not blueprints, but rather resources out of which a new progressive agenda might conceivably be developed.

Are we capable of social learning? Are we capable of moral vision? What can we possibly mean by a good society under modern circumstances? What would the political institutions of a good society look like with due allowance for local differences and circumstances? What is the political economy of a good society? What is its public culture? There is no one answer to these questions. But these are the kinds of re-envisionings that I believe are required, and there is no blueprint that can do it for us.

As we undertake this task, it seems to me above all we must be alert to—and reject—elitism in all of its forms. The critique of Bolshevik-style vanguard elitism comes very easily, I suspect, to many people. But there is a form of elitism that is somewhat harder to avoid or even recognize. And that is upper-middle-class or intellectual elitism, which frequently manifests itself in contempt for the working class, or to be somewhat more traditional about it, the petty bourgeoisie.

What I am suggesting as an urgent task is real attention to the experiences of economic marginality, of cultural conservativism, and of the virtues of localism and particularism that frequently characterize groups and indeed classes that stand at some considerable remove from the characteristic experiences of the upper middle class.

In this connection, the problem under current circumstances, at least in America, is radically conflicting images of the 1960s, which might be deemed a cultural class war. No effort to construct a new progressive agenda can take a meaningful step forward without attending to that cultural class war and the profound overlay that it has imposed on more traditional lines of economic division, at least in American society.

In the course of this re-imagining of the progressive agenda, we have to be willing to learn from liberalism. And one of the things that is necessary to learn from liberalism is the inevitability of the pluralism of competing worthy values.

There is simply no guarantee that everything any individual cherishes or that is collectively cherished can be realized simultaneously within the same political program. We need a constant awareness of what, for instance, Isaiah Berlin has talked about over and over again: the ineradicable tension at the heart of our personal and our public life.

There is another kind of lesson to be gleaned from liberalism, and that is that the liberal tradition contains within it resources out of which an understanding of shared public purposes and of more and less worthy individual ends can be constructed. It is very important not to caricature liberalism, as either a theoretical tradition or as a lived way of life, as simply equivalent to economistic individualism. It is much richer than that.

In his deservedly influential book, *The Spheres of Justice* (Oxford: 1983), Michael Walzer has suggested that it is useful to think of political communities as a whole as divided into different spheres of activity, each constituted by different patterns of conduct and different principles of legitimation. I would like to suggest that this set of ideas be combined with ideas articulated a few years earlier by Daniel Bell in his work, *The Cultural Contradictions of Capitalism* (Basic Books, 1976). Bell raises the very pertinent question of whether the different spheres of modern society fully cohere and whether, for example, developments in the economic sphere might not have unexpected and indeed negative consequences for culture, politics, and eventually even economics itself.

The heart of the communitarian message can be formulated in three theses:

1.

A good society has as one of its constituent elements a rich set of opportunities for satisfying human connections. The natural home of such connections is to be found not so much in national politics, the politics of the nation-state, as it is in what the social theorist Herbert Ganz has called micro societies: in particular, family, neighborhood, local schools, voluntary associations, and the workplace.

These micro societies are elements, though not the totality, of what is now being called civil society. They require special kinds of bonds of intimacy, continuity, and stability. Their characteristic language is a language of commitment, responsibility, duty, virtue, memory, solidarity, and even love rather than the discourse, valuable in its own right, of choice, rights, personal freedom, and individualism.

2.

The kinds of bonds and connections characteristic of well-functioning micro societies are now undergoing a triple assault. The first is an assault at the hands of economic growth and change, a familiar topic in both European and American social theory. The second assault—and this is a somewhat less familiar topic—is at the hands of collectivized social provision; this is the topic of Alan Wolfe's splendid book, *Whose Keeper?, Social Science and Moral Obligation* (Berkeley, 1989), which explores the real world of social democracy, especially in Scandinavia. Finally, the third assault is at the hands of what I will call cultural radicalism, which consists of a critique of limits, a critique of particularism, and a critique of traditional or bourgeois virtue.

3.

In the re-envisioning of a progressive agenda, progressives must rethink the entire problematic of microsocial connections in light of this triple assault upon them.

And so I leave you with three questions.

First of all, what is the progressive stance toward economic growth if such growth is increasingly incompatible with the protection of the forms of production on which, for example, neighborhoods and communities have historically depended?

In his latest book, Christopher Lasch has baldly stated that the stance of progressives in the late twentieth century must be firmly against the entire commitment to economic growth. I believe frankly that in this path lies political disaster. There must be a new way of thinking through the role of the state in trying to stabilize and compensate communities that are otherwise exposed to the full force of economic growth. But the answer does not lie in forms of closure, forms of protectionism, whether of goods or capital or people.

The second question is: what is the progressive stance toward social provision in light of its tension with micro social bonds, as well as with the limits of public support through the tax system and the growing sclerosis of the public sector, at least in the United States and perhaps in Europe as well. The appropriate new progressive agenda must involve simultaneously a commitment to social provision and a thorough rethinking of the mechanisms of the bureaucratic welfare state by which social provision has historically been delivered.

Lastly, what is the appropriate new progressive stance toward cultural radicalism? As a political program, cultural radicalism has been a complete political disaster. The war against bourgeois morality initiated in the 1960s, or at least reinitiated in the 1960s, must be ended. If progressives wish to rebuild governing coalitions that include the working class and not just talk to one another, they must make their peace with substantial elements of traditional morality, including family, neighborhood, law-abidingness, social contribution, patriotism, and respect for religious sensibilities.

I close by quoting an extremely important sentence by Norman Birnbaum. "A modern and multicultural society requires a common set of moral expectations and moral language, if it is to remain a society and not a haphazard association or even assemblage of groups and persons ready to do cultural and economic battle with one another at the least inducement." I think that is nothing more and nothing less than the truth of the matter in our current situation, and it is that truth to which communitarianism as I understand it is principally devoted.

9. Neo-Hegelian Reflections on the Communitarian Debate

Terry Pinkard

I will offer some very general reflections on why certain communitarian ideas have been raised in the national debate and why the communitarian agenda on its own cannot be the full story of what we should be doing and thinking. It strikes me that we ought to begin with the very general question: why is it that communitarianism has suddenly been appearing on the political and philosophical landscape in the way that it recently has? In trying to answer this question, I am going to do three things. I am going to begin with an anecdote, end with a slogan, and in the middle I am going to say a bit about Hegel.

The anecdote I have in mind has to do with a news report I saw on one of the network evening news programs. It was a story about a group therapy session for some women who had been betrayed by some men they had trusted, specifically some professionals to whom they had gone for help. The story was, to be brief, that all these women had been seduced by their priest or their physician or their therapist or their lawyer and so on, and it went on about professional ethics in America. But what was striking about this report was the gap between what the people being interviewed in the story were talking about and the rather impoverished moral vocabulary in which they and the reporter were talking about it. They were talking about things like the responsibility that individuals have toward each other in specific social settings, about very elemental human things like trust and betrayal, about the problems of social setting of unequal power, and about the ways in which people manipulate and exploit other people. And yet, when one listened to them talk about it, it seemed that they understood this only in terms of markets and choices. They had paid some professional for help, he had led them to something other than what they originally wanted, and the only ethical issue involved, at least judging from the language used, seemed to be that of whether there had been consent. After all, they were adults, and nobody had actually coerced them into doing anything, so the moral issue seemed only to be whether they had "really" consented, with the implicit assumption being present that if they had consented, then they could not hold that anything wrong had been done to them.

What struck me as I was watching this particular story was the way in which it was such a fine example of the impoverishment of moral vocabulary. Instead of talking about trust and betrayal, the individuals talked only about whether there had been any coercion, often straining the bounds of their own story so that they could work in the idea that somehow they had "really" been coerced. It was a fine example of people using the language of markets and choice to talk about political problems such as inequality of power and deeply ethical problems such as the betrayal of trust. It is this awareness of the impoverishment of moral vocabulary that has set the stage for the kinds of issues that have driven the revival of contemporary communitarian debate.

One of the ways in which one might understand this impoverishment of moral vocabulary had been raised by a leading communitarian, Charles Taylor. Taylor thinks that we can distinguish between a kind of intuitively felt identification of the issues, a sense of what we all experience, and that way in which we can articulate those issues to ourselves. The idea is that we know that something is going on here, we know what betrayal is, we know when somebody is betraying our trust and manipulating or humiliating us, but we have no adequate conceptual way of articulating this to ourselves or to others. All we have is the language of individualism and autonomy. We thus try to fit our experience into the rather cramped vocabulary of autonomy and choice, and we find ourselves coming up with various kinds of somewhat implausible scenarios about why some form of betrayal is "really" coercion or why some kind of choice "really" wasn't a free choice and so on.

It seems to me, as it does to many others, that something deeper is going on here than merely a violation of some individual's choices, and it has to do with what I would call a kind of irrationality of our current social space. By a social space, I understand technically that set of licensed inferences that individuals in a determinate form of life find themselves entitled to draw. In a less technical sense, I mean by "social space" simply that set of basic beliefs and accounts that we give ourselves as to why we take certain beliefs to be true and why we think that certain actions are required. Worries about truth, about status, about whether one is behaving properly, about whether one is being treated right—all these things have to do with one's sense of what kinds of beliefs, desires, and actions license what in one's world. (Compare all the questions: "Can somebody else get away with calling you those names?" "Does the government have any legitimate claims on my property?" "What kind of clothing is appropriate for me?" "Is the scientific account of the world the true account or is it only a partial account?" All these have to do with what neo-Hegelians like Robert Pippin call our need for reassurance that what we take to be good reasons really are good reasons.) Hegel held that to be a human agent at all is to be able to locate oneself in such social spaces, that is, to learn to move within that inferential space. Thus, when there are basic and abiding irrationalities and contradictions in the social space in which individuals find themselves, those individuals will each find their own self-consciousness to be at odds with itself. In such cases the individuals will find themselves alienated from who they are and what they are doing. To appropriate a phrase from Jerome Segal, they will find themselves not to be present in their activities in the sense that they cannot see what they do to be something that either expresses their self or is caused by some feature of their self. The question that Hegelians claim needs to be asked of contemporary social space is whether it is ringed with such tensions and contradictions such that individuals who become who they are by virtue of having their subjective lives structured by this social space can genuinely find themselves at home in it, be present in the activities structured by that social space.

In particular, we can ask this about modern social space, since the concern with modernity is central to the Hegelian story about things. Central to modernity is the question of whether a whole form of life or the individuals in it can be said to be self-determining (or "autonomous"). For example, consider one of the great philosophical starting points of modernity, Descartes' radical proposal that we construct a method to aid us in deciding what is true and false, and with the method being that of trying to doubt everything. To be sure, in many philosophy courses, this is often presented as if Descartes' problems were only a series of clever puzzles and problems with no social basis. But Descartes was after something deeper. In proposing to doubt everything, he was expressing a widespread feeling on the part of early modernity that it felt, as a culture, betrayed and fooled by the authoritative institutions. That is, the kind of medieval culture out of which his time was emerging had not led to where it was supposed to lead. Cartesian doubt and the insistence on method amounts, as Robert Pippin has argued, to the cultural claim that modernity won't get fooled again. The insistence on doubt and method is the idea that we should and we can provide our own cultural assurances as to what can be known and what can be done "on our own." We live in the aftermath of this kind of self-assurance, namely, a culture of individuals and societies "doing it on their own." This is the modern project of securing individual and cultural autonomy.

But modernity is not just a story about how individuals strived to become more autonomous. It is also a story of how certain social formations shaped who we came to be, and the failure of which has led to our current form of self-consciousness. There is also a story to be told about how, to use George Eliot's phrase, character is destiny. This has also been an element of self-conscious reflection in our political tradition. Rousseau, for example, was terribly concerned with asking about the consequences of a particular kind of society for the kind of characters it produces. In *Rameau's Nephew*, Diderot tried to show the vanity and emptiness of the pre-revolutionary culture and character of European life. This story about modernity does not fit in seamlessly with the story about autonomy. It is rather a story about the institutions of a culture, how they affect the structure of our desires, what we deeply want and what we think is possible for us in our lives. We can draw two very different and related pictures of this. On the one hand, we can have a very traditional society, one in which the possibilities of life are defined exhaustively by the social roles available. The German classicists and modern communitarians such as Alasdair MacIntyre have put forth the view of ancient Greece as a society in which people knew who they were and what they were to do and which was therefore wholly lacking in alienation. On the other hand, since the French revolution and the creation of the so-called "American Way of Life," there has been in modernity the idea that anything is possible, that individuals need not be restricted by the social roles (that even a common individual like Napoleon, the "little corporal," can by virtue of his talents and his will-power rise to become a world-historical figure). With everything possible, all seems to hang on individual decisions and motives. The result, as Hegel saw, was the creation of a moralistic society, in which the purity of motive and thought was the guiding thread and in which the virtues of sincerity and authenticity came to play central roles. If people are to be self-determining, and if everything is possible, then people need to be able to believe that they are really in charge of what they are doing. Since nobody can control the consequences of his actions nor how they will be received by others, the result is a set of individuals trying their best to control what they really can control, namely, their own motives and their own sincerity.

The problem with such pluralist societies in which the main virtues are those of sincerity and authenticity is that they rapidly deteriorate into hypocritical posings, with charges being thrown around on all sides as to who is "really" sincere and who is not, what is "really" authentic and what is not. The real hypocrisy and self-delusions of such a period are amplified by the mutual charges of the same kind. For modernity to hold together, it needs some bond other than the idea that "everything is possible" and that what really matters are the sincere and authentic actions of individuals. It needs some way of reconciling individuals to each other and to themselves.

There is a third story that we have to tell about modernity, which, in Hegel's view, is the Judeo-Christian story. Modern democratic pluralist societies are possible only on the basis of a kind of secularization of a Jewish-Christian morality. A pluralist society with democratic politics is only possible if some people are willing to recognize a kind of shared identity with each other and, more importantly, willing to see the possibility of reconciliation with each other, willing to acknowledge that nobody has any privileged insight into the good or even into their own hearts. The awareness that nothing is given in life, that nothing is self-evident, leads to the possibility of individuals learning that things are indeed up to them, but that a certain humility about one's own claims are in order. Rather than having only the politics of praise and blame, modern democratic societies also require the practice of the politics of reconciliation and forgiveness.

In order to understand what are the possibilities and projects of these pluralist societies, we need to be able to understand what it is that they take to reassure themselves about what it is they are doing. Hegel's view about these various projects has to do with the way in which a form of life tries to affirm and reassure itself that the kinds of things that it has come to take as a good reason for belief or action really are good reasons. The forms that such reassurance can take are many: the ideal of being a cultivated individual in court life in pre-revolutionary France, Greek epic and tragedy, autobiographical writing in the eighteenth century, early modern science, and nineteenth-century idealist philosophy. These practices are the social means by which the agents of that form of life reflect on who they are and on the social space—the standards of reasoning, thinking, and acting that they have historically come to accept as defining who they are individually and collectively—that these practices affirm or put into question. One of the features of modernity, so Hegel argues, is the way in which the social practices of affirmation and criticism have turned on themselves in a reflexive manner. That is, it is not enough to throw into doubt or to affirm the other set of reasons that we have come to take for granted, but the social practices of "criticism" themselves have come in for criticism as to whether they indeed are the proper tools by which to affirm or criticize these other practices. They no longer serve the immediate function of reassuring us—of defending rational faith, as Kant put it—that our ways of reasoning are in order. The complex order of modern life— with its bureaucracies, rule of law, competitive market institutions, constitutional order, and seeming daily chaos—requires a correspondingly more reflective set of justifications. Hegel thought that this role could only be played by academic philosophy, but there is no reason that it cannot also be played by a cohort of institutions, such as the media, film, and the overall intellectual life of the major research institutes and universities.

The problem with such complexity is that it threatens to undo the project of modernity itself. The kinds of individuals produced by modern institutions come to think of themselves as self-determining, as setting their purposes and ends in life for themselves (as the leaders of East Europe and the former Soviet Union discovered to their consternation). But in a complex, bureaucratic society, it becomes difficult for individuals to see how their own claims to personal self-determination fit in with the larger goals and purposes in the larger social life. Too many things come to seem to them simply like burdens that put limits on what they can do. In this way, modern life has still to come up with an answer to Rousseau's general problem: how do we reconcile the dependence of people on their society with the independence that they claim for themselves? This is properly a dialectical problem, in Hegel's sense; we have two opposite claims made on us which have to be integrated into one solution. Rousseau's own solution has proved notoriously to be untenable. Rousseau thought that since the whole structure of our desires were the result of socialization, we needed to construct a form of life in which "society" would socialize us in such a way that our sense of our own independence would be perfectly compatible with the dependence that we have in social life. For Rousseau and all those taken by this idea, the fundamental question has become that of the legislator and the educator, and, in Marx's words in his "Theses on Feuerbach," the issue of who would educate the educator.

Rousseau's idea proved to be the clarion call for the disastrously failed attempts at socialist dictatorship in the name of the proletariat in which the "new man and woman" would spring up. Interestingly, one of the fundamental assumptions shared by both the right and the left during the period of the cold war was in fact a Rousseauian assumption that society makes us up into the agents that we are, and that different societies will produce different people. The conservatives feared this was true, and that "humanity" (the kind of people they think ought to be) would be lost forever in Soviet indoctrination. The left shared the same view, except that they had a cheerier understanding of the kind of people that would be produced. The collapse of Marxist socialism seemed to throw that assumption into question.

In light of the failure of communism to completely indoctrinate its populace despite its virtual monopoly on the educational and mediating institutions of its societies, a number of conservative commentators have tried to resurrect the idea that there really is a "human nature" that communism tried to suppress and that eventually expressed itself in the revolt against it. These conservative commentators overlook, however, the ways in which socialist practice was not so much working against some inherent human nature as it was producing an irrational social space for its members. It first claimed that it would be more productive than the West, then, having failed at doing that, it devolved into a kind of asceticism, intoning against the overproductive deprivations of the West. It promised to put power (read: self-determination) into the hands of the "people" and then removed all power from them. In short, the socialist ideal promised a "kinder, gentler" version of the Western ideal but failed to deliver the goods.

There is no reason in the collapse of socialism, therefore, to abandon Rousseau's question, even if we abandon a lot of what Rousseau proposed in order to answer it. The false solution to the problems of capitalist society's problems have vanished. The basic problems are still with us.

We can turn to Hegel for a sharpening of the statement of that problem in the following way. The conflict in modern self-understanding is between the generally objective claims that we all assume to be true—that we all have certain basic rights to life, liberty, and property, and to have our rights respected—and the subjectivity of claims that agents make when they think of themselves as autonomously deciding for themselves what to do. This is, as it were, a conflict between moralist liberalism and liberal romanticism, or between bourgeois common sense and bourgeois self-creation. More pointedly, we could formulate the question like this: If the modern autonomous agent makes up her own mind in the sense that nothing counts as a good reason for her unless she elects to count it, then how could there be any objective claims about what we owe others?

The question concerns how we might reconcile the formal autonomy of modern agents with the seemingly objective status of the principles they invoke as rights-bearers. This is the source of the peculiarly modern problem of relativism, with its needs to reassure agents that they have objective rights and that they are the authors of their moral principles. In practice, almost all attempts at doing so have ended up doing one or two things: (1) they have abandoned the idea of there being any objective principles and focused instead on the concept of an agent's pure choice of principles (Nietzschean nihilism may be one example); or (2) they have ended up introducing some form of givenness into the picture, such as the conservatively communitarian assertion that "this is the way we do things, end of story" or by an appeal to some set of "natural rights," or by appeal to "basic intuitions" that we supposedly all share, or by appeal to some set of objective values to which our judgments must conform. All of these, however, must necessarily fail to reconcile agents possessed of a modern self-consciousness; none of the strategies can come to count as valid, as knowledge, for such agents. Such one-sided attempts leave the culture at odds with itself and the agents at odds with each other (each agent feeling himself as a split subjectivity, claiming objective rights for himself while at the same time claiming to be the source of the moral authority those rights have, which of course raises the possibility of denying them to others and having others deny them to him). In this way the personal and the impersonal point of view (what Hegel often calls the "individual" and the "universal") separate within the individual agents themselves. The agent cannot then find himself present in certain socially required actions, since they clash with his felt need for autonomy; the agent's subjective alienation becomes thus the mirror of irrationality in his social space.

This is particularly shaped by Hegel's other criticism of the way in which this conflict in modern social space cannot be solved. It cannot be solved by holding that we should leave such matters to "individual" conscience." Now, it is very important in modern pluralist societies that a large latitude of crucial things be left to decisions by individual conscience, for conscience is the appropriate place for those matters about which there can be no moral certainty. In our time, this now includes not only religious faith (the original locus for the modern appeal to conscience as the final arbiter of what to do) but also matters of sexual morality, personal relations, decisions about divorce, and even some matters of professional ethics. However, to say that conscience is the appropriate judge on those matters where there is no moral certainty is to say that it is only applicable in those cases in which there are important things "up for grabs." To go further and say that everything should be a matter of conscience would be to endorse the idea that everything is "up for grabs." In Hegel's view, this would be as unsatisfactory a doctrine for the modern world as the opposite idea that there should be no latitude for conscience, that "society" or (worse) the "state" could set moral doctrine on all matters. Moreover, this is something that we all recognize even if we do not articulate it in that way. That is, we all recognize that there are areas of moral certainty that stand outside of conscience. Questions such as "Should adults have sex with pre-pubescent children?" or "Is killing for turf OK?" should have such obvious answers that someone claiming otherwise on the basis of his "conscience" would be recognized as being simply in the wrong. But if that is so, what then is the status of this appeal to conscience and its relation to these moral certainties?

For Hegel, the way of securing these moral certainties as anchors for conscience—as those things that are simply required or simply ruled out—cannot lie in our elaborating some kind of moral philosophy that would put us in touch with eternal moral truths or give us a new version of the Cartesian idea of a "method" with which we could crank out unambiguous moral certainties. It must lie rather in the structure of mutual recognition of society—in social practices and institutions that make up what he called *Sittlichkeit*, "ethical life," a sense that "this is the way we do things" which provides the context around which our appeals to conscience, broad as they may be in the modern world, circulate and in which they find certain resting points. There must, that is, be a set of institutions that structure our desires and our expectations such that we have a firm sense of what sets boundaries to our consciences. Hegel argued that there were in fact three such institutions in the modern world that despite their various historical origins and checkered past could play this role. These were the modern bourgeois family (to which Hegel gave a decidedly patriarchal cast, but which need not be so taken), the modern market oriented civil society structured around the values and expectations of private associations and professional organizations, and the modern constitutional state.

In the bourgeois family (which even Hegel himself noted had to be constructed on a basis of equality between wives and husbands, however antiquated his conception of the equality of the sexes was), we have a structure for raising children and for providing for basic human needs and desires for intimacy, trust and reliance. This ties in with some more general points about social recognition and human nature. In a talk given in 1947 to the American Medical Association, Anna Freud discussed the question of why people often claim to hate doctors in general but say that they love their own doctors. They think that their own physician is the exception to the general rule that physicians are heartless folks, that their own physician is a wonderful, kind, caring person. Her explanation of this had to do with two fundamental features of all human beings. We all begin as dependent beings, requiring other people for our subsistence, requiring other people to care for us. As we grow older, we seek to become more independent beings. However, we never lose these two aspects of our nature: the desire for independence, and the desire to be cared for and to care for other people. Both these are essential to human nature. When people go to physicians, they're generally in the position of needing someone to care for them, and they go to physicians expecting them to care for them. Yet, people also tend to react to this by saying that the physician ought to take their hands off them because, after all, they are independent people, capable of making their own choices. In the ordinary case of the ambivalent attitudes that many people have toward doctors, one sees these two aspects of human nature in conflict with each other.

There is also the need for civil society. The family can be both nurturing and suffocating; it can care for the individual, but it can also stifle her. Civil society with its webs of free association in friendships, business acquaintances, careers, and the excellences (for which in principle professional organizations should strive) is that set of social practices and institutions that can provide us with some structured set of ideas having to do with reliance, responsibility, and trust. However, even in the best ordered of civil societies, where people find genuine identification with their various mediating organizations, a conflict of interests is always present, and it is entirely fortuitous if all interests happen to coincide. Therefore, there must be more to social space than just a collection of families and a civil society composed of families, individuals mediating institutions, and a set of legal institutions for administering the law and various public works. There must be a deeper form of ethical community, that of political community (what Hegel misleadingly called the "state"). A political community is about the common life of a people, that is, what structures their common point of view on matters of policy and public ends. Politics, after all, is fundamentally about this common life, or shared self-identity; it is about where the limits of our self-identities overlap. Indeed, the most pressing issues of politics are about how far down the common life goes—about just how much binds us together and how much should not be taken as common. To put it a different way: the most difficult issue in all politics is how far down the political goes into people's lives. The political community is thus that common point of view in terms of which people see their shared lives. The great discovery, as it were, of modern times was the limitation and the structuring of this common life and point of view in terms of constitutional principles and laws that preserved the integrity of family life and of the fragile bonds of a civil society held together only by threads of free association and freely accepted purposes of private associations.

Communitarians fruitfully enter the debate at this point, for they tend to focus on the common life (although not nearly enough on the free associations of civil society). The common point of view is not something that is achieved either naturally or at one fell swoop once and for all (however much liberal constitutionalists would like to think that a document like the American Constitution can perform this function). For there to be a common point of view, the citizens of a modern, pluralist social order must be able to see it and to see their own private concerns reflected in it. To do this, I would propose that we should focus on what I would call strategic goods, namely, those goods in which and through which we can project our values so that others can see them. Three examples of such strategic goods would be (1) the politics of education, which can't be handled from either a purely free choice or the purely conservative perspective; (2) health care, which also can't be handled by the utopians of the free market; and (3) the environment, because this requires the community to make various choices about what is going to surround it at the moment and what is to be available to those people who will follow us.

I said that I would end with a slogan. It seems to me that if you look at the progress of the last couple hundred years in American history, you can put it into three grand concepts. This country was founded on the principle of freedom, but the problem with this principle turned out to be that when taken alone, purely on its own, it could not answer questions about whether one person should be free to exploit another person, to humiliate another person or, worse, whether one person could be said to be free to own another person. The result was a very bloody war out of which emerged a rather Lincolnesque view of equality. That is, in finding out that freedom was not enough, we discovered that we also needed a concept of equality, the legal expression of which is the fourteenth amendment to the Constitution guaranteeing all persons equal protection of the laws and due process. Since 1964, though, about 100 years after the civil war, after we had finally passed the Civil Rights Act and the Voting Rights Act, we have come to realize that there was yet another problem, that of community. This was best captured by Dr. King's famous speech on the Washington Mall capping the march for civil rights when he talked not only about the freedom of individuals and the equality of individuals but also about the "content of their characters." This idea of the "content of our character" is not a matter of simply being free, for freedom does not come with a prescription telling us what to do with it, nor is it simply about the struggle for equality, for that too does not prescribe any direction in which to go after we have achieved it. We require some idea of how we ought to be doing things, how we are to maintain our sense of independence together with a recognition of the ways in which we are all dependent on each other. This can only be done within the context of a fully fledged "ethical life," a set of social practices that establishes the boundaries of what is to count for us as a proper object of moral reasoning and action.

So to conclude with the slogan I promised, communitarianism is now on the agenda because community will be on our agenda for the next 100 years. We have moved from Jeffersonian freedom to Lincolnesque equality to Dr. King's call for community. Hegelian reflections suggest that we need all three in order to be able to tell a coherent story about ourselves and about the direction in which our history ought to be moving.

10. From Socialism to Communitarianism*

Philip Selznick

My own departure from socialism occurred almost fifty years ago. In 1940 I broke with a small Trotskyist, Marxist-Leninist group and for a while belonged to the Norman Thomas socialists. However, by the time I returned from service in the army in 1946, I was convinced that the idea of socialism, at least for the United States, was no longer something I could really support. I retained very warm feelings for Norman Thomas, and felt a strong moral continuity with his concept of democratic socialism.

Nevertheless, I could no longer accept socialist economic doctrines, and since 1948 I have been something like a Truman Democrat. I take modest comfort from this long period of consistency, but I have not been happy with the attenuated moral vision that afflicts American liberalism.

Socialism had such a vision, but it carried too much ideological baggage, especially commitment to particular economic solutions. Although Thomas made some important modifications, especially in accepting the notion of a mixed economy, reserving government ownership for the "commanding heights," even that seemed to me insufficient.

At the same time, some of my old comrades, including some who in time broke with dogmatic and revolutionary forms of

* These remarks are based in part on a section of my book, *The Moral Commonwealth: Social Theory and the Promise of Community* (Berkeley: 1992).

Marxism, have clung to an image of socialism that seems more and more irrelevant, more and more attenuated. As one reads the pages of a magazine like *Dissent,* one sees that the socialist element becomes less and less clear. What we have is something else, a vague, not fully articulated sense that a moral perspective is needed, one not quite grasped by contemporary liberalism. Perhaps they have clung to a socialist identity out of a sense of piety, an unwillingness to discard the attachments that meant so much in their youth.

This is unfortunate, because it has meant that a fairly large number of people who might otherwise have helped to create moral and intellectual community have remained isolated from the mainstream of American politics. Without real justification, they have thought of themselves as necessarily radical—and separate.

The communitarian perspective offers an alternative. In important respects it carries forward the moral ideals of socialism, above all because it commits us to a strong sense of social responsibility. It suggests that the thin theory of community espoused by many liberals is not enough, that we need a stronger idea of community, one that will justify the commitments and sacrifices we ask of ourselves, and of one another, in the name of a common good.

However, we cannot be satisfied with this continuity, this residue of socialist morality, this affirmation of socialist roots. The communitarian perspective must go further. It must be more ecumenical, more open to other, related perspectives. Communitarianism reaches out to ideas that socialist groups have avoided. And that is, for example, the relevance of religious ideas, including Catholic social doctrine, Protestant social gospel, and the ideas of religious socialists such as Buber and Tillich. The communitarian perspective is also more sensitive to the values of tradition, to the funded experience of the community, and to the continuities of conventional and critical morality.

Not long before I made my break with Marxism-Leninism, I engaged in a debate with Irving Howe. I argued for the proposition that Marxism should no longer be taught as the official doctrine of the organization to which we belonged. What I was suggesting in that rather quixotic effort was another alternative, a different way of thinking, one more congenial to the American spirit and the American intellectual experience. I had in mind the philosophy of John Dewey.

There are signs today of a rekindled appreciation for what was once considered a crowning achievement in American thought. Dewey was a great spokesman for communitarian liberalism. He combined a spirit of liberation and social reconstruction with a strong commitment to responsible participation in effective communities. In his view, communities are effective insofar as they encourage uncoerced communication and insofar as they can apply intelligence and experimentation to problems of collective life. An important aspect of Dewey's thought is the connection he drew between democracy and community. He had a conception of communal democracy—which is not his term but the way his ideas have been characterized by various writers

Let me outline four principles of communal democracy. These may help to clarify the meaning of communitarianism. Communal democracy looks to the sovereignty of the people as a whole. Therefore it requires the protection and integration of minorities. And this means that it is profoundly anti-majoritarian. Although majority rule is one way of expressing the will of the people, it is not the only way, nor is it a self-sufficient way. Majorities may *represent* the community, but they are not the community. Without full participation, without the opportunity for everyone to have a say in creating, for example, the moral environments with which we are concerned, communal democracy is lacking.

The second principle of communal democracy is the primacy of the community over the state. Here the idea of civil society is especially relevant. This principle has very important constitutional significance. It suggests, for example, that a constitution is always in some sense open-ended—toward history, toward the future— because the rights and responsibilities of citizens can never be fully enumerated. For example, we can never state completely what the elements of due process are, because those elements must reflect changing historical circumstances and the needs of social life.

The encounter with totalitarianism in the twentieth century has reaffirmed a doctrine that emerged with special clarity from the political struggles of the seventeenth and eighteenth centuries: the idea that the containment of despotism requires a counterposition of state and society. If freedom is to be protected, government must be seen as derivative and instrumental—as the agent of the community, not its creator. On this view, governments are instituted for limited purposes, and they may be removed for cause. The people reserve for themselves fundamental rights of self-preservation, and fundamental liberties that have their roots in the experience of communal living.

A third principle of communal democracy looks in a different direction—toward the responsibility of government for the health and well-being of the community. Although the moral primacy of the community vis-a-vis the state must be protected, we must also recognize that the community itself may weaken and even atrophy. We cannot ignore needs that may arise for the repair or regeneration of social life. The viability of a community and its institutions cannot be taken for granted. It may be deeply divided along racial, ethnic, or ideological lines. Nor can government remain indifferent or idle when social conflict becomes social torment. Hence there is a need for positive government. A chief focus of that government should be the enhancement of community.

Social democracy is not necessarily communal democracy. Social democracy may or may not embrace concern for the vitality of community. It may be strongly individualist and statist. The programs of the welfare state are mainly designed to serve individual needs. (This is partly due to administrative convenience.) Guided by principles of equality and personal autonomy, they display only passing concern for the integrity and well-being of groups and institutions, that is, for the spontaneous arrangements of civil society. As government moves in to supplement and replace private ordering, the fabric of community is weakened. Kinship, religion, locality, employment, friendship, social networks, voluntary associations: all diminish in relative importance as resources for care and as centers of moral obligation.

Although the ideology of social democracy (or welfare liberalism) has often included affirmations of community, its operative ethos has been, in important ways, anti-communitarian. This slant stems mainly from the welfare liberal's commitment to rational organization and general rules—in a word, to bureaucracy. When liberalism becomes bureaucratic its spirit tends to suffocate. Bureaucracy, if unrestrained, reduces clients to passive dependency and, when interests conflict, gives the benefit of the doubt to the system.

The alternative is not a rejection of government, let alone of rationality. Rather, it is for the architects of the welfare state to transform their vision of how governments fulfill their responsibilities. If government will pay more attention to communal values and civil society, it will more clearly perceive and more adequately protect the needs of individual persons. And if it will adopt post-bureaucratic modes of organization, the welfare state can become more limited, more accountable, and more humane.

The fourth principle of communal democracy is the continuity of social and political participation. In John Dewey's conception of democracy-in-depth, the consent of the governed is active, critical, and participatory. It is self-preserving, not only in guarding freedoms and advancing well-being, but also in creating responsible persons who can govern their own passions and transcend their private or parochial interests.

Communal democracy must be distinguished from mass democracy. Mass participation is unmediated, undeliberative, and unstable. Its level may be high or low, excited or casual. Mass decisions are likely to be poor in quality and vulnerable to manipulation. In communal democracy, by contrast, people are tied into stable networks, understand their own interests, and are not readily moved by transient appeals or superficial impulses. The American electorate is a mass, some of the time and with respect to some issues, and is communal at other times and with respect to other issues. This variation accounts for many of the puzzles political scientists have encountered in analyzing voting and public opinion.

There is no substitute for an active, committed citizenry. The political process must be open to direct participation by individual citizens—not only that they may choose among parties or candidates but also that they may decide on major issues, including the shape of the process and the public agenda. At the same time, every form of direct participation must be mediated in some way. It must be filtered through a process that will take into account—and restrain—the potential degeneration of civic participation into mass participation. The former builds on community and enhances community; the latter distorts and subverts it.

Civic participation transcends the particularities of history, language, kinship, locality, and occupation. It creates new identities and new solidarities. It does not follow, however, that political democracy is the sole creator of community, or that it can be effective without a nonpolitical infrastructure of association, interdependence, and moral education. A democracy is weak and volatile if citizens are badly divided, or if many are incapable of participating or are shut out from participating, in the rewards and obligations of work, education, and family life. Citizenship cannot flourish—the call to deliberation will not be heard—if the main sources of personal responsibility are attenuated or lost.

11. On Labels and Reasons: The Communitarian Approach–Some European Comments

Otto Kallscheuer

Is there a common idea of the "left" in Europe and the United States? And should this idea be a "communitarian" one? Or is this "just another label"—as many people (especially in Eastern Europe) have also come to think about the common label "left" (used by both social democrats and communists)? Is there in the United States a coherent "communitarian" school of political thought, moral philosophy and even of economic analysis? Does this "communitarianism" have well-defined rules of methodology (in research) and membership (who is to be regarded as a "communitarian" and who not)? One might doubt it—even if the rumor about American "communitarianism" was not only commented on in American journals, e.g., *The Public Interest* (as a more or less disguised version of "socialism" or "postmodern populism"[1]), but has also already been the occasion for articles and debates in major European newspapers, e.g., the *Frankfurter Rundschau* in Germany.[2]

---

1. See *The Public Interest*, N. 104, Summer 1991, 122ff. (Reviews by Carl F. Horowitz and Vincent J. Cannato).

2. Most recently see the debate on "Communitarianism," Dec. 1991 on the "humanities"—page of the *Frankfurter Rundschau.*, now also published as a book: Chr. Zahlmann, ed. *Kommunitarismus in der Diskussion* (Berlin 1992).

Many American scholars regarded in Europe as "communitarians" do refuse this special label—preferring other labels like "populism" (Lasch), "communalism" (Barber), "civic republicanism," etc., obviously indicating various and rather contrasting philosophical and/or political sensibilities within the community of communitarians.

What I modestly could contribute to this debate is nothing more than a few comments on how Europeans might see—and approach—"communitarianism." To judge whether this picture conforms to reality, to which extent there really is in the American political and philosophical debate a "school," a "family," or a "club" of communitarian theorists, is up to you.

Seen from Europe—especially, but not exclusively from the German viewpoint—the communitarians are mainly social scientists or political or moral philosophers. Also, the (until now) rather few European commentaries or critiques of communitarianism come mostly out of the departments of philosophy.[3] The communitarian approach has not yet arrived in European economics departments or business schools.

With this impression—because it is just an impression—I obviously don't want to deny the transdisciplinary importance of recent efforts in the area of the "new social economics," prominently represented by Amitai Etzioni.[4] As far as I—not being an economist—can understand this "socio-economic" approach, it is aiming at a re-integration of the so called "pure" economical rationality in the social (that is, moral and institutional[5]) context of any economic activity. Consequently new social economics criticize the back-

---

3. Most recently see Jürgen Habermas, *Erläuterungen zur Diskursethik* (Frankfurt/M.: 1991), 100ff. See also Maurizio Passerin D'Entreves, *Modernity, Justice and Community* (Milan: 1990). Axel Honneth, ed., *Kommunitarismuss* (New York-Frankfurt/M. 1993).

4. See A. Etzioni, *The Moral Dimension:Towards a New Economics* (New York: 1990) (first published 1988). For European reactions see the special issue "La socio-économie — une nouvelle discipline," of *La revue du MAUSS. Mouvement Anti-Utilitaire dans les Sciences Sociales,* N. 9 (Paris, Fall 1990) with articles by Etzioni, Swedberg, and Joriot.

5. On this see Mary Douglas, *How Institutions Think* (Syracuse: 1986) (but obviously this is a classical Durkheimian thesis).

ground metaphysics of neoclassical economics (and rational-choice theories): the context-free homo oeconomicus—the "rational fool," to quote Amartya Sen[6]—as the only relevant or prominent subject of economical science.

I do not know whether all members of the recently founded Society for the Advancement of Socio-Economics would adopt (or accept) the label "communitarians." But certainly the new social economics and the communitarians in political and moral philosophy do have certain family-resemblances (*Familienähnlichkeiten*, to use the notion of Wittgenstein), not only with the idea of the left (and this will be my first point), but also with a general tendency in social philosophy and philosophy in general: a "movement" or shift aiming at a recontextualization of "pure" or procedural reason. I will return to that later (in the second point), before ending with an open question on what communitarianism might mean today—politically (the third point).

Let me say one word to the key-word "left." The French existentialist social philosopher André Gorz has recently proposed a definition of the left (he even used the word "socialist") as follows. What is left of the left after the collapse of communism? It is, says Gorz, the never-ending effort or task to put social limits on the otherwise "imperialistic" economic rationality: that is, on the tendency of the economic subsystem to dominate all other spheres of social activity, evaluation, and judgment.[7] (This kind of critique of pure market rationality conforms very well to Michael Walzer's or Alan Wolfe's definition of "market imperialism,"[8] but also Pope John Paul's criticism of the "idolatry of the market."[9] Obviously this is a

6. Amartya K. Sen, "Rational Fools: A Critique of the Behavioral Foundations of Economic Theory," in *Scientific Models and Men*, H. Harris, ed. (London: 1978), 317-44.

7. See André Gorz, *Critique of Economic Reason* (London: 1989), ch. 10; Gorz, *Capitalisme, Socialisme, Ecologie* (Paris: 1991), ch. 1 and ch. 5. Cf. my remarks in the afterword to the German edition, André Gorz, *Und jetzt wohin?* (Berlin: 1991), 175ff.

8. See Michel Walzer, "Liberalism and the Art of Separation," *Political Theory*, Vol. 12, N. 3 (August 1984), 315-330; Alan Wolfe, *Whose Keeper? Social Science and Moral Obligation* (Berkelely: 1989).

9. John Paul II. Litterae Enciclicae "Centesimus Annus," in *L'Osservatore Romano*, May 2, 1991, N. 40.

very old criticism, which in some respect has already been put forward by Aristotle or St. Thomas.[10])

Limits to economic rationality, then, can be considered as a left idea. But why just limits—couldn't we get rid of this kind of rationality totally, given its inherent "imperialistic" dangers? The answer is no. According to André Gorz, to suppress the economic rationality altogether is either impossible in modern complex industrial societies, or might lead to a totalitarian society, whose economy is ordered by command[11]—that is—to the kind of socialism that failed. A modern society cannot (without becoming despotic) suppress either "exchange" or "authority" or "persuasion" as forms or methods of social coordination (to adopt the terminology of Charles E. Lindblom[12])—but the task of the left is to prevent a domination of one subsystem (be it market imperialism or ideological tyranny) within the overall complex of spheres of social activity.

What's left then? A somewhat liberal idea, but a strong version of it: checks and balances—not only between the branches of administration, legislation and the courts, but between the various spheres of social activity, judgment and distribution which are economic, political, cultural, and religious life. Pure, or as Etzioni might say, "cynical" market rationality must be embedded in social responsibility and framed by democratic institutions. Economic values have to be counterbalanced by other—and for the left this should mean egalitarian—values. But the 1991 *Centesimus Annus*, the social encyclical of the head of the Catholic church, is also moved by an analogous critique of "pure," unframed capitalism (*capitalismus effrenus*, as John Paul II puts it). And the problem with Roman Catholicism is, then, that the non-economic moral values that the Pope would like to be embodied in social practice and political institutions are not likely to be pluralistic ones, stemming from Thomistic "natural law."[13]

---

10. Aristoteles, *Politics* 1257 b; Thomas Aquinas, *Summa Theologiae*, Pars la Ilae, quaestio 78.

11. Gorz, *Critique of Economic Reason*, ch. 4.

12. Charles E. Lindblom, *Politics and Markets: The World's Political Economical Systems* (New York: 1977).

13. On this see the chapter "Ecclesia Militans. Capitalism, Catholicism and Democracy" in my book: Otto Kallscheuer, *Glaubensfragen* (Questions of Faith) (Frankfurt/M.: 1991), 177-234.

If that is the task of the left—and I'm aware that instead of quoting *Critique of Economic Reason* by the French existentialist Andre Gorz I might have quoted as well the American book *Spheres of Justice* by Michael Walzer[14]—then, indeed, the left has to adopt a pluralist methodology in social theory and consequently also a pluralist methodology of social reform. *Ex definitione* a monocratic system—be it state-communism or Caesaro-papism[15]—could not be called a left one, exactly because the left is aiming at an integration of the economic, political, and social spheres (*società economica, società politica* and *società civile* in the Gramscian terms). One can only re-integrate, incorporate, recontextualize, etc. subsystems or forms of rationality that are also and at the same time preserved. Without separation (of economy, administration, social life, religion, science, etc.), there could be no connection—because there would be nothing left to be connected.

This sums up my general, and perhaps even too obvious remarks on the political coordinates (or the value system) of the "left": the reasons indicated by that label. But what has all that to do with the more specifically philosophical communitarian debate? From the viewpoint of European philosophical controversies the connection—or the room for "overlapping consensus" (John Rawls)—between left reasons and communitarian questions has something to do with the controversy on modernity.

I have tried to define "the" (or better: a democratic) left by its efforts to reconnect divided spheres and reasons of social life under the guideline of egalitarian ideals (leaving out the question of how "complex equality" should be conceived, a problem I cannot treat here).[16] And we might see in this way left politics—and left values in general—as dealing with the social consequences of modernity. If modernity is seen as a process of autonomization of several spheres

14. New York: 1983.

15. Which might be structurally identical: cf. Ernest Gellner, "La société civile dans une perspective historique," *Revue internationale des sciences sociales*, N. 126 (August 1991), 527. See also Otto Kallscheuer, *Gottes Wort and Volkes Stimme - Glaube Macht Politik* (Frankfurt/M. 1994) Ch. 2.

16. See Walzer, *Spheres of Justice*, and Ronald Dworkin, "What is Equality?" *Philosophy and Public Affairs*, Vol. 10 (1981), no. 3 and 4, for different approaches to this problem.

or subsystems of rationality—economic rationality (the market system), political rationality (legitimation and administration), religious belief, scientific rationality, privacy (as a reason not to be governed by other forms of rationality) etc. ... —then a democratic left would tend to integrate or connect those subsystems under the guideline of egalitarian values. This would be achieved without suppressing the "liberal walls" (Walzer) of separation between market, political democracy, religious liberty, the freedom of opinion, and the right to choose a personal or group-specific lifestyle.

With these background considerations in mind, it is of highest interest to observe in recent philosophical discussion (and within "humanities" in general) something like a "movement"—or, more modestly speaking, a shift—toward recontextualization of "pure" reason: be it the reason of science or the reason of moral philosophy.[17] I have already mentioned socio-economics and the rediscovering of the "moral dimension" of any economic activity.

Within academic philosophy I might mention the programmatic book of Stephen Toulmin, *Cosmopolis*, on "the hidden agenda of modernity" (as its subtitle goes), which is not just another book on the history of ideas but also a kind of manifesto on the politics of rationality. Toulmin adopts a kind of hermeneutical methodology in his reconstruction (one might also say: archeology) of modern reason, aiming to restore the political, religious, and existential context (Toulmin speaks of "subtext") of classical rationalism in the sixteenth and seventeenth centuries, the period and "space of experience" of religious wars in Europe, when and where the "pure" reason of the Cartesian cogito and Newtonian physics originated. He does not want to dismiss modern rationalism totally. Obviously it is as impossible (or self-defeating) to forget or destroy the achievements that modern scientific rationalism has brought to our western civilization as it would be impossible (or self-defeating) to destroy market rationality. However, Toulmin says we have to correct or to connect them, in order to contain the risks of morally or ecologically "blind" scientific growth. And by his historical "recontextualization"—so Toulmin maintains—we could (and should) also relearn the "reasonable"

---

17. See Bernard Williams, *Ethics and the Limits of Philosophy* (London: 1985).

(as opposed to "rationalistic") and more ecological, tolerant, and pragmatic virtues of Renaissance Humanism that seventeenth century rationalism once suppressed.[18]

I will not comment on Toulmin's diagnosis and therapy of modernity (the therapy might not work even if the diagnosis fits), but will mention only other recent works on moral philosophy (e.g., Bernard Williams' brilliant book on *Ethics and the Limits of Philosophy* or the works of Charles Taylor[19]) or on social anthropology (Clifford Geertz, Mary Douglas, and others), that stress the moral and institutional contexts of rational procedures as well as individual decision making of human beings in society.

The "family-resemblance" with the communitarian approach in recent American philosophy—*ceterum censeo*: as seen from the European viewpoint—seems to me the following: "Communitarianism" seems to be less a "school" of thinking—not to speak of a "club" with defined membership rules—than a common kind of reaction in political and moral philosophy to modern individualism.

Individualism is seen by communitarians[20] also as a social tendency, which in social macro-theory may also be explained by the ("functional") autonomization of spheres and (sub)systems of action and reason in modern society, "producing" the disintegration of shared social values in the "life world" (Habermas, *Lebenswelt*). This is ultimately enforced by the growing mobilities in social life[21]—and as a methodological option within social science and moral philosophy. Communitarians would like to counter as well the overall social shift toward "unconnected," context-free individualism in society—by means of communal (or "strong")

---

18. See Stephen Toulmin, *Cosmopolis: The Hidden Agenda of Modernity* (New York: 1990).

19. Charles Taylor, *Philosophical Papers*, Vol. 1. and 2. (Cambridge: 1985); Taylor, *Sources of the Self* Cambridge, MA: 1989.

20. But not only by communitarians. See e.g. Jürgen Habermas, "Individuierung durch Vergesellschaftung," Habermas, *Nachmetaphysisches Denken* (Frankfurt/M.: 1988), 187ff. (especially 234ff.)

21. On this see M. Walzer, "The Communitarian Critique of Liberalism," *Political Theory*, Vol. 18, N. 1 (Feb. 1990), 6-23. Walzer here speaks of the "Four Mobilities": geographic, social, marital, and political.

democracy and the strengthening of bonds of civic solidarity[22]—
and the individualistic methodologies (and background ideologies) in social science.[23]

To simplify my remarks, if the process of modernity can be seen
as a "production process" of individualization in society, with the
consequence of loosening shared normative orientations of all
members in modern societies, then there are two possible *prima
facie* reactions to this process. Either we can accept, even hail or
adopt this tendency within social philosophy (by this means enforcing it), or we might condemn it, trying to return to some (real or
imagined) status quo ante.

• Postmodernism—or deconstructionism—would adopt the
first view. If (to quote Marx's *Manifesto*) "all that is solid melts
in the air," if modernity itself has already deconstructed the
"great tales" (Jean François Lyotard: "les grand récits") of
progress, liberty and justice, then postmodernists say we
should welcome this evolution and try to further it within
(and by means of) philosophical discourse.

• Vice versa: Aristotelianism—or other kinds of (in the Roman
Catholic sense) "natural law" fundamentalism, as is present in
the recent social encyclical of John Paul II, would like to
restore an older, more integrated moral order of society.
Obviously, aristotelianism or neo-Thomism are not the only
forms of this reaction to the loosening of common (social,
civic, or moral) bonds in contemporary societies. One might
also mention Christopher Lasch's recent plea for a revitalization of the American working and lower middle-class "populist" virtues of limits, self-respect, and family—against the
culture of critical discourse of the "new intellectual class."[24]

22. See Benjamin Barber, *Strong Democracy: Participatory Politics for a New Age* (Berkeley: 1984); Robert Bellah et al., *The Good Society* (New York: Knopf 1991). Etzioni,
The Spirit of Community, (New York 1993).

23. See Alan Wolfe, *Whose Keeper?* and "The Return of Values," *Tikkun,* Vol I., no. 2
(1986).

24. See Christopher Lasch, *The True and Only Heaven. Progress and its Critics* (New
York: 1991) and the debate in *Tikkun,* Sept./Oct. 1991.

Tertium non datur? Does this alternative exhaust the philosophical possibilities of reacting to the modern disintegration of social bonds? Or is there a third way—which would mean to accept the process of modern individualization and fragmentation of social spheres, but to try to reintegrate modern society by means of a process of self-government, which would develop the pluralism of life-spheres without abandoning the democratic hopes of (classical) modern philosophy in a common good?

Our problem with American communitarians—viewed with the glasses of European philosophy—is that it is not at all evident for us which one of the two (or three) options mentioned above they would like to adopt. If we take the two major representatives of "communitarianism" within moral philosophy, then Aliasdair McIntyre might be seen as an example of an antimodern critique of modernity, whereas the books of Charles Taylor might be read in Europe as belonging to the third alternative listed above: that is, developing a reflective self-limitation of an otherwise destructive modernity, without abandoning the pluralism fundamental for any democratic society. (And this would obviously fit the rather generic definition of the "left" I mentioned earlier).

Or, to quote two representatives of political thinking, Christopher Lasch's last book is likely to be read by a European political scientist—who might even accept most of his diagnosis about the "illusions of progress" (Georges Sorel)—as a somewhat romantic vision of American populism, whereas Benjamin Barber's "strong democracy" might be read—even by those who are skeptical about the practicability of all his proposals for "communal" democracy—as an effort to correct a merely privatistic vision of representative democracy without abandoning the essential division of power in a democratic state.

For Europeans the bothersome thing—or, to put it more politely, the healthy American provocation—about the communitarian approach lies precisely in one difficulty (which, as it turns out now, is not only a problem of labeling). Communitarians criticize the all-too-optimistic, individualistic, and rationalistic self-interpretation of modernity, but they (often) do this with reasons that come out of a tradition of either civic-republican or solidaristic (or both) norms or values that stem from the core of the modern

Enlightenment project itself. (But one might even recall some much older background stories on the grammatics of emancipation and social criticism—like the one of prophet Amos[25]).

In moral and political philosophy, communitarians seem to concentrate their criticism on either the methodological fiction or (even more) on the substantive ideal of the originally a- or presocial individual in the mainstream traditions of modern ethical thought: be it the utilitarian or neoclassical "context-free" and utility-calculating subject; be it the Kantian subject, governed by the *a priori* rules of "pure" practical reason; or be it (last, but not least) the subject under a "veil of ignorance" in the Rawlsian version of contractualism. It should be noted, however, that John Rawls recently has modified his theory of justice in a somewhat less contrafactual-hypothetical way, now much more stressing the cultural tradition of the "liberal community" in American democracy itself.[26] So even this opposition between "Kantian Liberalism" and "Communitarianism"—often referred to in European philosophical "labeling"—might look stronger than it really is.

This communitarian criticism of the individualistic background metaphysics of the (neo)liberal mainstream rejoins European traditions in moral philosophy. Hermeneutics (Hans Georg Gadamer), phenomenology (especially Paul Ricoeur), as well as the communication or "discursive" ethics of the New Frankfurt School of Jürgen Habermas might agree with at least one critical point of communitarianism. The concept of individual liberty— the key concept of the Enlightenment tradition of emancipation— cannot reasonably be conceived within a purely individualistic conceptual framework. If—to quote the classical German philosopher Marx—"the positing of the individual ... in his nakedness is itself a product of history,"[27] if human beings can individualize

---

25. See M. Walzer, *Interpretation and Social Criticism* (Cambridge, MA: 1987), ch. 3.

26. See John Rawls, "Justice as Fairness: Political not Metaphysical,"*Philosophy and Public Affairs*, Vol. 14 (Summer 1985). On this see Habermas, *Erläuterungen zur Diskursethik*, 125ff.; Richard Rorty, "The Priority of Democracy to Philosophy," German translation in: Rorty, *Solidarität oder Objektivität?* (Stuttgart: 1988).

27. "Die Setzung des Individuums *als eines Arbeiters*, in dieser Nacktheit, ist selbst historisches Produkt," K. Marx, *Grundrisse der Kritik der politischen Ökonomie* (1857-58) (Frankfurt/M.: 1968), 375. In quoting I left out the emphasized words "as a

themselves only within history and society, then without the networks of social communication even the most individualistic lifestyle would be impossible.

If individual liberty is not only understood as a more or less formal "opportunity concept" (that is, "negative liberty" in the classical definition of Sir Isaiah Berlin) but also as a "human agency" of moral actors,[28] then this "exercise concept" (Charles Taylor) of human liberty presupposes a conception of the self that is already a social one. "One has to be a member of a community to be a self" (George Herbert Mead). This social construction of the individual self could not be grasped within atomistic models of moral philosophy or sociological thought, but has to be understood as embedded in discursive networks of moral traditions—of a socially shared moral world—in order to reconstruct "a picture of agency in which individuals create their own moral rules through the social interactions they experience with others" (Alan Wolfe).[29] The political ethics of civic republicanism as well as the approaches of communitarians or of "communicative rationality" (Habermas) underline the necessary embedding of individual emancipation in a more or less "thick" environment of a socially transmitted "moral world," which is our real social world—and the only world where social criticism and social reform are possible.[30] So even the "liberal" liberty—one might conclude—would be impossible without the "liberal community."[31]

Liberty needs community, then. But now the problem arises as to which community should be referred to when we speculate about conditions for the possibility of equal liberty in modern plu-

---

worker" (see also the English translation by Martin Nicolaus, Pelican Marx Library 1973, 472).

28. See Charles Taylor, "What's Wrong with Negative Liberty," in: Taylor, *Philosophical Papers*, Vol. 2.

29. Wolfe, *Whose Keeper?*, 212. Wolfe goes on: "A sociological approach to moral obligation focuses neither on the individual standing outside of society nor on society as if it were not composed of individuals, but instead on the way individuals and society interact to make moral order possible" (213).

30. See Walzer, *Interpretation and Social Criticism.*

31. See Ronald Dworkin, "The Liberal Community," *The California Law Review* (1990), here cited from the Italian version: *Teoria Politica*, Vol. 1, no. 1 (1990), 27-56.

ralistic societies. And even if I do suspect that this question does not arise only from the European (or my German) viewpoint on communitarianism, I might try to exemplify my problem as a problem of translation.

For German ears the "community" referred to in the expression "communitarian" is a rather ambivalent notion, because it has two different meanings. First, it covers aspects of the meaning of the German word or concept *Gemeinschaft*, which might be the local community, the religious community, "*die Gemeinde,*" the ethnic community or even the communities "in fusion" (in the Sartrian sense[32]) of social or cultural movements. But the "community" referred to—especially when referred to in order to (re)construct the "good society"—might also be the translation of the word/concept *Gesellschaft*.[33]

Politically speaking, *Gemeinschafts*-comunitarianism would stress multicultural (multireligious, etc.) tolerance among the various "communities," whereas *Gesellschafts*-communitarianism would accentuate more the political virtues that prevent a disintegration of the political community into mere economic corporate interest groups or (and I shall limit my remarks to this problem) ethnic tribalism.[34] In the German philosophical tradition, the first communitarianism, that is, the pluralism of cultural and/or ethnic communities, might be identified with the cultural pluralism (some critics even say relativism[35]) of Johann Gottfried Herder—who (it is valuable to be reminded) was one of the first multicultural immigrants crossing Europe from the Balticum to the West (which then was revolutionary France). The second, republican- or civic virtue-communitarianism might be analogized with the political *Sittlichkeit*;

---

32. See Jean-Paul Sartre, *Critique de la Raison Dialectique,* (Paris: 1961).

33. See the classic book of Ferdinand Tönnies, *Gemeinschaft und Gesellschaft. Grundbegriffe der reinen Soziologie,* first published in1887 (Darmstadt: 1979).

34. And might be identified with the M-Version (the Montesquieu-Tocqueville tradition) of the "Civil Society" conception — as opposed to the Lockean tradition (the L-Version). See Charles Taylor's paper on the "Civil Society" conference of Pope John Paul II at Castelgandolfo, German translation in: *Europa und die Civil Society. Castelgandolfo-Gespräche 1989,* ed. K. Michalski, (Stuttgart: 1991).

35. For a defense of Herder against the verdict of being a "relativist" see Isaiah Berlin, *The Crooked Timber of Humanity* (New York: 1991), 70-91.

that is, according to Hegel, is the level of "ethical life" specific for a modern state and modern citizenship and necessary for the constitutional existence of political liberty.[36]

If I were a Hegelian, I might be tempted to come to the dialectical conclusion that what we need for a liberal and pluralistic left would be a communitarianism integrating both *Gemeinschaft* and *Gesellschaft*. What we need is both a modern equivalent of the Hegelian political *Sittlichkeit*, democratic citizenship in a somewhat "strong" sense of political participation (as stressed by Benjamin Barber), and also a vision of multicultural pluralism, of difference and diversity as positive values for radical democracy.

Unfortunately, I am not a Hegelian philosopher. But—apart from my personal taste (de gustibus non est dubitandum)—the historical fact in Central Europe is that in the last two centuries the Herder and Hegel heritage never really did integrate, they never developed *Wahlverwandtschaften* (elective affinities). Today, "the day after" the break down of communism, the erupting nationalisms claim "national" (which equals ethnic) community first and are fighting bloody wars for ethnic segregation and homogenization. A political integration of the real-existing cultural (ethnic, religious, linguistic, etc.) pluralism by constitutional rules—the kind of political community that in Germany Jürgen Habermas defines as "constitutional patriotism"—today seems to have little chance in Central or Eastern Europe after forty or more years of communist *Sittlichkeit*.[37]

---

36. On this see the excellent book by Allen W. Wood, *Hegel's Ethical Thought* (Cambridge: 1990).

37. On this see the articles in: *TRANSIT. Europaische Revue*, no. 7 (1994), "Macht Raum Europa."

Part III

ECONOMIC POLICY AND SOCIAL JUSTICE

12. Economic Policy and the Role of the State — The Invisible, the Visible and the Third Hand

Elmar Altvater

It is evident that, among other factors, the functioning of the welfare state as well as the institutional richness and democratic reach of the civil society depends heavily on the economic efficiency of a given society. Now, the question is: what does economic efficiency depend on? There are several different answers, each of them depending on their theoretical background. Neoliberals or neoclassical economists stress the meaning of the "invisible hand" of a free-market system as the crucial prerequisite for achieving the best distribution of productive factors, of finding the best path of innovation and evolution, and for realizing the highest possible speed for economic growth, i.e., material welfare provision. Of course there are many doubts about this answer, even within the neoliberal discourse. But although there may be no best distribution, no best path and no highest possible speed of growth, deeply convinced liberals hold that there is no better solution than that produced by the anonymous market mechanism.

Yet, obviously there are market failures that may hamper the achievement of the best or at least the second best solution of economic problems. Of course, there are the problems of regulated prices and of entry and exit barriers to markets, which might result in a disequilibrium and waste of economic resources. There is also the familiar problem of myopia of market agents. The horizon of market decisions in terms of time is by its very nature restricted: market agents have difficulties calculating effects beyond the time schedule of the marginal efficiency of capital. The same happens in terms of space. Markets generate external effects beyond the spatial reach of producers or consumers. Last, but not least, markets can only allocate and distribute commodities, so they fail in allocating and distributing the great bulk of non-commodities, namely public goods. The theoretical and consequently political reliance on market mechanisms by means of "deregulation" therefore may impoverish a given economy and may even reduce the economic growth rates and slow down innovation and evolution. After ten years of deregulation in the United States or in Great Britain, many economists today criticize the negative effects of deregulation on international competitiveness of deregulated economies

Hence another traditional answer seems rather convincing. Instead of relying on the invisible hand of the market, there is some need of a "visible hand," in other words, state intervention. It should be mentioned here that the term "visible hand" has been used by Alfred Chandler in a somewhat different way. He stresses the decisive role of management of modern business enterprise insofar as it is replacing "what Adam Smith referred to as the invisible hand of market forces":[1] the visible hand is that of "managerial capitalism."

In the context of the discussion presented here, however, the "visible hand" is that of the various public institutions following other "logic" than the big business enterprises. The best known and most elaborated concept of this "logic" is of course the "Keynesian message," a policy of full employment and of a welfare state.

For a long time, in fact, Keynesian and Beveridgean state interventions have been rather successful in terms of high employment, economic growth, and welfare. But here, too, the effects of state intervention are tentatively producing counterproductive results, so that the statement of failures of the state becomes a plausible argument. The causes of the erosion of Keynesian economic policy are manifold. Each of them may be interpreted as a negative

---

1. Alfred D. Chandler, *The Visible Hand* (Cambridge and London: 1977).

consequence of the success of and not as an inherent flaw in the mechanism of Keynesian state intervention. First there is internationalization of capital, undermining the regulating capacity of the traditional nation-state. Yet, the internationalization of capital is a result of the high dynamics of the world market after World War II in terms of growth rates of world trade, of foreign investment, and of international capital transfers, managed by the globally operating banking system. The growth of capital in time is always connected to the expansion of capital in space, so that high growth rates stimulated by Keynesian state intervention enhance the expansion of capital beyond the nation-state. Yet, the result of these processes is the "loss of interest sovereignty," so that in the course of internationalization the nation-state loses one of its most efficient policy instruments (control of the interest rate by means of monetary policy) for the market mechanism.

The growth of the national product is always a qualitative process, in the course of which not only ecological changes take place, but also capital intensity also increases. Changes in the latter exert a fatal influence on employment, since the monetary equivalent of capital investment has to increase in order to create a given number of jobs. This might not only be senseless ecologically, but also imprudent in terms of economic efficacy. This occurs especially when technological progress does not prove to be Harrod-neutral, since with growing capital intensity, capital productivity decreases.

Therefore, a shift occurs from an orientation toward the "quantity" of labor to an emphasis on the "quality" of labor. In Keynes's words, "When 9,000,000 men are employed out of 10,000,000 willing and able to work, there is no evidence that the labor of these 9,000,000 men is misdirected. The complaint against the present system is not that these 9,000,000 men ought to be employed on different tasks, but that tasks should be available for the remaining 1,000,000 men. It is in determining the volume, not the direction, of actual employment, that the existing system has broken down."[2] Contrary to Keynes, Joan Robinson stressed the importance of social and economic changes leading to the quality orientation of labor; what matters is having not just any job, but a qualitatively sat-

2. John M. Keynes, (1936), *The General Theory of Employment, Interest and Money* (Macmillan repr. 1964) p. 379.

isfying job. Only if the mere quantity is relevant, might Keynesian policy work. However, if people do not simply expect jobs *sans phrase*, but want qualitatively interesting, socially useful, and ecologically reasonable jobs, Keynesian political concepts must fail, unless they are modified to some kind of a "Keynes-Plus Project." This is not an "economics of full employment," but an economics of qualitatively satisfying employment, comprising strategies of worktime reduction as well as the social control of private investment.

Last but not least, economic growth produces social changes, not only in terms of stratification of the working class, but also in regard to social and individual values, habits, and norms. Economic growth may produce increased economic and social material welfare by deteriorating communitarian structures and security networks, or by destroying parts of the natural environment. Due to these by-products of economic growth, a reluctance toward further commodification and monetization may emerge, a reluctance extended to the traditional instruments and the output of the Keynesian welfare state. New social movements emerge, no longer willing to accept the Keynesian message of (quantitative) growth and any employment increase at all. On the contrary, they begin to try other forms of production and consumption, and consequently other forms of distribution and exchange.

There is a third answer to the question, stressing the institutional factor of a given economic system. Not just the invisible and the visible hand matter, but also a "third hand" (Diane Elson). The "third hand" comprises all non-market networks for diversified quality production[3], such as public goods, which have to be produced by society and societal agents, since they cannot be supplied simply by the market mechanism or as the intended output of state actions. These public goods are social peace, competence of private management and public administration, skills and qualifications of the work force, an ecologically healthy environment, and a functioning material and immaterial infrastructure.

---

3. Wolfgang Streeck, "On the Institutional Conditions of Diversified Production," Matzner and Streeck, eds., *Beyond Keynesiansim: The Socio-Economics of Production and Full Employment* (Aldershot: 1991).

Further important factors of non-market networks include, as Streeck points out, "redundant capacities." They are a necessary condition for flexible reactions to market signals. This factor is a well-known ethnological term. The best strategies for survival in a hostile environment are "leisure-preference" and "retardation of productivity-increase." Only insofar as a community disposes of its reserves, i.e., redundant capacities, does it remain capable of surviving. It is quite obvious that the market forces produce at their full capacity in order to minimize individual costs. Therefore, redundant capacities can only be provided by means of some social decision making, i.e., by overcoming the constraints of individual rationality and by introducing criteria of social rationality.

Non-market networks may be interpreted as a regional structure of Marshallian "site effects," i.e., of productive channels for external economies and advantages for all regionally producing and consuming units. By definition, site effects, or external economies, are non-market processes. The more a given economy is embedded in a social structure, favorable to the production of "economic commons," the more they exert positive results. The "tragedy of the commons" (Hardin, Daly) is a widely acknowledged phenomenon; but without the possibility of economic units recurring to economic commons, the productivity of the whole process falls behind.

This deliberation naturally brings us back to the importance of a developed and rich civil society for an efficient economic system. Therefore, we may conclude that the invisible as well as the visible and the third hand should not be grasped as alternatives, but as necessary ingredients to an articulated social entity. The notion of civil society utilized here refers to the concept of Gramsci. He distinguishes between *società politica* and *società civile* as different institutional sets linking state and society. The first comprises the "hard core" of the power structure of a social and political system (police, army, etc.); the latter refers to institutions generating social consent. It is important to note that consent is not merely psychological, but is inscribed into material institutions and depends on the performance of the economy.

In reality, this conclusion has the following meaning in the context of an analysis of economic stance and the policy of a nation:

Today the "invisible hand" may be described as the "reality principle" of the world market, because if one speaks of markets, it is important that this refers to the developed world market. Commodity trade, capital investment, and financial flows at the end of the twentieth century are globalized to a considerable extent. Of course, the distribution and allocation of factors and income flows are exerted world-wide by means of the market's functioning "invisible hand." But on the other hand, everyone recognizes that on the global level the allocative capacity of the market is limited due to political interventions, regimes, and interferences of power structures. Therefore, the most important contribution of the "invisible hand" to economic efficacy is the exercise of a "hard budget constraint." Thus, by means of scarce money, companies dispose only limited amounts of money, for which they have to pay a determined interest rate, formed on the market for financial assets. Interest rates are the most important market signals for individual companies. According to these, they produce a surplus sufficient to pay interest on invested capital. Otherwise companies will perish, i.e., they will be punished through bankruptcy.

As Janos Kornai pointed out, the existence of a hard budget constraint is the most important precondition for investment decisions, following the economic principle, and thus for the improvement of economic efficiency. Moving interest rates rule decisions made over producing an economic surplus in terms of money, on the level of a given enterprise. Monetary obligations are an effective power to force single business enterprises to follow market rules of surplus production. This force may of course be perverted into a relation of violence, well-known from Hollywood movies, in which an indebted person is blackmailed by Mafia-like organizations into performing morally questionable and even criminal acts. I might add that on a national level the hard budget constraint of the world market exists as the "loss of interest sovereignty." The service on foreign debts exerts an efficacious pressure on the selection of production technologies, product variety, employment, price level, real wages, etc. The requirement to service the foreign debt rules economic and social policy to such an extent that nations may fall back into a state of economic stagnation, social involution, ecological disasters, and political ungovernability. Paradoxically, the hard budget constraint in the case of foreign indebtedness of nations is often not exerted by market forces alone, but by political institutions like the International Monetary Fund or the World Bank. They are the institutional incarnations of the hard budget constraints; they use political pressure on nation-states, in order to force them to adjust and restructure their economic system. The budget constraint, at first glance a pure market signal exerted by scarce money in a considerable number of cases, turns into the "violence of money" under which social systems of indebted countries are suffering. Therefore, on the one hand the hard budget constraint of the market is a powerful means of enforcing economic rationality. But on the other hand it also compels individual firms and even nations to commit to socially, ecologically, and even economically problematic activities that undermine its rationality.

Thus it follows that the exertion of market signals in modern times rationally only works as long as political institutions intervene in the process of economic and social evolution and adjustment. Especially on the global level the traditional contradiction between economic and political principles remains a decisive characteristic of the capitalist world system. Even if limited in its efficiency, the visible hand still exists in the economic sphere of the world market: control of trade relations, technology transfer, capital flows, migration fluxes, to give just a few examples. Since the global economic system is constituted by the many nation-states, a wide space for political interventions still remains. The reach of political interventions depends of course on the economic, political and military power of nation-states vis-à-vis other nation-states, so that powerful nation-states wield a considerably higher degree of sovereignty than less powerful nation-states. Therefore, the policy resources of a nation-state also depend on its comparative power in the global system. Some nation-states set rules that others have to follow. As the regime theory or the theories of hegemony and of the capitalist world system convincingly reveal, in modern times there seems to be no other way than basing the comparative power structure of nation-states on a secure foundation of consensual rules and norms integrated into a network of international institutions. In order to have the visible hand free for interventions, the nation-states have to participate in the "international game" of states, following the rules of a certain historical regime or hegemonic order. Only insofar as the international environment is settled can the nation-state use its "visible hand" for the regulation of the national economy by means of a certain kind of "social democratic supply-side policy," e.g., by promoting technology, qualification measures, and environmental protection and supplying the economy with all those already mentioned non-market factors such as social peace and material infrastructure.

As has already been pointed out, the latter is only possible insofar as an institutional network of a civil society exists. The civil society of course does not serve the economy, but it is a necessary component of an articulated social entity, which without civil societal institutions cannot be efficient and therefore will fall back into international competition, forced by the invisible hand of the world market. The relation between the market, the nation-state, and the institutional network of a civil society is not a simple one and not without contradictions. First, there is the problem of the spatial incompatibility of societal organization, political institutions, and economic processes. The market today can only be described as the world market of commodities, capital, and financial flows. The state, on the contrary, remains a nation-state. The institutional network of a civil society is usually regionally or locally bound. The articulation of global, national, and regional spaces in a given social system is a crucial element of economic development. For instance, world market tendencies may foster industries in certain regions. However, it is not certain that industries producing for the world market also promote regional and national development. Whether this effect occurs depends on the capacity of industries to produce "linkages" of different dimensions: consumption as well as financial linkages or backward or forward production linkages.[4]

Moreover, the efficiency of linkages depends on the kind of products (staples or industrial products), since they determine the degree of processing, and therefore the amount of regionally-produced added value. Other important factors influencing the production of linkages by means of site or district effects, are the already mentioned competence of managements of business

---

4. Albert Hirschmann, "A Generalized Linkage Approach to Development, with Special Reference to Staples," in *Essays in Trespassing*, (Cambridge, London, New York: 1981) p. 69-97.

enterprises and state bureaucracies, skills of the work force, social peace as the output of a special organization of industrial relations, etc. It is the interrelationship between economic processes and social institutions that for the most part contributes to regional and national development, despite the (asymmetrical) dependency on the world market. Therefore, regions may fall behind due to world market tendencies if the institutional network of the economy is too poor to mobilize the necessary district effect. There are many examples of successful regional development as well as of its failure in recent history, all of them closely connected to tendencies of reshaping the geographical structure of the world economy. The manifold investigations and studies of successful regional development, be it in the "third" Italy or in California or Baden-Württemberg in Germany, have shown that the existence of the non-market institutional network of a civil society is one of the decisive and most favorable factors for the relocation of industries. Interventions of the nation state are certainly important also. They either support these tendencies or they hamper their realization. This is no trivial assertion, since the nation-state is always bound to the contradictory interest structure of a given society and economy. Consequently, all interventions of a nation-state have contradictory effects. Promoting export industries by means of devaluating the national currency may prejudice industries depending on imported inputs. This trade-off may be migitated by mediating between different and sometimes contradictory interests in the framework of the institutional set of a civil society.

Is a civil society a prerequisite for economic efficiency? Yes. But a civil society only emerges and develops as long as communitarian and democratic participation is possible. The market is only democracy-prone as long as economic and political liberalism are based on the same historical roots of modernity emanating from both the Industrial and the French Revolution in the late eighteenth century. State intervention, (that is, the visible hand) by its very nature has an authoritarian bias. If, however, that authoritarianism destroys the institutional structure and traditions of a civil society, it undermines economic efficiency. There is only one guarantee for economic efficiency as well as for democratic participation: the efficacy of the third hand and its institutional prerequisites in the form of a developed civil society.

To conclude the argument, a project to increase the efficiency of the economic system and to enhance social welfare must rely on a strategy of "socializing the market"[5] through state interventions and the functioning of the institutional network of a developed civil society. This conclusion is theoretically relevant, since it demonstrates clearly that institutions are important. This conclusion also has political meaning. The economic and political difficulties in Eastern Europe, for instance, demonstrate that nothing seems to be easier than establishing a market system, setting the invisible hand free. But it is also obvious that nothing is more difficult than avoiding an informalization and demoralization and even criminalization of the market system, the emergence of some new kind of "mafia capitalism." This difficulty obviously goes back to the absence of the institutional framework of a civil society. Therefore, strategies of transforming the centralized planning systems of Eastern European countries should not only rely on market mechanisms, but also on the necessity of democratic institutions and of non-market networks. Only the social ensemble of the invisible, the visible, and the third hand is historically apt to increase economic efficiency and democratic participation.

5. Diane Elson, "Market Socialism or Societalization of the Market?", *New Left Review*, Nov./Dec. 1988, no. 172.

13. Industrial Policy—Will Clinton Find the High Wage Path?*

Jeff Faux

Bill Clinton's charge that "we are working harder for less" was repeated at campaign bus stops all the way to the White House. Echoing a decade of policy debate among Democrats, he talked of the need for America to seek a "high-wage" path through the new competitive global marketplace. With his election, "industrial policy" has crept back on to the national agenda: the question now is not whether the government should guide the private sector to become more competitive, but how.

It's still too early to judge Clinton's answers. But, although he is pointed in the right direction, political and ideological timidity seem to be restraining him from taking the steps needed to move the country along a high-wage path. If so, Americans in 1996 will be working even harder for even less. And the Democrats will have missed an opportunity to stimulate their own political recovery.

After years of denial, the political and academic mainstream now acknowledge the long-term decline in real wages. The effect on opportunities for those who do not graduate from college (75 percent of the work force) has been dramatic. In 1992, real wages for male high school graduates with up to five years' work experience were 27 percent below their 1979 levels.

What to do about declining incomes for the middle class, who, in Clinton's words, "work hard and play by the rules," was a major

*This article first appeared in Fall 1993 issue of *Dissent* magazine.

theme at the post-election Little Rock economic summit. Economist Robert Solow of MIT and John Sculley, founder of Apple Computer, led off the discussion by defining the long-term economic problem as one of sluggish productivity, lack of innovation, and obsolete work organization—particularly in the manufacturing sector. America's choice, said Sculley, echoing the title of an earlier report written by Clinton adviser Ira Magaziner, is between "high skills" and "low wages."

Postulating "high skills" as an alternative for "low wages" tells us something about the politics of the industrial policy discussion. It is an accommodation to the sensibilities of the business participants for whom high wages do not typically top the list of priorities. Stressing high skills rather than high wages avoids the question of how the proceeds of rising productivity are to be distributed.

Nevertheless, raising the issue represents progress. It signals an understanding that in addition to its "macroeconomic" responsibilities for maintaining overall levels of production, the federal government should also concern itself with the composition of output and the way that it is produced. Macroeconomic spending and monetary policies determine the size of the Gross Domestic Product (GDP) and, thus, how many jobs there will be. Industrial policies affect the quality and wage levels of those jobs. In particular, industrial policy implies that a healthy manufacturing sector is essential for a high-wage strategy. By itself the market—because of its short-term horizons—will not make the necessary investments to keep that sector prosperous.

This idea challenges the notion that has dominated U.S. national economic policy since the end of World War II—and the discipline of economics since the early nineteenth century — that a nation must make do with whatever "comparative advantage" (its natural resources, its location, the energy and intelligence of its population) God and history have given it.

But by the late twentieth century, different factors of production—technology, worker and management skills, and workplace organization—have become more important to the ability of an advanced nation to compete. These are factors that can be improved upon by shrewd public choices. The idea is still resisted in most university economics departments, but in the 1980s it spread among younger academics, journalists, and think-tanks, and seeped into the consciousness of Democrats in Congress and state houses.

As the presence of Sculley and other high-tech entrepreneurs at the Little Rock summit suggest, this view has now spread to important segments of the business sector. A decade before, the high-tech business people were scornful when some labor leaders and industrialists talked about industrial policy to save mature industries—auto, steel, chemicals, textiles, and so on—whose markets were being eroded by foreign firms subsidized by industrial policies in their home markets. Irving Shapiro, then head of DuPont, Lane Kirkland, president of the AFL-CIO, and investment banker Felix Rohatyn advocated that the U.S. government increase subsidies to these sectors through a variety of policies, including a national development bank. But the high-tech crowd, confident that they were in expanding world markets, dismissed industrial policy as a bailout of economic dinosaurs who simply couldn't cut it in the new global marketplace.

Their political allies—"Atari Democrats" like Gary Hart— joined the new Right Republicans and the press in ridiculing these ideas. Soon the Democrats retreated; Walter Mondale, an early advocate of industrial policy, abandoned it and made deficit reduction the centerpiece of his failed 1984 campaign.

But in a few short years many U.S. high-tech firms found themselves outspent and outmaneuvered by Japanese and European companies whose home markets were secured by protectionist policies and who had access to government-subsidized capital.

Following a well-established tradition, these corporate free-marketeers went to the Republican administration for help. Instead of sympathy, they got lectures from Reaganite bureaucrats who refused to believe that government-subsidized foreigners were outcompeting America's private sector. Gradually, the high-tech community began to look elsewhere for political support. They found it among Democrats on Capitol Hill, Democrats who began to argue that industrial policy was needed to maintain U.S. technological competitiveness. Their efforts created the government-sponsored SEMATECH Consortium of computer chip producers, an increase in funding for technology programs at the Department of Commerce and other civilian agencies, and removed the word "defense" from the Defense Advanced Research Projects Agency (DARPA), now known as ARPA. Bush's resistance to these ideas gave the Democrats a wedge to drive between parts of the business community and the Republican party. When Bill Clinton was nominated, many Silicon Valley entrepreneurs defected to him.

After his inauguration, Clinton did several things to lay a foundation for industrial policy. One was to take up the suggestion of adviser Derek Shearer to create a National Economic Council to coordinate the many federal agencies whose functions affect the domestic economy. Another was to choose economist Laura Tyson—a well-known advocate of industrial policy—to be the chair of his Council of Economic Advisors. A third, initiated by an act of Congress, was to organize a "commission" of representatives of government, business, academia, and labor to design competitiveness strategies for the troubled airline industry. Legislation is currently pending in the House of Representatives to create a second commission focusing on the auto industry.

The ideological walls have been breached, but it is not clear how far into the citadel of laissez-faire the Clinton administration is willing to storm. The shared dissatisfaction with Reagan and Bush among manufacturing executives and labor leaders conveniently obscured class and political differences among supporters of industrial policy. Business's vision is one in which U.S.-owned firms—wherever they might locate their production—are subsidized and deregulated to make them more competitive with their foreign counterparts. Labor's vision is of an industrial policy that will help create high-paying jobs in the United States. One labor leader who attended a meeting with fifteen business representatives and the president reported: "Clinton asked what we should do. The fifteen business guys said deregulate more and cut the deficit. I said regulate more and invest to create jobs." During the campaign, Clinton could play to both camps. But now that he is president, he will have to make choices, and it will require a much higher level of statecraft to keep the coalition together. We know now he chose the former path.

Given widespread ideological resistance to government interference in the marketplace, creating a full-fledged industrial policy will not be easy. For the immediate future, industrial policy is likely to involve a mosaic of government actions rather than a single unified economic plan. To make genuine progress toward building such a mosaic in four years, Clinton will have to fit together five policy pieces. Ranked according to their ideological acceptability in the current political climate, they are

(1) increased government subsidy for civilian research and development;

(2) a national system for training and retraining workers;

(3) a managed trade policy;

(4) finding a substitute for the Pentagon as a driver of industrial growth; and

(5) the reorganization of the workplace by empowering frontline workers.

The good news is that the Clinton administration has taken some steps in all five areas. The bad news is that most of the steps are tiny.

The shift of federal dollars from defense to civilian research and development actually began during the Bush years. In 1988, for example, the military share of R&D spending stood at nearly 68 percent; by 1992, it had fallen to under 59 percent. The limits here are budgetary rather than ideological. There is bipartisan agreement that the federal government should subsidize research that would benefit no particular firm and development that would require private firms to put up some of their own money. Given the political consensus, it is not surprising that the administration has moved most quickly to continue the trend. In Clinton's 1994 budget, the largest share (58 percent) of federal R&D funds still favors the military, but the civilian share will rise faster than the military share.

The chief advocate for expanded training is the new Secretary of Labor, Robert Reich. Since co-authoring (with Ira Magaziner) the book that first put the case for industrial policy on the map, Reich became somewhat of an apostate. In a world economy, Reich now maintains, there is little practical distinction between domestic and foreign firms. The only way for us to gain comparative advantages is to create a superior labor force that will attract global capital.

Up to now, the bulk of government-sponsored training programs has been devoted to training the poor and disadvantaged and, to a lesser degree, retraining the unemployed. Reich would have the government take responsibility for a continual training and upgrading of the entire labor force—including the 90 percent who are employed. In his presidential campaign, Clinton proposed a U.S. version of the French system where businesses are subjected to a special training payroll tax (Clinton proposed 1.5 percent of payroll), which is forgiven if they spend an equivalent amount on employee on-the-job training.

But the president has already backed away from this idea. The new taxes associated with his deficit-reduction and health-care plans now make it too tough for him to demand yet another business tax. As a result, there is no significant increase in resources going to upgrade employed workers in the Clinton economic plan, although some more money will be provided for training the disadvantaged.

Expanded training and research and development programs will have some positive long-term effects on the performance of U.S. workers and firms. But these are largely activities that improve "supply-side" skills and capital, rather than create jobs. The common complaint about training among workers is "training for what?" Without the prospect of jobs, the average worker fails to see the logic of going through the expense and trouble to learn new skills. This was dramatized in the middle of the Little Rock economic summit when the President took calls from television viewers. After a long session in which the assembled cabinet officers and experts extolled education and training as answers to the problem of too few good jobs, a woman with a masters degree called from Boston to say that she has been looking for full-time work for two years. Another call was from an unemployed man in Los Angeles who was a tool-and-die maker—about as high-skilled a blue collar job as one can get—asking how more training would help him. The cabinet officials were silent. The president counseled patience.

Lack of skills does not seem to be the central problem for the unemployed and underemployed. For example, the Bureau of Labor Statistics (BLS) reports that in 1980 some 12 percent of U.S. college graduates worked in jobs that clearly did not require a college education. In 1990, the number was close to 20 percent.

The greater problem is inadequate demand for labor—particularly in the high-wage manufacturing sector. And it is a bit eerie to hear Clinton and his advisers, when pushed on this question, repeat George Bush's assumption that the answer is to increase U.S. exports.

The Clinton people are not knee-jerk free-market zealots like those in the previous administration. Bush's trade policy for Japan consisted of fierce denials that the huge U.S. trade deficit with that country was a problem, and political stage whispers to the Japanese urging them to voluntarily reduce their surplus with the United States. It culminated in Bush's tragicomic trip to Tokyo in 1992, when he brought to Japan a group of overpaid and underperforming auto executives to demand that the Japanese buy more U.S. cars.

Clinton's people are much more savvy; they are bargaining for an improved trade balance rather than pledges of allegiance to free trade. It is in this area that Laura Tyson's influence has been greatest. Her presence has steadied the hand of U.S. trade negotiators. The issues are unresolved and made more complicated by a Japanese government weakened by scandal; for the first time in memory, U.S. and Japanese trade officials are negotiating on the basis of interest rather than ideology.

On the other hand, Clinton's embrace of Bush's North American Free Trade Agreement (NAFTA) with Mexico and Canada moves in the opposite direction. This agreement will encourage U.S. producers to solve their competitiveness problems by pursuing cheap labor, rather than take the more difficult route of making higher quality goods and services more efficiently. During the election, Clinton stipulated that he would approve NAFTA only after negotiating side agreements on labor and environmental standards. But under the influence of his more conservative advisers, the administration proposed side agreements that do not even meet Clinton's own criteria. Given NAFTA's unpopularity in the polls and the widespread skepticism in Congress, Clinton had to spend a large share of his political capital to win the vote. Business and the free-trade press hailed the victory, but it will prove Pyrrhic if it results in large defections from his working class base.

The trouble with trying to solve the problem of inadequate markets through exports is that every nation in the world is trying to do the same thing. The competition for world markets has become severe, exacerbated by the deflationary macroeconomic policies pursued by international lenders. But even if the G-7 nations could agree on an expansionary global policy, neither NAFTA nor a willingness by Japan to open its markets a little wider nor a successful completion of the Uruguay Round of trade negotiations will provide a market stimulus great enough to support expanded U.S. manufacturing in a way that will generate high-wage jobs.

Robert Heilbroner has suggested that we may be in the economic trough of a long-term cycle of technological innovation. The 1930s were such a period, in which the initial exploitation of the automobile industry, which drove much of the investment of the 1920s, had been exhausted.

It took the tremendous technological energies expended in World War II to bring the economy to a new level of investment opportunities. Thus, the jet airplane not only created a booming new aircraft industry, it made possible the explosive growth of tourism, worldwide. The computer and the expansion of the welfare state—in health care, housing, and education—are other examples. But these are largely exhausted, and while inventions keep coming, we have not yet seen the development of large new sectors.

One might argue that this is all the more reason to allow more money into research and development. But just as training cannot be isolated from the question of "what for?," neither can research and development.

If technology policy stops with simply subsidizing research and development, it might do more harm than good to the economy. America is not deficient in basic science or in the ability to invent. A whole series of recent successful "Japanese" products came originally from U.S. minds (including the fax, the flat-panel display, the VCR, and the video camera). But we have not been producing the products for market. And one can argue that unless the government is prepared to assure that the results of its R&D subsidies will be produced in America, we should stop the subsidies.

Where do we find the engine of growth of demand for high-technology production in the United States? At least in part from the same source that has generated much of the demand for high-tech production for most of this century—the U.S. government.

Critics of industrial policy assert that U.S. business culture precludes the establishment of strong government institutions like the Japanese Ministry of International Trade and Industry (MITI). The idea of Washington bureaucrats telling large corporations where they should invest and threatening regulatory retribution if they do not is simply not credible.

Rather, industrial policy in the United States has been "mission" oriented. It has been successful when applied to specific national goals creating an internal barge canal network, a transcontinental railroad track, a weapons system, or a space program, supporting the small farmer, establishing an aircraft industry, and so on. For most of the last half-century, the Cold War military mission has been the driver of national industrial policy. Now the defense budget is shrinking. But there is little prospect that, left to itself, the private economy will generate industries that can play the role that defense has played as the major source of support for cutting-edge industrial technologies. As economist Ann Markusen observed in an EPI report entitled "Converting the Cold War Economy," defense industries embody much of the leading edge technological capability of the U.S. These industries have posted the highest rates of manufacturing output growth in the last two decades, and they account for the lion's share of net manufacturing trade receipts. They employ disproportionately large shares of the nation's scientists and engineers. Even sectors such as computing and semiconductors, which have successfully developed extensive commercial markets, still rely heavily on military contracts for basic research and innovation funding.

In recent years NASA and the Departments of Agriculture, Housing and Urban Development, and Health and Human Services have all established their own versions of the military-industrial complex—complete with networks of bureaucrats, businesses, banks, labor unions, and influential members of Congress—which have created small investment "klondikes" of economic growth.

Despite the popular view of these activities as pork barrels, they have been essential for the creation of private investment opportunities. And as they have shrunk as a share of GDP, our growth rate and standard of living have declined. Economist David Aschauer has estimated that had the U.S. economy maintained the rate of public investment in infrastructure that it supported in the early 1970s, private-sector investment and productivity would have been raised by 20 percent and 50 percent, respectively.

Investment in infrastructure has a dynamic quality that is missed in the conventional conception of public works. For example, the shrinking of public spending on transportation does not just show up in potholes, worn bridges, and traffic congestion. It has meant that the United States has missed a generation of progress in the development of high-speed rail technologies. High-speed trains are now clearly the superior mode of public transportation for distances under six hundred miles. They relieve congestion. They do not require airport expansion, or construction of new airports, which environmental standards now make all but impossible. Their energy efficiency is three times that of autos and four times that of airplanes.

The United States is woefully behind in this industry. Japan's bullet trains, which go 130 mph, are thirty years old. Newer models have exceeded 200 mph. They are now working on the next generation of systems—including "Maglev" technologies in which trains are powered by superconducting magnets and are capable of speeds up to 300 mph. Europe will soon have a network of trains that can move at 200 mph connecting major cities, and Germany may be even further ahead of Japan in the development of Maglev technology. Meanwhile, the fastest U.S. passenger trains can go only 125 mph, and that exclusively on the New York-Washington Metroliner. Other routes of the small and antiquated Amtrak system top out at only 90 mph.

High-speed rail could be an investment "klondike" of the twenty-first century. Nations all over the world will be buying sophisticated cars, equipment, and computer technologies from firms in first world countries that can produce and install them. But the absence of a market for rail transport in the United States is accompanied by the absence of an industry. Today, only one relatively small American company, with limited capacity, can produce rail cars. Forgoing the public system in America has meant forgoing the private market.

In the last six months of the campaign, Clinton seemed to understand the political potential of the theme of public investment. Earlier, he made a middle-class tax cut the center of his economic program. But this crude attempt to outbid George Bush as a tax cutter was ridiculed by his opponents on both the left (Harkin) and the right (Tsongas) and ultimately left the voters uninspired. This set off an argument within the campaign, with Reich, Magaziner, and Shearer on the side of a public-investment strategy, and a group representing the conservative Democratic Leadership Conference in favor of tax cuts. Clinton decided for Reich and company, and began to pepper his speeches with talk of public goals that might be substituted for the Cold War. He spoke of high-speed trains, vertical lift-off, short-haul aircraft, automated highways, and advanced environmental systems for recycling and waste treatment. And he picked up Al Gore's favorite project—the creation of a national information network "to link every home, business, lab, classroom and library by the year 2015."

Clinton's pro-investment advisers understood that there was a power in these ideas that went beyond a list of programs. Creating jobs by building high-speed trains, investing in technologies that clean the air and water, and giving everyone the opportunity to master the computer could be the building blocks of an alternative economic vision that could rival the abstract picture of a laissez-faire future painted by Reagan and Bush, which, in the absence of any competing vision, is implicitly accepted by most Democrats as well. Its concreteness would enable middle-class voters to see, in some tangible way, where a social democratic path might take them. Not Utopia, but as far as one could imagine the U.S. Democratic party venturing in this decade.

But after the election, this vision began to fade. After the defeat of Clinton's modest stimulus package in spring 1993, to paraphrase a description of FDR, Doctor "Invest-in-the-Future" became Doctor "Reduce the Deficit."

The once promising high-tech public investment strategy of the campaign was scaled back in the first Clinton budget: $2 billion for high-tech transportation infrastructure R&D, and $1.5 billion for manufacturing technologies. Worse, once deficit reduction took priority, the administration's commitment to even this level of funding dwindled, allowing the various appropriations subcommittees to downscale virtually all of the president's high-tech proposals.

The last piece in the industrial policy mosaic is the reorganization of the workplace. Politically, it is the most difficult, but it has the greatest long-term political potential.

U.S. industrial power over the past century was marked by a specific management system—symbolized by the mass-production assembly line. The system of pyramidal hierarchies, known as "scientific management" or Taylorism (after engineer Frederick Taylor), required that those at the top of the pyramid break down tasks of those at the bottom into smaller and smaller pieces. Ideally, the movements of those who actually do the work are programmed minute-by-minute.

The size of the U.S. market made this system ideal for the production of identical mass-produced items. (Henry Ford once said the American public could have the Model T in any color it wanted so long as it was black.) Today, a global market has given the same advantage to corporations located anywhere there is a large supply of trainable labor. Since in most other countries labor is cheaper, the U.S. no longer has an advantage in assembly-line-type work organization.

For any advanced nation, the high-skill, high-wage path now requires an ability to compete on quality, design, and capacity to speed the product to market. Nations that want to pay high wages have to target their goods and services to market "niches"—segments that will pay for quality goods and thus generate sales with large enough margins to pay high wages. This requires an organizational system that can modify its product or process rapidly to adjust to changed market conditions. This in turn requires putting more responsibility in the hands of the front-line worker.

Inspired by the success of Japanese, Swedish, and German firms, and pushed by business schools, American business has been experimenting with horizontal organization for more than a decade. But old ways die hard. Despite the hype of business magazines, most of their efforts are largely cosmetic. In a new study for the Economic Policy Institute, Eileen Appelbaum and Rose Batt report that most of the efforts at reorganizing the U.S. workplace have been piecemeal and tepid, and therefore have had a small effect on workplace performance. U.S. business is still responding to global competition by shrinking, and cutting wages.

Still, the idea of workplace democracy is spreading. And politically, the idea has enormous potential. It brings a democratic vision to the place where most Americans spend the best years of their lives. It captures the spirit of teamwork and even patriotism in this era in which economic competition has emerged as a major national concern. Clinton seems to understand it. The campaign manifesto "Putting People First" states: "We are determined ... to create an environment in which workers at the front lines make decisions instead of simply following orders."

The administration has already made some positive moves. Labor Secretary Reich has revived the Department of Labor's program to promote labor-management workplace cooperation (it had been dismantled by Bush) and appointed a very able former assembly-line worker with an MBA from Harvard to run it.

As with the other pieces of the industrial policy mosaic, God is in the details. In this case, the most important detail will be the administration's attitude toward organized labor.

Many of these efforts have been thinly disguised employer-initiated strategies for preventing, or undermining, unionization of plants in industries such as textiles, autos, steel, communications, shipbuilding, and even public services.

Yet, there is increasing evidence that unions provide an essential element of what it takes to create a high-performance workplace—a sense of equality between labor and management. A study by David Levine and Laura Tyson identified four conditions that made for an effective high-performance workplace: (1) productivity gains are shared with employees; (2) workers have employment security; (3) there is a sense of group cohesiveness; and (4) whether workers have guaranteed rights. Economists Richard Freeman of Harvard, Paula Voos of the University of Wisconsin, and others have concluded that efforts to create high-performance workplaces are more successful when workers are represented by a union.

Herein lies the problem for American business. Most of these efforts at a cooperative workplace have been half-hearted because they conflict with another, at this point stronger, management objective—to get rid of labor unions. By and large, managers have never come to terms with the idea of sharing power in the workplace. Inspired by twelve years of anti-union sentiment in the White House, they have become even more hostile.

Like most other Democrats, Clinton has been happy to "sup at Labor's table" at election time, depending on labor's money and organization. But when it comes time to rule, labor's seat at the policy table is well below the salt. The degree of support the administration gives to labor-law reforms that reverse the anti-union bias of the past twenty years may be the clearest indication of how progressive Clinton's industrial policy will be.

No one should bet the farm on a progressive outcome. The administration's shift from an investment strategy to a deficit-reduction strategy can be read as an ominous decision to sacrifice the interests of the industrial sector in order to accommodate Wall Street. It may be that under Clinton we will have more public consciousness about industrial policy with even less cash to pay for it.

The hope for something better lies in the assumption that the president wants another term. Someone is soon going to have to ask Bill Clinton what he intends to say to the majority of voters in November 1996, who, in the absence of a bolder industrial policy, will be working even harder for even less.

14. Redefining the Role of the State to Facilitate Reform in East and West

Ottokar Hahn

As a statement of principle, the Marxism and Leninism as applied by Lenin and Stalin have nothing to do with socialism. They are complete perversions of the great vision of socialism. And instead of creating a free society of equal chances and international solidarity, they established an especially crude form of capitalism and of national supremacy.

The former Soviet Union had become one of the few countries in the world where the partition between the classes, the ruling class of the Communist Party and the underprivileged class of the proletariat was extensively elaborated and shown openly to the outside world.

But the consequence of the bankruptcy of Marxism/Leninism is now a bias against socialism in general. Today, many more people are busy developing principles to convert socialist countries to capitalism than vice-versa. In fact, you can hardly find anyone nowadays in Europe to defend socialism at all. Socialism is considered as an ideal only for dreamers, bureaucrats, and lazy men. Capitalism has become, in the general impression in Europe, the leitmotif of our time.

The utmost you can expect in actual discussions today are hints toward a third way, and examples like China and Cuba seem rather to be limited and depend on special conditions.

So the real question today is whether we go back to a laissez faire policy or whether there is a role for the state in the economic policy of the future and, if there is, whether this role is a transitional or a permanent one.

For most Europeans, there's no doubt these days that capitalism has proven to be the better economic system compared to the state-controlled economies of the East, and that we have to help Eastern and Central Europe to change to a market economy and capitalism as soon as possible. The only dispute in Europe is about the choice between the shock therapy intended to be exercised in Poland, or a more gradual approach such as policymakers in Hungary and the former Czechoslovakia favored, which allows them to analyze the economic situation and their targets, and try to find the most effective remedies before taking the next steps.

In my view, this more gradual approach might take a longer time, but it has so far avoided the huge social problems that exist today in eastern Germany and Poland. It is clear that at least during the transitional period, the role of the state is more important in this gradual adaptation to market economy than in the case of shock therapy. But even in the latter case, the state has to intervene massively with tax reliefs and of enormous subsidies for redundant workers.

I am convinced that the gradual approach of Hungary and the former Czechoslovakia will lead to less friction than eastern Germany and Poland currently experience.

In the former Soviet Union, it was not possible to choose shock treatment, because there is no money for this, nor was the gradual approach feasible, because there was no clear consensus about future economic policy. The disorganization of the state destroyed the existing system of production and distribution of goods so that living conditions continuously worsened instead of improving. Whether decentralization will bring better results is still an open question. Many experts doubt that economic liberalization can work in this region in the foreseeable future, since no basis for a market economy has ever existed there before. Psychology and education will have to change radically if the new policy makers decide in favor of a Western-style economic policy.

Perhaps the Chinese third way would have been appropriate for the former Soviet Union. But in the past, not even privatization in the agricultural sector was allowed, which has been the basis for China's economic improvement so far. And today the pressure from the West by the IMF and the EC is so strong in favor of complete liberalization that there will be little margin to develop new models for the economic policy in the former Soviet Union.

This leads me to the questions: Where are we in the West going? Is it really a laissez faire policy that is needed? In Western Europe we are talking intensively about deregulation and liberalization. The political aim is to achieve free market conditions everywhere, and to complete the so-called internal market within the EC after 1993. But does this mean that the state will disappear completely in economic policies?

For the EC Commission and for the majority of EC members, even now for post-Thatcher Britain, it is clear that there will certainly be a role for the state in the future as well. The degree might differ for each of them according to the principle of subsidiarity.

On the basis of the White Paper in 1987, the EC decided to do away with the technical, financial, and bureaucratic barriers between the member states and the state ministries' influence in economic policies in general. While this is still the official line of thinking, it is clear that the effect of the liberalization is not the same in all member states. Britain, with its high degree of deregulation, has today more economic and social problems than Italy, with its high percentage of state-controlled industries, or Germany with its enormous public investments in infrastructure, social welfare, and education.

Leading industrialists and economists confess now that competitiveness not only depends on wages, taxes, and interest rates, but on the entire environment including the role of the state, society, and even culture. If we look to Japan, we can see that the strong influence of the MITI and the Ministry of Finance on the economy led to the success of the Japanese economy. And the most successful competitors with Japan, Taiwan and Korea, are supported massively by the interventionist policy of their respective governments.

Lacking a similar assistance by their governments, European enterprises decide more and more to cooperate with them and to form strategic alliances with them. In the United States, there is a discussion going on about "reregulation" and the negative effects of Reaganism, which led to social unrest in certain areas. The huge budget deficit and the foreign trade deficit has led to reflection on the role of the state.

Although the concept of socialism seems to be thoroughly discredited, the return to a state-free capitalism or laissez-faire policy in the West is quite unlikely. In Central and Eastern Europe, two different approaches can be seen at the moment. The ex-GDR—and Poland to a lesser extent—opted for shock therapy, replacing the centrally planned economy with a market economy overnight. The social consequences have been harmful and require enormous financial correctives.

Hungary and the former Czechoslovakia have taken steps toward a market economy and rely still, to a large extent, on initiatives and controls by the state. In my experience, such an institutional framework facilitates acceptance in countries where strenuous measures are necessary. The entire reform process would be helped by a mid- and long-term strategy, a point very difficult to explain in these countries after their departure from the planned economy. In addition, priorities and the sequence of measures must be be decided in accordance with the Common Market to which these countries adhere by their Association Agreements concluded with the European Union.

Whether these developments, trends, and different approaches to shape a more social and democratic society in Central and Eastern Europe should be defined as social democracy is questionable. Certainly, the label "socialism" will not be accepted there and will have rather negative connotations for a some time to come. The former communist and socialist parties have been renamed and try quite successfully to create this new image.

A new theoretical approach and another fresh terminology is needed to develop the society of the future. Laissez faire is not the solution, but what will be the leitmotif of the next decades? How will we deal with the huge social and economic deficiencies, not only in the East, but also in Southern Europe and the Third World? Sooner or later, and I hope sooner, we shall have a new vision, a new Utopia. For us, as well as for the generations to come, it is not sufficient to appeal to individual well-being alone; we must contribute to the implementation of better society for all people. And for this, we need a clearly defined role for the state with all the checks and balances that democracy requires.

15. Between Social Darwinism and the Overprotective State — Some Reflections on a Modern Concept of Social Welfare Policy

Johano Strasser

Until very recently, there had been a violent discussion going on in all highly developed industrial societies on the limits of the welfare state, and even today the topic plays an important role in the scientific and political debate in Western Europe — and North America. Ironically, this debate was started in the early 1960s (M. Friedman, F.A. Hayek) and resumed with special vehemence in the 1970s (Wilbur J. Cohen/M. Friedman, J.M. Buchanan, etc.) in a country which, compared with the standard of social welfare in, e.g., Sweden or Germany, might perhaps be counted among the "underdeveloped" welfare states: the United States. In the course of this debate it became fashionable among conservative politicians all over the world to conjure up the ruinous consequences of the welfare state for the freedom of the individual as well as for the functioning of the economy. The "deterring example" referred to was, in the first phase, Sweden, but soon other countries with (then) social democratic governments such as Great Britain, Denmark, the Federal Republic of Germany, and Austria followed.

This debate on the limits of the welfare state is at least partly just another sequel of the longstanding controversy over state intervention vs. market regulation. However, it received an extraordinary practical relevance in the face of the prolonged economic difficulties that started to trouble the world economy in the middle of the 1970s and the growing financial problems in almost all sectors of the welfare system. The neoclassical assertion that the economic crisis was essentially due to excessive welfare expenditure led, at least in some cases, to severe cuts in the welfare budget in countries where governments with this ideology took over. Social democrats, on the other hand, trying to defend the welfare system, sometimes found themselves in a dilemma. Although they held that the neoclassical assertion was utterly wrong, they reluctantly pursued a similar policy of budget reduction since the only other alternative they saw, i.e., raising fees and taxes, appeared to them to be unfeasible. For a long time, the defenders of the welfare state were thus up against the wall — partly because, after Keynesianism had lost its splendor, they simply did not possess a valid and explicit answer to the neoclassical understanding of economics, and partly because they did not realize that the financial problems were, at least to some extent, due to structural problems of the welfare state and called for a thorough reform of the system itself.

Meanwhile, thanks to the obvious failure of Reaganomics to tackle the problems it claimed to solve, but thanks also to such outstanding books as Amitai Etzioni's *The Moral Dimension,* a new and more complex understanding of the economy and the role of state intervention seems to be growing. Nevertheless, it should be clear that there is no chance to return to the social welfare policy conducted by most West European countries in the 1960s and early 1970s. It is very unlikely that the high economic growth rates needed for that type of policy can be obtained regularly over the next ten or twenty years and it is even more unlikely that a drastic increase in taxation, which would be unavoidable, could be made acceptable.

Hence, there is a necessity for the advocates of the welfare state to rethink their premises and to come up with new organizational forms and methods in the field of social welfare. After a first phase during which the fanatics of the invisible hand on the one hand and the advocates of the traditional welfare state model on the other dominated the discussion, a second phase followed with the more sophisticated critics of the traditional welfare state model coming to the front. The criticism put forward by authors such as Hans Achinger, Christian von Ferber, Franz Xaver Kaufmann, Frieder Naschold, Elisabeth Liefmann-Keil, Ivan Illich, Bernhard Badura, Peter Gross, Pierre Rosanvallon, and Patrick Viveret (I might also include in this list American authors like Alan Gartner and Frank Riesman), cannot and should not as easily be shrugged off as the anti-welfare rhetoric of neoclassical market partisans. On the contrary, it should be taken very seriously because it clears the ground for a reform of the welfare state, which may help to guarantee a high level of social security and justice under changed economic conditions.

In the following, I shall deal with some fundamental problems of the modern welfare state as I see them. After that, I shall try to point out in which direction steps might be taken in order to solve these problems and thus improve the existing system of social welfare so that it provides for more security and justice as well as for more autonomy of the individual. Although my view of the problems and my suggestions for solutions are, quite naturally, often determined by special experience with the situation in Germany I think that, nevertheless, some of what I have to say may also be of interest and perhaps even use to people in other countries.

I start with a short analysis of some problems and deficiencies of the welfare state model that all have to do with questions of efficiency and financing the system. Since my aim is to give some hints toward an improved paradigm of social security and welfare, I shall not go into too many details here.

Although in welfare states such as Sweden or West Germany social welfare budgets have been raised dramatically in the last 30 or so years there is no indication that the pressure of social problems, or rather the demand for social welfare measures, has decreased. Whatever this may mean in detail, it seems to me to be quite obvious that the capacity of the system to solve problems is far from being satisfactory and that therefore the amount of money spent on social welfare — in some European countries social welfare spending comes near to one third of the GDP — cannot be taken as a proper standard of social well-being. Taking the cost of social welfare as an indicator or equivalent of something like social quality of life would be as misleading as to identify the cost of maintenance and repair of a car with the pleasure it offers to its owner. It is a harassing fact that in spite of an extraordinary expansion of social welfare measures in most West European countries, the pressure of social problems has not substantially decreased. In Germany, for example, after a short period of relative "social detente" in the late 1960s and the early 1970s, new social problems arose and old problems were aggravated in spite of massive efforts to overcome or to alleviate them.

No doubt, part of the problems in the field of welfare policy had to do with the prolonged crisis that started to make itself felt in the middle of the 1970s, and present difficulties must at least partly be attributed to the turbulence of German unification. After all, a high rate of unemployment over many years creates considerable problems for every welfare system. The rate of unemployment having been fairly high in Germany for the last ten to fifteen years, it seems that due to the breakdown of the East German economy even more people will be forced to rely on unemployment benefits or other forms of public transfer income in the coming years. And, of course, the growing rate of unemployment leads to substantial deficits in public insurance systems such as the old-age pension fund. In Germany every 200,000 unemployed causes a loss of contributions to the old-age pension fund of one billion DM (approx. US$600,000,000). In addition to this, unemployment reduces the tax income and thus also the financial capacities of the welfare system.

In such a situation it may appear quite natural for politicians to resort to incentives of economic growth as the only way out. The connection between economic growth rates and the financial situation of the welfare system is so obvious that it may seem to be quite plausible to concentrate all efforts on the recovery of the economy as an overall solution to the problems in question. However, relying on economic growth as a solution of the present problems of the welfare state is in more than one respect insufficient and shortsighted. First, it is highly improbable that growth rates of 3 to 4 percent per annum, which are said to be necessary to solve the financial problems, can be reached in the near future even if all the incentives that the monetarist and Keynesian arsenals provide are applied. And it appears to be almost impossible to obtain growth rates of this size over a long period of time. Second, economic growth does not necessarily go hand in hand with a diminution of unemployment, especially not if we go on following the line of technological development that aims at further rationalization of the old type and automation in key sectors of the economy. Third, the further expansion of the economy most probably entails a long trail of ecological and social problems which may well thwart all the high aspirations connected with economic growth. Last, the financial problems of the welfare state are only partly due to insufficient growth rates. They are to a large extent the result of structural problems that would sooner or later lead to financial predicaments even if it were possible to return to the high economic growth rates we began to regard as normal after World War II.

The indirect way of solving the problems of the welfare state by stimulating economic growth does not work any more. The only alternative left to the dismantling of the welfare institutions and the lowering of standards of social justice, as advocated by neoclassical economists and their political adherents, is a thoroughgoing reform of the welfare system and its relations to other societal subsystems. Part of what has to be done in this respect becomes apparent if we take a closer look at the structural side of the financial problems of the welfare state.

Before we go into this, I want to stress that there is one structural aspect of the financial problems that cannot be eliminated. This is what Baumol and others after him have called the "cost disease." Since, to a large extent, social welfare consists of personal services, it is completely impossible to rationalize the "production process" in the social welfare system in the same way as this is done in the non-personal service sector and in the goods sector of the economy. If the standards of efficiency applied in other economic fields were transferred to social services this would simply destroy their special kind of "productivity." To put it very bluntly, replacing nurses, teachers, doctors, and streetworkers by machines and technical control systems would destroy the character of the services in question instead of making them more efficient.

This does not mean, however, that efficiency is of no relevance in this field. On the contrary, if we investigate into the causes of the dramatic increase in welfare costs we will easily see that there are many ways in which this subsystem can be made more efficient in the proper sense, i.e., without violating or denying its humane purposes. In order to show this I will take the health system as an example.

In Germany, as in many other countries, the costs of the health service system have soared to vertiginous heights during the last two or three decades. I shall discuss here some of the most important causes of the "cost explosion" in the health service system because I think they can be used to show what is fundamentally wrong with the traditional concept of welfare policy.

(a) The first cause is the radical professionalization and monetarization of services that were formerly fulfilled in the family, in the home, in the neighborhood, etc. What Polanyi called "The Great Transformation" generated belated effects in the sphere of personal services. In Western Europe this process accelerated palpably after World War II. The massive social deracination as a consequence of the war, the enormous geographic and social mobility forced upon people by the sweeping economic development and the ensuing degradation and destruction of smaller societal units, the seemingly unavoidable centralization of almost all public and private structures, and, last but not least, the special attraction of what Europeans came to regard as the modern "American way of life" favored the ever-increasing absorption of nonprofessional services by the professional and monetarized system. In the course of this development even very simple and personally gratifying activities were transferred to professionals.

There can be no doubt that such a development is in the interest of the professional service groups, such as doctors and dentists, and of their suppliers in the pharmaceutical and medico-technical industries. These groups are, of course, not primarily interested in the health of the people; they want to sell their services and products. For them the best method to increase income and social prestige is to make more people become more dependent on the special services and goods they offer. In this respect, the process of professionalization and monetarization of the health service is at the same time a process that makes the consumers of such services more and more dependent on professional services and finally destroys their capacity to help themselves. Thus the system produces much of the demand it pretends to gratify.

(b) It is also in the interest of the service professionals and their suppliers to propagate and apply a definition of the problems to be solved that is adapted to the special strategies they have to offer. Thus doctors normally define illness as a defect in the individual, denying the social and socio-cultural aspects of the problem. The diseased person is artificially isolated from his societal context and treated as if his disease had nothing to do with the natural and social environment he lives in, with working or housing conditions, with income relations, in short, with the quality of social life. Of course, this is not just a deplorable mistake. It is a kind of systematic blindness in a system that allows special interest groups to define the problems they are expected to solve. It is highly profitable for doctors and dentists and their industrial suppliers to isolate the individuals to which they offer their services and goods. If they admitted that disease in many cases is, at least partly, generated by the societal context they would have to admit that the adequate action to be taken belongs, at least partly, to the societal or political sphere. Doctors cannot modify working conditions, provide for better housing, improve the environment, change income relations etc. As a sociological group they are not even interested in political action to this effect because this would necessarily have negative effects on their "market position." It goes without saying that a therapy that relies to a large extent on a false or incomplete definition of the problems must be highly ineffective and thus extremely costly.

(c) Although there has been much rhetoric about medical prevention, it is a fact that the services offered by the health system consist almost wholly of compensational treatment. Of course, treatment of this kind is necessary and will still be necessary after radical changes in our lifestyle. Nevertheless, the extent to which the health system fails to provide for adequate prevention is striking. Again, this is largely due to the patterns of interest mentioned before. Real prevention, i.e., primary prevention of disease, would mean changing the living conditions of people, which is beyond the field of action of doctors, dentists, and their industrial suppliers. As soon as we try to eliminate the causes of disease (as far as this is possible), this calls for political action and therefore collides with the special income, prestige, and profit interests of the medico-industrial complex. This complex, therefore, has tried very hard to redefine prevention to coincide with its particular purposes. Prevention as offered by the medico-industrial complex is very often nothing but a series of technical check-ups applied to people with a maximum of machinery and a minimum of personal care. As long as we do not concentrate on eliminating (as far as possible) the causes of disease, the demand for medical treatment will continue to increase and hence also the costs of the medical service system. Quite contrary to the many legends about the glorious success of modern medicine, the truth is that, in the majority of cases, the forms of disease have changed, but disease has not been pushed back substantially. There is even overwhelming evidence that the accelerating deterioration of natural and social environment causes an epidemic growth of so-called "civilization diseases" that may well turn the tide on medical progress.

(d) One of the most harassing phenomena in this context is the fact that medical treatment and medication in themselves are important causes of disease. In many cases the health system as it is tends to aggravate problems rather than to solve or alleviate them. Hiatrogenic disease is the most obvious indication of an increasing counter-productivity of the health service system.

Apart from the aforementioned general causes of the "cost explosion" in the health service system there are many special causes that differ largely from one country to the other. For the sake of brevity I shall not deal with them here.

Summing up what was said before, we may say that the modern health service system, in spite of its high reputation, is a striking example of an ineffective and very expensive way of dealing with problems. However, what has been said of the health service system holds, to some extent, true of all sectors of the social welfare system. The system as it has developed in the course of time, especially in Western Europe, may be characterized as follows:

1. It is over-professionalized and tends to monopolize certain service activities which could be taken care of with more efficiency either in cooperation with the recipients of the services or by the people themselves.

2. It is prone to individual and group interests on the part of the producers of services and at the same time tends to neglect the interests of the consumers.

3. It tends to make the recipients of the services dependent and to curtail or even destroy their capacity to help themselves.

4. It defines the problems according to established strategies and producer interests, thus arriving at an incomplete and often misleading analysis of the problems to be solved. In addition to that, problem analysis and subsequent action normally stop short at institutional border lines so that the system tears apart what belongs together and operates in a highly artificial segmented reality.

5. It focuses almost all its energies on compensation, while prevention, above all primary prevention, is almost completely neglected. Thus the question of how to cope with the rising demand for its services almost never leads to the more important question of how to cope with those structures and processes that produce the permanent increase of demand in this field.

6. It uses methods and organizational forms that are highly incompatible with many of the tasks it has to fulfill.

For all these reasons, the welfare system is inefficient, very expensive, and shows a growing tendency toward counter-productivity. On top of this, it radicalizes a central characteristic of modern capitalism/industrialism, i.e., the dependence of people on professionalized service systems, and undermines their self-reliance. In the long run, this may well become a serious danger to freedom, especially in connection with other dehumanizing trends in the development of our type of society. The overprotective state is to a large extent the natural product of the dynamics inherent in the capitalist/industrialist society. The traditional concept of the welfare state, as it evolved in Western Europe, must be questioned today not only because of its unrealistic economic premises, but also because of its tendency to absorb the autonomous activities of individuals and groups.

In order to avoid misunderstandings, I have to stress here that I do not favor neoclassical concepts of a minimal state with all their illusions about free individuals in a largely depoliticized society. On the contrary, I hold that it is inevitable to politicize some decisions (e.g., in the field of technology development, in the economy, etc.)

that according to the neoclassical economic ideology should follow the indications of the invisible hand. However, I think it necessary and possible to reshape political intervention so that there is more room for independent and self-determined activity for individuals and groups without neglecting the idea of social justice, and that such a reshaping of political intervention may, at the same time, contribute to solving the financial problems of the welfare state.

To start with, I want to make it very clear that, in my opinion, the neoclassical alternative to the welfare state — individualization of social risks, reprivatization of social services, and replacement of political and juridical regulation by market regulation — would not solve the problems discussed here, but would rather radicalize them. The special inefficiency (over-professionalization, dependency of the consumer, false definition of problems, neglect of real prevention, etc.) is not due to the fact that the welfare system is partly state-organized. If the health service system were completely privately organized the discussed causes for inefficiency would most probably act even more powerfully. Apart from that, a strategy of reprivatization and market adaption of the social welfare system would necessarily lead to gross injustice, thus being a denial of solidarity rather than another form of organizing it.

In order to safeguard social security and justice, while at the same time avoiding the malfunctions and structural problems inherent in the traditional concept of the welfare state, social welfare policy, in my opinion, should be modified along the following lines:

(a) The basic risks of life, such as disease, disablement, unemployment, and old age, should be borne by the society as a whole. Otherwise we would act contrary to the most elementary principles of social justice. Private efforts to safeguard against these risks with savings and/or private insurance initiatives can never offer the same degree of security, equality, and freedom from discrimination guaranteed by a general public insurance system that includes every individual of a given society as contributor and possible beneficiary. Additionally, private charity cannot provide fair conditions for those who are not able to look after themselves. In this respect, I think, the modern welfare state has generated models of security that are still without alternative for those who need them most desperately. However, what is basically well-contrived can and has to be improved in detail. For that purpose, I think, we should concentrate on solving two problems: unequal treatment of persons with identical problems and the inflexibility of the system.

The different insurance systems existing today, for example in Germany, have developed over a period of roughly a hundred years. This long development was, of course, not a planned and systematic process, but full of conflict, contradictions, and compromise. As a result, the system shows many irrational traits that even those who profit by them can no longer justify. One of these is the fact that, very often, identical cases are treated in a widely divergent ways. To give a few examples:

1. State officials and farmers are by far better off concerning their old-age pension than workers and employees. While state officials do not pay any contributions at all and farmers pay very little, workers and employees have to pay their full share.

2. People who are disabled by an accident are entitled to benefits by far exceeding those granted to people who are disabled at birth.

3. People who are out of work for more than a year have to put up with a considerable reduction of unemployment benefits, as if they deserved punishment for refusing to work.

4. And above all, women, in many aspects of social security, still have to put up with conditions far worse than those for men.

In order to abolish injustices of this kind it may prove necessary to change the financing of the security systems so that transfer payments and other gratifications are no longer mainly or exclusively based on contributions paid during what formerly was regarded a normal working life. Another consequence is that more justice in this respect cannot be brought about without eliminating all those unjustified special arrangements for particular groups which have complicated the insurance system over time. Thus, reforming the insurance system in order to enhance justice and equality would at the same time contribute greatly to simplifying the system and making it more transparent to the public.

Whereas, on the one hand, the insurance system has grown to excessive complexity by complying with the demands of special interest groups, it tends, on the other hand, to oversimplify and over-generalize the problems it has to deal with so that it is insufficiently adapted to the real needs of the people. I want to illustrate this point by an example that shows that more flexibility does not automatically mean reduced security and that flexibility may also contribute to solving the financial problems of the welfare state.

The main source of the financial problems of old-age insurance is the demographic trend in which a steadily diminishing number of gainfully employed have to secure the old age pensions of a steadily growing number of retired people. At the same time, recent inquiries reveal that one of the most serious problems of elderly people in our type of society is the feeling of uselessness, of not being needed by the society they live in. This problem is likely to become even more serious if the age of retirement, as some trade unions demand, is further reduced. The obvious solution would be to offer the possibility to combine a reduced working income with a reduced old-age pension, thus leaving it to the individual to decide how much work and how much leisure is good for him or her. In Western Europe we are just beginning to experiment in this field. In Sweden a law was passed some years ago allowing workers and employees to choose their own combination of work and retirement between the age of 60 and 70, i.e., five years before and after the normal age of retirement. I think that this is a good example of how greater flexibility can be reached without any loss of security. And, in addition to that, it may prove to be a necessary step to avoid the financial breakdown of the old age insurance systems.

(b) Effective prevention is not only necessary for moral reasons, but also because it helps people to live their own lives and because it contributes, in due course, to making social welfare less expensive. Some important measures of effective primary prevention have already been mentioned: improving the environment and preventing its further deterioration, improving working and housing conditions, and changing the income relations in favor of those 20 to 30 percent who are at the bottom of the scale. It should be added here that, in a situation of high unemployment, it must of course be a prime aim in a concept of preventive social welfare policy to create jobs for those out of work and/or to distribute fairly the volume of necessary work via shorter working hours and measures to encourage and facilitate female employment. Without going into further details I want to stress some general implications of a preventive social welfare policy which may help to mark the difference to traditional social welfare politics. A concept of preventive social welfare politics must necessarily go beyond the individualistic approach to social problems. Trying to eliminate, as far as possible, the causes of social problems implies changing societal structures and processes and the relations between people. Such a concept cannot be limited to the sphere of action traditionally attributed to social welfare politics. Economic policy, technology development, communal development, etc., quite naturally belong to its sphere of action. Parallel to this, the concept of social security and social well-being has to be widened so as to encompass not only what Franz Xaver Kaufmann called "systematic security," for instance the security offered by an insurance system, but also the socio-cultural side of security, i.e., security founded in reliable relations between individuals in the context of communities and informal groups.

(c) The overprofessionalization of the social welfare system and its tendency to make its recipients dependent are, as has been pointed out, important causes of inefficiency and, at the same time, constitute, at least in the long run, a serious danger to freedom. For these reasons, a thorough reform of the welfare state should imply measures to activate the addressees of welfare measures, to encourage cooperation of professionals and non-professionals, and to assist people in solving a good deal of their problems themselves or in cooperation with others.

The importance of activating the addressees of social services becomes apparent if one realizes that personal services represent a unique type of production, quite unlike that in the goods sector and in other services. In personal services the producer cannot be strictly separated from the consumer. On the contrary, to assure an effective production, the producer and the consumer have to cooperate, i.e., the addressee of the service must necessarily play an active role in the process of production. To some extent this knowledge is common sense. It is almost a truism that a patient will not recover from his disease unless he makes an effort by himself. You cannot help a drug-addict if he does not try very hard to leave the vicious circle he is in. Freedom cannot be brought to people unless they actively seize it and make use of it. The problem, however, is that the traditional welfare state, up to now, has grossly neglected the "productive power of participation" (Naschold) instead of systematically encouraging it. That this should be so is due to false organizational forms and methods as well as the dominant influence of private interest groups in the system. This deplorable situation can only be changed if the welfare state is thoroughly democratized in the interest of the addressees of its services.

Of course a complex society cannot do without a large amount of professional services. But in many cases, the service systems of the welfare state could be operated both less expensively and more in harmony with the needs of the people if they made use of the possibilities of cooperation between professionals and nonprofessionals. I mentioned before that, according to recent inquiries, many elderly people look for opportunities to do something useful for the community. Shorter working hours facilitate such activities for many younger people, too. This growing potential should be used by the society instead of producing additional social problems by frustrating those who look for more humane and gratifying forms of social activity. It is necessary to change the legislative framework and the institutional forms of the social welfare systems in order to give this kind of cooperation a fair chance. As things are in Western Europe, cooperation between professionals and non-professionals, which once was prominent in the welfare institutions of the workers' movement, is now to be found almost exclusively in the welfare activities of the churches and of informal groups. The welfare state, which, to a large extent, is the product of the workers' movement, relies almost completely on professional services.

Very often, what people really need is not professional service but a real chance to solve their problems by themselves. However, the opportunities to do so are by no means distributed equally. Therefore it is necessary that public aid be directed toward the end of giving more people a fair chance to solve their own problems. In my opinion, a modern concept of the welfare state should above all do away with all paternalistic structures and methods and concentrate on activating the citizens of the welfare state. The general idea behind all this is that treating people equally in equal conditions is not enough. Since we are dealing with persons, who for moral reasons should be treated as subjects rather than objects, the overall aim of social justice should be to strengthen the subject position of the individual in his social context rather than making him an object of welfare.

16. Civil Society and Social Justice

Günter Frankenberg

The Paradox of Solidarity

Solidarity as a voluntary act of recognizing others as deserving one's esteem, care and support is possible in a secular society where the responsibility to help is not always already commanded by religion, tradition, or status (noblesse oblige). Yet, solidarity seems to be almost impossible in a society based on contractual relations governed (a) by the principle *pacta sunt servanda* and (b) by the idea of liberty that establishes a system of limited irresponsibility (the limits being contracts and some obligations for "dependents"). That is why societies that we have come to regard as modern do not rely on social solidarity but rather on some kind of insurance system or welfare regime that externalizes the costs of the market economy by means of a mixture of risk distribution, economic compensation, poor relief, and social control. Typical of these welfare regimes are the following traits:

1. The underlying dualism of civil and/or political rights (freedom) and of social rights (justice) implies that "social entitlements" are not genuine individual rights but mere programs for government action.

2. In the German context the program of social rights/justice is constructed as self-executing mandate laid down in the constitution and partly removed from social conflicts.

3. The welfare state program is oriented toward reintegrating the recipients into the labor society and is executed by a

social bureaucracy on the basis of contributions paid into an insurance scheme or means tests for welfare payments.

4. The most striking critical feature of the welfare state is the clientelization and the demoralization of citizens in the welfare labyrinth.

The critics of the welfare state have generally accepted the dualism of freedom and justice and, to a lesser degree, the notion of social justice as a matter of state action. They have focused, instead, on the way this governmental task has been executed, criticizing its operation as "social control," political disenfranchisement, or "colonization of the life-world" and its results as unjust or problematic for the proper functioning of capitalism. Consequently, therapies have shifted between nationalization and privatization, between restricting or expanding welfare expenses and services, and have tried to strengthen the legal position of the claimants, or to shift power and funds from the state agencies to self-help groups and non-state organizations.

Civil Society and Non-Regressive Answers to the Welfare State

I would like to redirect the critiques and therapies for the welfare state. The starting point is the theory of secularization, which then informs the concept of civil society and may help to solve the seeming paradox of solidarity.

Secularization is usually discussed as a problem of how to establish and legitimize political authority in a disenchanted world. Yet this view is too limited. Secularization affects not only the question of authority in modern society but also the problem of social integration. In the absence of a plan of salvation, or any laws of evolution (progress, decay), and after the breakdown of the traditional hierarchies, social ties, and responsibilities, a new symbolic social bond has to be constructed. The question is not only how societies can govern themselves (self-rule, law-rule), but also what constitutes their unity. Liberalism has answered these questions with a model guided by market rationality: the social contract as the precondition for an endless series of contractual relations. The dangerous supplement to this model has been referred to as "the social question." The welfare state was invented as liberal society's last resort—the only medium through which the society of individuals could act upon itself.

A theory of civil society addresses the problem of rationalizing social integration and political legitimacy. It attempts to correct the "liberalist" misunderstanding and negation of solidarity and its externalization in the form of the welfare state. Central to this approach is the concept of public freedom as practiced in the public sphere, where citizens articulate their opinions, organize and bring to the fore their interests, and try to shape their polity. This notion of secular, radically pluralist politics is informed by the experience of a conflict-ridden society bereft of any transcendent authority that might guarantee consensus or harmony. Hence all resolutions of conflicts are always temporary.

The civility of social struggles presupposes a "basic convention"—a horizontal and mutually binding promise of the members of civil society to accept one another as different but politically equal, and which has to show in the way they resolve their conflicts. This implies free access to the public sphere for everyone and conflict settlements that respect everyone's physical and psychic integrity. The spirit of such a "convention" depends on the willingness to tolerate others as different and as political opponents rather than banning them from the public sphere as political enemies. Hence, a basic convention of this kind is more demanding normatively than a mere *pacta sunt servanda* agreement. The "other" is regarded not just as the abstract partner of a contract, but as constitutive of individuality and autonomy. Without others, one cannot be recognized as an autonomous self; without others there is no life in society. Individuals need others to be able to identify themselves.

Mutual recognition therefore includes the obligation to enable every other member of society to support the "basic convention." This thought has already played a minor role in the French Revolution: that a society of individuals cannot look the other way when the autonomy of its members is threatened. Political or public freedom and social rights therefore do not reside in totally different, disconnected spheres, but constitute together the status of the citizen in a civil society.

Public Freedom and Social Justice: Civil Solidarity Instead of a Welfare State

There are at least two ways in which public freedom and social justice can be regarded as coexisting. First, social rights can be considered as necessary conditions for the enjoyment of public freedom. Without a modicum of social security—minimum income, shelter, food, and clothing—citizens are virtually deprived of their chance to participate in a polity's public life. Second, the freedoms of political communication may be seen as the necessary conditions of active citizenship, joined by social rights as the sufficient conditions. This argument presupposes that the enjoyment of public freedom as well as the duty of mutual support are part of some kind of basic convention. It avoids the unrealistic idea that every aspect of social life is governed by the requirements of political communication (which would imply that we owe welfare payments, public housing, or a winter coat to our public freedom). Moreover, this argument makes it quite clear that social rights interfere with the autonomy of those who have to contribute to the transfer of wealth: the self-imposed restriction of autonomy to enable autonomy. While the first alternative suggests that social rights come automatically as the functional annex of political rights, the second alternative stresses the fact that social rights and justice are a project that has to stand the test in public debates, rather than be grudgingly accepted as an abstract constitutional mandate or functional imperative.

This kind of basic security for all citizens could indeed be called "social security." It would no longer combine economic compensation with social control but with political empowerment, thus informing the recipients that they are not clients but members of a civil society who are equally entitled to public support. Such social security would create a *cadre d'appartenance*, a thin and vulnerable social bond between the members of society.

Civil Solidarity and Group Solidarity

Similar to social movements that organized the protest against nuclear war or the destruction of natural environment, similar to the workers' and women's movements, quite a few association and

self-help groups have broken through the asphalt of the bureaucratic organization of social services. They have made visible the
social structures that are usually severed by the individualist structures of market competition and commodity production or
excluded from a bureaucratic perspective. Thus, at the margins
and in the niches of the society of individuals we see a civil society
of greater density. Instead of exaggerating the achievements of self-
help and totalizing the idea of group solidarity we should connect
community and community (or group) membership on the one
hand with society and the status of citizenship on the other to
increase the "visibility of the social" (Rosanvallon) and to clarify the
conditions of solidarity. While citizenship calls for some kind of
basic protection, the recognition of pluralism and of social security
as a communal task calls for efforts such as a genuine "social law"
that enhance a non-statist type of solidarization.

17. American Social Reform and a New Kind of Modernity

William Sullivan

The United States, as has been said for at least 100 years, is different from Europe. And it has been different, it has been said over and over again, because of the importance of the doctrine of laissez faire in the United States. This has been a society in which mobility and expansion (perhaps we could call it the frontier thesis in many ways) have played the role that politics and political negotiation and conflict have played in European societies. So, as it has often been noted, even labor in the United States never had an estate consciousness; rarely, in fact, has the labor force or the working class in the United States, been the same people for more than a generation or two. And, consequently, the sorts of democratic politics that evolved in Western Europe have never evolved in the same way here.

We have had what Michael Harrington used to call 20 years ago a kind of invisible social democracy centered largely in the Democratic Party, but it has been always a social democracy developed within the encompassing world of laissez faire.

The great exception to that, or rather the great alternative to laissez faire, has been the Cold War. For the last half-century, the United States has been a mobilized continental society and has become a far more corporatist society than it had ever been before. But this corporatism has been largely in the form of a war corporatism.

Another way to describe the important difference is that while America has had something like a half-recognized corporatism, certainly capital, labor, government have been seen and organized in various ways as definite groups. This has been historically first under the tutelage of not the state, but capital itself. The American industrial economy at the turn of this century was reorganized by the financiers before the regulatory state was put into place. And that, it seems to me, is a second major difference between the United States and virtually any other industrialized democracy.

Now within that broad context, there have been three major periods of American reform that are continually recycled as analogs or models, which is why I think it is worth mentioning them.

The first one is the period that began in the 1890s and ran up to and including the Great War, and that is the period of progressivism, in which the regulatory administrative state was formulated as a possibility. In reality, that model—which we see as corporatist but also as having strong democratic elements—was only generalized to the national scene with the New Deal and World War II. During this period the rudiments of a national welfare state—of a very peculiar kind, however, I might stress—were put together.

This second period, the New Deal and World War II, has been the one reviewed again and again by social reformers in the United States for the last 50 years. And it is frequently invoked today. I want to suggest, however, that the nature of the changes in the world and the social context we face today are far more sweeping than the changes of the 1930s or 1940s, so that the more relevant analogy, actually, is the more progressive moment, not the moment of the New Deal and the war. I will elaborate on that later.

The third great period of reform is the one that all of us have seen and lived through, and that is the period of Civil Rights and the new left—the '60s—as we say. The outcome of these reforms has been disappointing. American politics today—and I think we need only look at the traditional party of social reform in this country, the Democratic Party, to see this—embodies very little of the sense of corporate solidarity or social responsibility that is intrinsic to the notion of social justice. Along with our laissez faire philosophy, American society has been characterized for a long time by a pervasive anti-institutionalism; a pervasive sense, in fact, that institutions are essentially constraining and not enabling, that organized structures are obstacles to be overcome or instruments to be used, but cannot provide the basis of life context to be cultivated. And this is perhaps at its most extreme in the politics of the new left.

What this has amounted to, however, is to allow the politics of interest, or the politics of the interests, to become the dominant form of American political life. So the American state has evolved in a most peculiar way, in which the state has become involved in virtually every area of social and economic life during the last half-century, and yet is perceived both by those at the top and those who must encounter it as somehow inept, not able to focus. It has become diffuse and frustrating. It is a highly porous state. It is a very large and distended state.

The anti-institutional quality of American life is evident in this realm perhaps more than anywhere else. It shows itself in the difficulty that Americans have had on focusing on sociocultural conditions, upon which the American social system depends. The result of not tending to what we might call the social infrastructure or the institutional infrastructure of our social life has been finally a kind of perfection of the politics of interests, a further development of the philosophy of laissez faire that some commentators now refer to as the politics of secession. That is, every group, every family, every individual who has the means and the wherewithal, wants and attempts to withdraw from the common realm, to privately secure for themselves what they think, perhaps rightly, is not available in public.

So we have, for example, the extraordinary phenomenon of the American development of the suburbs, or as some have now referred to them, "edge cities." It is a phenomenon both like and unlike comparable developments in Europe. The difference is that they become, as they are often described, special services districts. They are, in effect, private governments designed to promote and provide social services for those who can afford them, leaving the common provision to become ever poorer.

Now, this is a very abbreviated, abstract way of presenting what I think is actually a very complex and important story. But I think this goes some distance in explaining why the party of social reform in the United States today appears to others and often to itself and its own counsels as simply a conjury of interests, a party that seems unable to present a compelling image of American society, let alone global society, based on something that we might recognize as the ties of solidarity and social justice.

The new historical moment has both negative and positive possibilities. The negative possibility we are well aware of on both sides of the Atlantic. In the United States, it means the breakdown of the American growth coalition into this politics of secession. On both sides of the Atlantic, it marks a realization that the attempt to use the state, the regulatory and administrative state, to correct the abuses of the market is not a panacea.

What happens in these cases, from the point of view of social justice, is that the society—the capacity of citizens to understand and to nurture their society and their common ties as active participants—is weakened rather than strengthened. That is to say, civil society for the public realm contracts rather than expands as the result of a well-intended effort to improve social justice. And this is the negative of the present historical moment, that the old hopes, the old programs, the old perspectives, simply carry little conviction.

What is the positive? The positive perspective is that we are also witnessing if not the breakdown, at least certainly the crisis of the corporate governmental organization of the national economy. The national economy of the United States, like that of most other states, is far more porous and open and interconnected to the world than it has ever been before.

This creates both great dangers and difficulties as well as a significant possibility. The possibility, to put it in very abstract terms, is this: that we find—certainly in the American discussion—a new awareness of the critical role of what is often referred to as human capital. That is to say that all national societies today find that their future hinges on their capacity to nurture and develop a skilled and interactively effective work force. Again, this is of course a highly economistic way of talking and thinking. It is to see civil society as essentially a kind of enterprise society.

But, nonetheless, within that context, there is more than the beginning of the understanding that the development of human capital, the development of human skills itself, depends upon something that could be referred to as social capital. The potential for human individuals to actualize their skills and capacities is dependent upon the viable function, the vital functioning of social networks, social institutions ranging from the family through educational institutions to the workplace and, indeed, beyond that to the regional and national community. And that is a very important possibility.

It remains, however, merely an inchoate possibility. The need, in the very broad sense, is as much a cultural and a political need as it is a social and institutional one. Part of that need is to go beyond the thinking of materialist theories of historical progress. Here I would face the fire of lumping both liberalism in its traditional form and Marxism in its traditional forms as parts of this, which is to say that theories of progress that assert that self or class interest can be trusted are the engine of moral progress. Very briefly the critique is that these theories provide no restraint, neither upon social tyranny—whether it be the tyranny of interest, the tyranny of parties, the tyranny of the state, the tyranny of the classes—nor upon ecological depredation, and that the two in fact issue from the same fundamental root.

What is required is an overarching—and in that sense universal yet at the same time locally-rooted—moral order that stresses and that in fact can cultivate the disposition of solidarity, the traditional virtue of the left, and responsibility for common ends.

Such an understanding, then, would be part of a postmaterialist social justice. It is postmaterialist in two senses. First, such a notion of social justice must fit with the new possibilities of what is sometimes described as the postindustrial form of economy that fits with the more flexible forms of work and knowledge that are required in such an economy. This conception of social justice does not simply look to distributional arrangements, which have been a traditional concern of social justice in the welfare state, but rather sees social justice as involved with participation and the development of human capacities in a variety of areas.

It is postmaterialist in a second or cultural sense as well, in that it moves beyond the instrumental conception, the instrumental focus on achievement to an emphasis upon solidarity and responsibility for the whole. And here the civic tradition, both civic humanism, republicanism, and the other forms of this general family of thought, are of great importance. In the American tradition, this emphasis upon participation, the development of human capital through improved social capital and democratization, was expressed most powerfully in that analogous era at the turn of the century, and by no one more effectively than John Dewey.

The purpose of this emphasis is to attempt to develop what we might think of as a democratic infrastructure. If, in fact, in the new postindustrial global economic order, the provision and development of infrastructure—both material communicational, and educational—is so vital, then by extension it is equally clear that the reestablishment of bonds of solidarity and the creation of new bonds that have never before existed require a large and complex infrastructure of institutions, institutions that are understood not primarily not as instruments but as educational contexts.

This kind of a view of a democratic infrastructure is certainly deeply rooted in the American reform tradition. It reaches back not only to figures such as Dewey, but also before that to visiting Frenchman Alexis de Tocqueville.

We have then a kind of march of bureaucratization in the state, but also the beginnings of a counter movement or counterbalance in civil society, in the public realm outside the state, very interestingly carried by informal groups and religious communities.

In the American context this suggests that what is needed, and what the fate of social justice actually hinges upon is the development of those forms of cooperation between professionals and nonprofessionals, and indeed cooperation on a much larger scale than simply that which is perhaps today only found in the realms of informal groups and the activities of the churches and others. This must be focused upon and then injected into the central institutions, the institutions of power within the political economy itself. That is to say, the space of civil society needs to be reclaimed and opened up within the institutions of the economy and the state. Americans must understand the need for democratic infrastructure in a way that has not been typical of the American tradition. We must see that institutions share with us, that they teach us and inform us, but that we as citizens acting together are also able to shape those institutions. If this is to be accomplished, then it seems to me that the

American reform tradition has to similarly expand its understanding of itself and its possibilities to include both the traditional solidarity of the left and also the informed and responsible leadership that must be part of any such reform coalition and movement.

And this suggests a cultural program that holds forth a new vision of a kind of modern society that does not revert to traditional forms of solidarity and hierarchy, but is also not simply a further extension of the institutions of industrial life. This society would combine high levels of skill and high levels of human development with the kind of vital community and social life which the left has always, in its heart, most wanted and desired.

Part IV

THE INTERNATIONALIZATION OF POLITICS AND ECONOMICS AND THE CHALLENGE OF NATIONALISM, IMMIGRATION, AND MINORITY CONFLICT

18. East European Reform and West European Integration

Peter Glotz

The political world has been changing radically since the Central European revolution of 1989. Instead of traditional bi-polar conflict, we now have the potential for multi-polar political conflict. Small wars have once again become a real possibility. Ethnic and social conflicts in Central and Eastern Europe are brewing into equally revolutionary and explosive mixtures. Despite these changes, however, Western Europe's political classes are still sitting impassively at yesterday's gambling tables, placing their bets as though oblivious of the fact that "Rouge" and "Noir" have become almost indistinguishable after the historic downpour. They mutter strange codes under their breath (CSCE, CFE, EC, WEU, NATO, etc.), but can we be sure that these letters still stand for the same concepts that they did three years ago?

The situation in Eastern Europe has already become far too complex to just carry on business as usual. "Don't mention my name," a close advisor of President Vaclav Havel once said to me, "but if we were already members of the EC, I would say 'Let the Slovaks go.' The only trouble is that they (the EC) won't have us for a while." And the elegant, well-educated, appealingly honest, and radically neo-liberal Vaclav Klaus vehemently defended the British position: Poland, Hungary and the former Czechoslovakia must be accepted as full members by the EC and all "socialist utopias" must be relinquished. By "socialist" he meant plans for monetary and political union. The "Brussels Bureaucracy" should be trimmed and the national parliaments should retain their powers as far as possible. As a German "modernist" I was put right in my place. While some of the Eastern Central European countries indisputably belong to "Europe," the Community's expansion to the East could at the same time make it impossible to finally overcome nationalist pride and create a European confederation. What should we do? European policy has come to a dangerous crossroad. The disintegration of the Eastern bloc, German unification, and the economic decline of the superpowers represent an existential challenge for the EC with its "two-track," divided approach to this mixture of dangers and opportunities. The attempt by many European political leaders to confront the radicalness of these alternatives with hollow opportunism and also with frantic management will be short-lived.

The New Situation in Europe

Since 1989, the formerly dominant trend toward supranational structures (single market, monetary union, political union, etc.) has been confronted by a secular counter-trend in the form of belated nationalism of the Eastern European middle classes, which have now been freed from Marxism-Leninism. A thoroughly international colloquium of soothing voices was formed in the meantime, promoting hope that this nationalism is nothing more than a fit of fever, a healthy reaction by these societies' immune systems, and the storm will have passed in three or four years' time. But how? The Western trend toward Europeanization is primarily the result of the economic and ecological needs of highly developed industrial societies on their way to powerful information and service sectors. Only the former Czechoslovakia and Hungary could manage such a step and even then only with help from the West in the form of "Marshall Plans," that no-one is working on and certainly nobody is able to actually carry out. The European Community is facing a dilemma: if it opens the doors to embrace Eastern Europe, it will not only prevent the emergence of statesmen such as Pilsudsky or Horthy, but will also hamper further steps toward the development of supranational structures. In terms of industrial policy, this will rob it of the opportunity to become a world player instead of being the playing field. What is even worse, however, is that Europe as a relatively loose league of nations will remain vulnerable to old Entente structures engaged in an utterly "neo-classical" pool game of power politics played with variously colored balls across all frontiers. The new possibility of "small wars" (such as nationality conflicts resolved with military aid) following the (de facto) end of nuclear parity certainly does not indicate the existence of a smoothly functioning "European security system," and the uncertain future of the former Soviet Union as a vital security element makes the situation still more ominous.

The German Question

This fundamental dilemma is further aggravated by the German question. Eurocratic etiquette turns this into a taboo subject, but everyone knows that after six or eight years of struggling to integrate its Eastern states, united Germany will once again reclaim its central position as the strongest economic power in Europe. Either it will have ceased to be a separate historical figure, a "state" measuring up to other "states," because it will have become integrated, or it will become the supreme regional power in Europe—which, given the German sense of guilt, will probably lead a new and endless round of familiar confrontations (albeit in different forms) given even the best intentions of all involved (and that is hardly to be expected).

French President François Mitterand appears to have realized this state of affairs most clearly, although it is only mentioned behind closed doors in Germany. Former Foreign Minister Genscher acted in full knowledge of the danger: both the Federal Chancellor and the Opposition leaders provided him with more or less cover, while the Bavarian CSU and the right wing of the CDU raised for a long time more critical voices, albeit only occasionally. It is hard to say how this constellation will develop as the first economic straits become apparent and right-wing populist forces apply more pressure.

Unification has certainly changed the Germans' psychological attitude toward Europe. The fronts have changed: formerly modern capital, the political class and part of the educated class constituted the protagonists of Europeanization. Apart from the small postmodern fraction (with leanings toward Enzenberger and

Nenning), the literary and social-scientific intelligentsia remained just as passive as the greater majority of the public at large. Only the (small) farmers' pressure groups and a handful of ecology supporters openly campaigned against "Brussels." The result was that Kohl's government could tolerate or even support Delors' activism.

Now, however, the first nationalist circles are forming within the intelligentsia with an aggressive esoteric literary nationalism (centered around the literary supplement to the *Frankfurter Allgemeine Zeitung*, the magazine *Merkur*, and isolated renegades from the student movement of 1968) and a more pragmatic English nationalist school, of which the renowned historian Christian Meier may be considered a representative ("Far-reaching plans for union should be treated with great skepticism; sometimes we can make faster progress at a slower pace."). These groups do not have any grass-roots support at present, but if an anti-migration mood geared toward a German "identity" and self-assertion becomes more widespread as a result of high unemployment in the Eastern part of the country, it will not only have a voice this time, but also spokesmen who will have to be taken seriously.

Herbert Kremp, well-known commentator and journalist from the Springer publishing house, is a good example of these spokesmen and how they present their arguments. In an article written in June of 1991, he argues that the idea of politically uniting the West, "the industrial hearts of Europe," is "a form of self-assertion against the Soviet claim to hegemony and the bipolar American-Soviet world directorate." He claims that this "philosophy of the core of Europeans, the deep-thinkers" (Delors, Mitterand and Kohl) died in the meantime. The idea ceased to be a plausible motif of power politics following the spread of political freedom across Eastern Europe. If pursued further, however, it had to degenerate into a European directorate over Germany."

However, it is still difficult to describe the naked national desire for power in Germany, and so Kremp adds a "social" argument. The intensification of the European Community "which closed its eyes to Germany's state of siege" automatically means limiting EC membership to the Eastern European countries. And that means missing "the great objective of economically and politically safeguarding the newly won freedom in Eastern Europe." It would therefore be better to kill two birds with one stone. Europe should be limited to a "free trade area" in order to thwart the "central purpose of integration, namely control over Germany" and at the same time do the world a favor by integrating Vaclav Havel, Lech Walensa and other heroes of the Central European revolutions into Europe and the West.

What does that mean? It means that Delors' strategy still stands a chance of success in Germany, although time is running out. Sooner or later, Germany could cease to be the European locomotive unless certain things are accomplished first (a smoothly functioning Economic and Monetary Union could serve as a point of no return).

The Different Sides to Europe

It can be justifiably said that the Europe of "Brussels" often argues in a technocratically limited manner. Wolf Lepenies, the rector of the Berlin Institute of Advanced Study ("Wissenschaftskolleg") who has just conjured up a "Collegium Budapest" and who is one of the few German intellectuals to pursue the cultural, scientific, and political dimension of "Europe" (unofficially), has discovered a wonderful quotation by Jacob Burckhardt: "If necessary, the Europeans will sacrifice all their specific literary and cultural heritage in favor of 'non-stop night expresses'." If that were to become the prevailing train of thought, we would have to join Enzensberger and Nenning in the trenches of regional cultures. Preferably those in the Danube basin.

There is of course more to Europe than just the EC. Europe is a cultural claim. The elements of European tradition compiled by the Jewish religious philosopher Eugen Rosenstock-Huessy are open to discussion: he listed the Greek, Roman, and early Christian experience, the national and religious schism of 1648, the dream of sovereign nations and nation-states, self-enlightenment and, above all, individualization as the product of Renaissance and reformation. But criteria are vital for anyone seeking to find a way through the jungle of European terms and institutions; otherwise they will end up with arbitrary power politics. And if we then conclude that Europe needs the Americans (militarily, for instance), that certainly does not mean that America "is" Europe ("CSCE" Europe). Whoever failed to understand that Catholic Croatia (which belonged to Hungary for a thousand years and to Austria-Hungary for four hundred years) is fundamentally different from Byzantine Muslim Serbia, will never be able to settle or even mediate the deadly contradictions in the artificial former state of "Yugoslavia."

It means, for example, that a European Community intending to standardize the diversity of regional cultures, literary heritages, and traditions in Europe is doomed to fail. Any dogmatic "liberalism" set on using EC directives to standardize the variety of television, literary, or film promotion would simply be "un-European." The cultural and linguistic diversity of Europe (including the totally "irrational" preservation of the Ratho-Romance, Basque, and Gaelic languages) is a part of our identity.

It also means that what is and what is not "Europe" cannot be defined arbitrarily. "Pragmatic" boundaries can of course be crossed, for instance by including Turkey in the European Council in order to tie the country to certain democratic principles. Turkey has European traits: the Kemaslistic nationalism that has given rise to Kurdish suppression is totally and utterly European. However, it is also an Islamic country, which is why European universalism, with its Christian roots, cannot simply be imposed there. Should it simply be dispensed within parts of "Europe"? It is not necessary to recall Europe's historical and cultural traditions in every individual institutional decision, but the structures created will not be able to survive and be peaceful in the long term if the former are disregarded entirely. Romania, Bulgaria, Serbia, Albania, and Macedonia make up a completely different world from Bohemia, Lithuania, Hungary, and Poland. Anyone who lumps these countries together in an "Eastern bloc without communists" is bound to fail, for they are anything but a "bloc."

There are many sides to "Europe." European policy is a game played with many balls: Europe as a forum for cultural diversity, a system for peace, an economic area. The variety of institutions is equally large: some are solidly established, such as the EC, the European Council, and NATO; others are interim organizations, such as the WEU and EFTA; there are regional and sub-regional forms of cooperation, such as the Pentagonal, the Nordic Council, the trilateral cooperation between the former Czechoslovakia, Hungary, and Poland, and finally the pan-European networks, such as CSCE. The Neapolitan *arti di arriangiarsi*, the art of arrangement, is needed in order to manage this diversity. Nothing could be more obstructive to a European union than the German sense of order, which would put an overnight end to everything that overlapped; or well-meaning attempts to please some fifty nations in a single stroke.

One question remains and must be taken seriously, namely whether it is actually possible to guide the political fate of a geographic Europe (Western Eurasia) from a single location. The happiness created by the liberation of an Eastern bloc held together by force is one thing; the question as to the viability of a common policy for this "Europe" is quite another one.

Vertical or Horizontal Expansion

This problem is currently being debated in terms of horizontal or vertical expansion in the Europe of the European Community. And quite rightly so. The development of supranational structures in the EC was bound to be delayed, if not actually prevented, by the rapid integration of the Eastern Central European states. When could a country like Poland survive economic and monetary union with France and Germany? Would the consideration of a defense policy within the EC in the long term not be blocked by including Russia's neighbors, since Russia cannot presumably be expected to tolerate the expansion of other alliances up to its Western borders? And would the EC not become a deformed monster? The EC members have long transferred important powers to "Europe." They would lose a great deal of their democratic legitimacy if they allowed these to roam freely on the no-man's land between the European Commission and the Council of the Ministers, instead of assigning them to the European Parliament in a democratically correct process. Anyone hanging on a rope in a crevice has the choice between going forward or back. Remaining motionless may be picturesque, but it can also be deadly.

Usually treated as a problem of time (when will the EC accept Austria, Sweden, and the former Czechoslovakia?), the debate over horizontal versus vertical expansion remains superficial and illusory. It is self-deceptive to claim, as the EC does, that the goal is a politically united Europe, while simultaneously insinuating that a Europe extending from Brest (on the Atlantic coast) to Brest (Brest-Litovsk on the former Soviet border) could be ruled by a parliament in Brussels or Strasbourg. Either the "political union" would only be a loose league of nations with a merely symbolic and ornamental parliament, or the larger "geographic" Europe would have to be understood as a plurality of national associations (federal states, confederations, or alliances). Why? Because a "European Parliament" worthy of its name and representing five hundred million people speaking forty to fifty different languages has long ceased to be a "utopian dream" and instead has become an obsession. Even Austria-Hungary in 1913 was an orderly community compared to this monstrosity.

Proponents of the nation state can derive great satisfaction from these arguments. They will claim that this is their chance. Poland will remain Poland, both culturally (in any case) and in terms of sovereignty; Germany will remain Germany, Great Britain will remain Great Britain. We will all meet in Brussels occasionally and coordinate our common interests. But there is also another possibility, namely François Mitterand's vision of a "Europe of different speeds" which may over the years develop into a "Europe of different degrees of intensification."

The "Europe of Different Degrees of Intensification"

We may argue over whether the economic, technological, and ecological developments of industrial and post-industrial societies is not generally forcing us to set up larger, supranational structures, just as centrifugal forces of the nineteenth century led to the creation of states or at least to the end of European city states. Be that as it may, constructive integration of Europe's largest nation state, Germany, into Europe's West, certainly demands pooling of sovereignty, as Jacques Delors, for more than a decade President of the European Commission, appropriately characterized the situation. Pooled sovereignty can be developed in stages.

Thus, it is perfectly conceivable for the EC to include countries like Austria, Sweden, or Switzerland in the mechanism of the single European market (i.e., the common European economic region), then a few years later followed by Hungary or Poland. The primary instrument available is an "Association." Yet a number of countries expecting to join the EC, maybe even some full members (such as Great Britain), may not be willing to support the final delegation of responsibility for monetary policy to a European Central Bank. In that case, France, Germany, and the Benelux countries could find themselves making up the core of the monetary union as soon as 1997. Anyone who has felt economically unprepared for a full participation (because of their rate of inflation or budget deficit) or who refused to "renounce sovereignty" would remain in a looser, less "intense" structure. British Prime Minister John Major considered it conceivable that the House of Commons could ratify such a treaty, even if London were not (yet) prepared to become part of the full monetary union.

The decisive question really arises over the development of the "political union." The European Political Cooperation (EPC), which has existed since 1970 and found its substantiation in the Uniform European Act of 1987, is not supranational in structure: unlike the Treaty of Rome, it employs intergovernmental methods whose primary characteristics are information, consultation, and consensus. The Gulf crisis has shown that these instruments leave the EC powerless, or conversely, that the Community of Twelve is so divided that Saddam Hussein can totally ignore its mediation attempts. Anyone who wishes to change this situation will have to be prepared to jump. Parallel organization should be established for a transition period, with one organization for economic integration, another one for political union, and a third one for security matters. In the long term, however, the Community will only be able to acquire political authority by acting as a single community, and that demands introduction of the majority principle (through several transitions). Many European nation states will clearly refuse to take this path, either temporarily or permanently.

Accepting this as the reason for relinquishing the goal of a European confederation would mean throwing Europe back to the arbitrary cabinet period of the years between the two world wars. In the meantime, European integration may have sufficiently developed in order to prevent military conflicts, at least on Western European soil, but the status of a loose league of nations will not only lead to "querelles allemandes," but above all to the superpowers, especially the United States, using Europe as a mediator.

For this reason, the European states should promote a political union worthy of the name and they should do so with the same resoluteness and efficacy as displayed by former British Prime Minister Margaret Thatcher when she was fighting for issues that she considered to be British interests. If necessary, the relevant EC treaty obliging the member countries to strive toward an albeit ill-defined political union will have to be revised. Some situations that require political decisions demand rough, overwhelming and seemingly violent political measures instead of angelic patience and diplomatic cunning. Such a situation has been created within the EC through the Central Europe Revolution of 1989 and German Unification.

Europe as a whole will always remain a multi-layered structure with pan-European institutions (such as an environmental agency, an arms control agency, a mechanism for mediating conflicts, a European University) in which all or almost all European states can participate, as well as regional (Northern, Southern, Eastern, or Central European) and functional forms of cooperation. Anyone striving toward a "Europe" must say good-bye to the idea of a uniform organization of European states stretching from the Atlantic to the Soviet border. It is precisely this European diversity that creates opportunities for a European confederation as a partner among partners and not as a model hegemonist.

The Europe of Regions

Political processes, which have been brought to a successful conclusion, demand a pragmatic capability for maneuvering and compromise, but they also need a leitmotif. Bismarck's vision centered on Prussia and not on "Germany as the European great power;" de Gaulle's version of a "Europe of Fatherland" was dominated by France and not a supranational Europe. The central ideas in the vision of Europe after the nation states is an intelligent combination of supranational and federalist structures, most vociferously proposed by Konrad Adenauer; the radical nature of his support is revealed most clearly in the (failed) EDU policy.

Adenauer consciously or unconsciously remained on familiar European territory: the imperial idea (in its original form, not as it was abused by Hitler) was certainly federalist. European federalism, however, draws its potential (and usually unrecognized) power from its continuing relevance today and not from the honored history of sacrum imperium. How else are the radical conflicts of Hungarians in Slovakia, Hungarians in Transylvania, Serbs in Croatia, Kurds in Turkey, Irish in Britain, Basques in Spain and France, to be resolved, if not through a combination of federalist and supranationalist structures? That is what adds weight to the words of Vaclav Havel's advisor: "If we were a member of the EC, I would say 'let the Slovaks go.'"

The albeit remote European utopia is a federalist Europe under a supranational roof of "multinational states" with extensive regional autonomy and a federal parliament to vote on matters of common interest (i.e., foreign and security policy, economic and ecological matters). An early version of this utopia is revealed in the struggle of German states to participate in EC legislature, as legislative powers are delegated "up" (to Europe) and "down" (to the regions) until the "nation-state" eventually disappears. It may take a long time for centralist nations, such as France, to accept this trend in historical development, but who knows? Corsican autonomy is a revolutionary yet very wise step for France. Perhaps Western Europe will learn from the Czech-Slovak, Hungaro-Romanian, Serbo-Croation or "Soviet" (e.g., Russo-Georgian, Osseto-Abkhazanian) lessons. The question is: does Western Europe want to learn from its Eastern counterpart? Has it not been expecting the opposite for the last millennium?

Either the European Community will take firm action soon, and will introduce supranational structures, or it will remain a loose league of nations, in which case Europe will revert to the former rivalry of hostile nation-states. I can find no more positive concluding sentence than the one by Ralf Dahrendorf, the leading German sociologist, now teaching in Oxford and a naturalized British citizen: "It remains an indisputable fact that the security vacuum and absence of law and order in Eastern and Southeastern Europe entail dangers that cannot be disregarded, namely violence and dictatorship. It is good in these hard times to bid farewell to the card houses of the past, to fasten our seat-belts and to create safe havens of freedom here and there." He is right, but it remains to be seen whether the Europeans will follow his advice.

19. Rooted Cosmopolitanism

Mitchell Cohen

The resurgence of nationalism after the collapse of communism startled many observers in the West. What could have been more stark than the contrast between Western and Eastern Europe? As the European Community pursued new modes of integration, nationalist virulence asserted itself in more than one of the previously communist lands. The bloody unravelling of Yugoslavia has been the most potent example, and the fear remains that the former Soviet Union could become Yugoslavia writ large. Evidently, Leninist and Stalinist dominion led neither to a withering away nor to the successful repression of national sentiments. At the same time, as the processes of integration have proceeded, xenophobia has intensified in Western Europe.

It is gradually becoming clear that nationalist aspirations were sometimes mistaken for democratic ambitions by Western observers of the momentous events between 1989 and 1991. Earlier, during the Cold War, both theorists of totalitarianism and Stalinists, each for their own reasons, tried to convince us that ideology was redesigning in its own image every nook and cranny of— and brain cell in— Soviet-style societies. It is now evident how wrong they were, how much more complicated history has been. Much seems not to have been remade, but frozen or stunted or integrated and used by these regimes. National sentiments is one example, and it is a particularly thorny problem for the left.

The left, historically, never came adequately to grips with nationalism and was often confounded by its intransigence. Consequently, its reemergence poses old quandaries anew. Marx's famous quip about modernity, that "all that's solid melts into air," would seem an appropriate metaphor for the last four years, save for one aspect of the modern world: national consciousness. Apart from circumstances in which nationalism served anti-imperialist purposes, the left has tended toward wishful anticipation of the dissipation of nations. For example, Eric Hobsbawm, one of the finest Marxist historians, wrote as recently as 1990: "The owl of Minerva, which brings wisdom, said Hegel, flies out at dusk. It is a good sign that it is now circling around nations and nationalism."[1]

The left, habitually, advanced two linked assertions about nations: that they are products of history and not embodiments of timeless collective essences; and they should be regarded as epiphenomena, that is, as secondary (if often bothersome) matters. It will become evident that I generally agree with the first point but think the second misconceived. Considerable contemporary scholarship—not only of the left—addresses precisely these issues. Anthony Smith, in his thoughtful book, *The Ethnic Origins of Nations* (1987), elucidates them neatly by means of a—Greek— ontological twist. He reminds us that Parmenides, the ancient Eleatic, proposed that "what is, is." He meant that change, "becoming," is illusion. A "Parmenidean" approach discerns in nations something inherent in human existence, something primordial which makes historical reappearances in varied guises, and which is in some way essential. The assumption is like that of Herder: nature creates nations. In contrast to Parmenides, Heraclitus of Epheus held that "all things are in a state of flux." A Heraclitian perspective on nations would emphasize their historicity. Nations, on this account, are a distinct product of modernity. They could not have come into being under earlier conditions, and will likely be transcended in the future. Thus Ernest Gellner, for instance, argues with characteristic erudition, in *Nations and Nationalism* (1983) that nations come of the transition from "agroliterate" to industrial societies, and Benedict Anderson, in *Imagined Communities* (1983), contends that however subjectively ancient nationalists perceive their nations to be, they are objectively modern.

---

1. Eric Hobsbawm, *Nations and Nationalism since 1780*, (Cambridge: Cambridge University Press, 1990), p. 183.

Smith seeks a middle ground between Parmenides and Heraclitus. He accepts the modernity of nations but traces their origins as far back as antiquity in what he calls *ethnie*, at whose core is a complex of myths and symbols tied to "the characteristic forms or styles and genres of certain historical configurations of peoples." All of them generate ethnocentrism, a sense of collective uniqueness and exclusivity that can be found, for example, in the oppositions between Greek and *barbaroi*; between Jews and pagan idolaters; in the self-conception of the Chinese as the Middle Kingdom; and in the Arab-Moslem notion of *Dar al-Islam*. In the West, an array of economic, political, and cultural transformations produced nations out of *ethnie*. So, rather than a break between premodernity and modernity, Smith perceives a political transformation leading from *ethnie* towards notions of common citizenship.

The "collective uniqueness" of a social entity is a problematic notion for Marxism, which ascribed the most salient features of human reality to social class and conceived the future to be embodied in a universal class whose interests represented those of humanity as a whole. The proletariat's victory was to give birth to a classless society—the first truly universal society. Nations and nationalism had to be viewed as epiphenomena. In the socialist future, with human "prehistory" left behind, there would be a new social individual dwelling amid socialist humanity. Nothing would mediate between the individual and the human community writ large.

Marx was radically Heraclitian. However, one can find in his writings on nationalism at least two paradigms, as Shlomo Avineri notes[2]. Before 1848 Marx believed that due to the universalizing tendencies of the capitalist market "nationalist differences and antagonisms between peoples are daily more and more vanishing" (*The Communist Manifesto*). National cultural distinctions among workers were, objectively, secondary matters—at best. As Marx wrote in his unfinished critique of Friedrich List (1845) "The nationality of the worker is neither French, nor English, nor German, it is *labor, free slavery, self-huckstering*. His government is neither French nor German, it is *capital*. His native air is neither French nor German, it is factory air."

---

2. See Shlomo Avineri, "Towards a Socialist Theory of Nationalism," *Dissent,* Fall, 1990.

In Marx's post-1848 paradigm, nationalism tends to be a superstructural device employed by the bourgeoisie in its pursuit of expanding markets abroad and domestic mastery. In the first paradigm, the natural course of capitalist development ought to lead to the withering away of nationalism; in the second paradigm, nationalism is sustained by capitalists, distracting proletarians from their class interests and leading to the intensification of conflicts among nations.[3]

Despite their divergences, the two paradigms are linked by Marx's insistence that "workers have no country." In both, nations and national cultures are viewed as historically created but, finally, as epiphenomena; Marx's ultimate vision is of a universal culture. It couldn't be otherwise if workers are the universal class, have no country, and breathe only factory air as their native air.

The difficulty is that this universal culture is something quite abstract. Here we may discern in Marx a problematic inheritance of Enlightenment rationalism. Now, few have been more incisive than Marx in criticizing bourgeois forms of abstract universalism, particularly concepts of the individual. He contrasted the Robinson Crusoe individual imagined by many capitalist ideologists with his own notion of "social individuals." In a trenchant passage in the *Grundrisse* he wrote that

> The more deeply we go back into history, the more does the individual appear as dependent, as belonging to a greater whole .... The human being is in the most literal sense a *zoon politikon* [political animal], not merely a gregarious animal, but an animal which can individuate itself only in the midst of society. Production by an isolated individual outside society ... is as much of an absurdity as is the development of language without individuals living together and talking to each other.

In short, the self-created rugged individualist is an ideological fiction.

But Marx did not go far enough, and he thereby encouraged an abstract proletarian internationalism in place of abstract bourgeois universalism. Among other things he should have said that individuals belong to greater wholes, not to a greater whole. Just as an individual is not an abstract entity, neither are the social realities through which one individuates oneself. The worker's native air may be factory air, and not French or German or English, but when the worker demands rights, it will be in French or German or English. By making a parallel between the producing and the speaking individual, Marx—unintentionally—implies the essential point. Societies are differentiated not only through productive relations but through language and culture, particularly national languages and cultures in the modern era. The most fruitful Marxist analyses of nationalism recognized just this. In *Die Nationalitätenfrage und die Sozialdemokratie* (1907), Otto Bauer argued that a nation is constituted by "common history as the effective cause, common culture and common descent as the means by which it produces its effects, a common language as the mediator of common culture, both its product and producer."[4] Instead of proposing a classless society that would negate or homogenize national cultures, he advocated a federal socialist state would provide national minorities with cultural autonomy on a "personal" (that is, non-territorial) basis. Consequently, Bauer avoided the class reductionism that leads to an esperanto vision of socialist culture—a vision no less one-sided than that of nationalists who cannot see beyond their own tongues.

However, it is not true that all nationalists have had chauvinist views of the world and that all expressions of national sentiment represent particularist evil. For one example, a central current within the history of French socialism has been quite nationalist when the nation in question represented the universal values of justice and progress: and anti-nationalist when "la nation" meant chauvinism and clericalism[5]. When Jean Jaurès rallied to the cause of the Dreyfusards, he refused to allow the right-wing to be identified with "la nation," and concurrently demanded of the left that it make the French republic, together with universal human values, its cause. Any assault on human rights had to be its charge, not solely proletarian interests narrowly defined.

---

4. Otto Bauer, "The Concept of the 'Nation'," in T.B. Bottomore and P. Goode, eds., *Austro-Marxism* (Oxford: Clarendon Press, 1978), p. 107.

5. See K. Steven Vincent, *Between Marxism and Anarchism: Benoit Mâlon and French Reformist Socialism* (Berkeley, Los Angeles and Oxford: University of California Press, 1992), p. 116.

Nationalists, like nationalisms, play different roles in different situations. As Avineri points out, in Marx's own day at least one socialist, Moses Hess, argued that nations should be conceived as mediators between the person and humanity. Hess, in response to Jew-hatred, espoused a socialist Jewish state as one link in an international chain of national redemptions. The title of his 1862 tract, *Rom und Jerusalem*, was not incidental, for Mazzini had made essentially the same arguments, though with republicanism in the place of Hess's socialism. Moreover, the apostle of Italian nationalism did not preach devotion to the nation alone, but told his followers: "You are men before you are citizens. ..." Like his Jewish counterpart, he saw the nation as a mediator between the individual and humanity; Mazzini and Hess both proposed their peoples' independence as sparks for universal liberation, and not solely as particularist enterprises. The agenda was not just a flag, but a pacific world of free nations. One may oppose their programs, find them bleary-eyed, ill-conceived or historically deluded, but they cannot be classified as belligerent exclusivists. It is true that neither Hess nor Mazzini elaborated their ideas with the trenchancy of the author of *Capital*. Yet they grasped something that the more formidable mind did not. Owls of Minerva can have their blinders.

To recognize the modernity of nations and to discard the notion that they incarnate timeless collective essences should not be translated simplistically into the proposition that nations and nationalism are nothing more than epiphenomena. While it is incorrect to speak of "nations" before, roughly, the fifteenth and sixteenth centuries, and nationalism before the French revolution, national cultures and national consciousness take on an autonomy beyond their origins, perhaps answering a basic human need not to be the Robinson Crusoes of extreme liberal ideology. In any event, it is as historically spurious as it is politically hazardous to homogenize nationalist movements and sentiments.

Let us take a contemporary example. I think it incumbent upon the left—and everyone else—to speak out forcefully on behalf of the Kurds. Not just forcefully, but honestly, which is impossible apart from advancing Kurdish national aspirations. Kurds sometime define their aspirations as autonomy (within Iraq or Turkey), sometimes as independence; social democracy is not their priority. Shall we tell them that Westerners will support them so that in a future era they can embody Western leftist ideas of universal humanity (whatever those are nowadays)? It is difficult to imagine a more condescending posture. And what should Kurds make of that part of the left which, preoccupied singularly with anti-imperialist indignation, draws attention to the Kurdish tragedy solely to indict American policy in the Gulf (as if Saddam Hussein would otherwise have been benevolent)? My point is simple: this is an oppressed nationality; Kurds are oppressed as Kurds and not as members of generalized categories. Their problem must be addressed in its specificity. Their national sentiments are legitimate, both intrinsically and as a response to oppression.

I do not mean to underestimate the murderous catastrophes wrought by nationalist fanaticism, especially in our century. (The Kurds themselves do not have entirely clean historical hands; should an independent Kurdistan arise, one would demand of it the same respect of minority rights Kurds should have been afforded in Iraq or Turkey.) Rather, I want to argue against conceiving nationalism as an either/or proposition: either all its forms to be condemned or all its expressions to be sanctioned. Both possibilities are inherently perilous. Michael Walzer has suggested what seems to me to be a sagacious alternative, that of domesticating nationalism's more dangerous impulses, seeking to integrate and counterbalance them within broader pluralistic frameworks. A useful historical model, as he notes, is religion—which, once a primary source of slaughter throughout Europe, was domesticated after its battered apostles reconciled themselves to multi-religious societies and, consequently, to tolerance. I would add that this ultimately meant resigning themselves to an important principle, one that is key to such domestication and to which I will presently return, that of the legitimacy of plural loyalties and therefore difference.

I employ the word "difference" with some hesitation since it is now encumbered by faddish, often vacuous, usages. This baggage aside, "difference" is a vital historical and contemporary question in American and European societies. It has also been a longstanding problem for the left, for much the same reasons nationalism was and rooted in that troublesome dimension of the left's Enlightenment heritage to which I alluded when discussing Marx. The

Friar tells Lessing's "Nathan the Wise": "You're a Christian soul! By God, a better Christian never lived." Nathan replies, "And well for us! For what makes me for you a Christian, makes yourself for me a Jew." A universal quality—reason—makes this identity of Christian and Jew possible. The tolerance suggested is based on equivalence, not acceptance of difference: the play is entitled "Nathan the Wise," not "Nathan the Jew." In later left-wing versions, membership in the universal class became the solvent of differences, on the way to a universal, classless society.

Yet, there are and will be "differences" not assimilable to sweeping universalist prescriptions. While much of the left conceived the classless society as the melting pot of humanity, a striking alternative was formulated by an American radical not long before the U.S. entered World War I. It was a moment in which nativist prejudices against immigrants intensified considerably in this country. Many of these newcomers were stirred by European events, often asserting bonds to their "old countries." This begot huffy indignation, especially on the part of American Brahmins; why, these immigrants simply weren't becoming proper "Americans."

In his July 1916 essay "Trans-national America," a young WASP named Randolph Bourne fashioned a remarkable retort. "As the unpleasant truth has come upon us that assimilation in this country was proceeding on lines very different from those we had marked out for it," he wrote, "we found ourselves inclined to blame those who were thwarting our prophecies. The truth became culpable." What was at stake was the relation between culture and democracy. "We act"—Bourne's "we" was dominant Anglo-America—"as if we want Americanization to take place only on our own terms, and not by the consent of the governed." Against the "thinly disguised panic which calls itself 'patriotism'," he proposed celebrating as culturally invigorating the hyphen in Polish-American, Irish-American, Jewish-American, German-American, etc. He went so far as to propose referring also to "English-Americans." [6]

Instead of a melting pot, Bourne envisioned "trans-nationality." This was "a weaving back and forth with other lands, of many

---

6. Randolph Bourne, "Transnational America," *The Radical Will: Selected Writings 1911-1918* (New York: Urizen Books, 1977) pp. 248-49.

threads of all sizes and colors. Any movement which attempts to thwart the weaving, or to dye the fabric any one color or disentangle the threads of the strands, is false to this cosmopolitan vision."[7] In a subsequent essay, Bourne argued that this thinking pointed toward "new concepts of the state, of nationality, of citizenship, of allegiance."[8] Here we find a multidimensional conception of political society and human relations, one that implies an important democratic principle: the legitimacy of plural loyalties.

Perhaps I am not stretching Austro-Marxist purposes too far if I suggest that they too accepted this principle by championing a class politics aimed at fashioning a federal socialist republic in which there would be systems of both territorial representation and national linguistic cultural—personal—autonomy. This was at odds with the radical universalism of Marx or Luxemburg (and with the expectation that the state would wither away).

The Austro-Marxist position was expounded in a specific context: a debate inside a socialist movement within a multinational empire. One can also find a notion of plural loyalty articulated by the left within a national movement, with the use, notably, of metaphors like Bourne's—threads and cloth. In the late 1920s and early 1930s, the growing dominance of the Labor-left within the Zionist movement was threatened by the right-wing "Revisionists" led by Vladimir Jabotinsky. The latter proclaimed himself a "pure" nationalist and denounced his adversaries as "*shaatnez*," a mixture of wool and cotton proscribed in Jewish garments by religious orthodoxy. The national raiment, in his formulation, had to be unsullied by foreign admixtures and universalistic notions such as socialism. David Ben-Gurion, then Labor's leader and later the first premier of Israel, proclaimed the very concept of *shaatnez* to be a deceit. A national movement without social conceptions was an abstraction, and Zionists, like any national movement, could be good or bad depending on the society it fashioned. He declared—changing the metaphor—that unlike the right, the Zionist left stood not in one circle (that of nationalism) but in many circles, and "when we stand in two circles it isn't a question of standing in two separate areas,

---

7. Ibid.

8. Ibid. See also Bourne's "The Jew and Transnational America," *Menorah Journal*, December 1916, pp. 277-84.

one moment in one and the next in another, but rather in what is common territory to both of them." He continued:

> In reality we don't stand within two circles alone, but within many circles—as citizens of Palestine we stand in the circle of a nation that aspires to its homeland, as workers we stand in the circle of the working class, as sons of our generation we stand in the circle of modern history; our women comrades stand in the circle of the working women's movement in its struggle for liberation.[9]

To stand in many circles is to accept the principle of plural loyalties. It must be readily conceded that ascribing to such a principle and practicing it are two different things. But for my purposes here, it is the theoretical point that is most salient, together with the fact that it has direct implications for concepts of citizenship. This was articulated with acuity by one of Ben-Gurion's colleagues, the American Labor Zionist thinker Hayim Greenberg, in his 1948 essay "Patriotism and Plural Loyalties." Greenberg took the example of an Italian speaking Swiss citizen. "He hardly knows himself how many different loyalties he harbors in various degrees." As a Swiss he owes fidelity to Switzerland; he is also a patriot of this canton. Whatever his "race," he feels a cultural and linguistic kinship to Italians in Italy. If he is Catholic he feels ties to Catholics around the world and in various regards accepts the "sovereignty" of the Vatican. And we should add: if he is a she, she may well have keen allegiances to the women's movement.[10]

How shall we regard this individual? As a bundle of prospective betrayals? Or ought we to accept, indeed value, the legitimacy of "pluralist-social relationships, attachments, sentiments and loyalties?"[11] The true democrat, maintained Greenberg, will seek not to destroy, but to harmonize such differences, which does not mean that they are easily harmonized.

---

9. David Ben-Gurion; (1933) "Ha-Poel ba-tsyionut" ("The Worker in Zionism), *Mi-Maamad le-am* (*From a Class to a Nation*) (Tel Aviv: Am Oved and Keren ha-Negev, reprint 1974/originally 1933) p. 249.

10. Hayim Greenberg, "Patriotism and Plural Loyalties," *The Inner Eye: Selected Essays*, Vol. 1 (new York: 1953), p. 179.

11. Ibid.

Plural dimensions of human identity often don't rest easily with each other, and sometimes not at all. Such discontents are the hobgoblins of what I would call "unidevotionalists," those vigilant and anxious beings who are endlessly obsessed with litmus tests of absolute loyalty. Alas, their questions and answers, always so earnest, are ever easy. For them it is unimaginable that an individual might actually face moral dilemmas, might confront legitimate conflicts of reality, might have to inquire of the rights and wrongs on contesting demands, might be compelled to assess the consequences of embracing this or that position. Unidevotionalists have their flag, they salute it; they legitimate only particularisms, usually just their own. Such one-sidedness—no less than that of abstract universalism—frustrates democratic pluralism, which demands refusal of singular answers (to borrow again from Walzer).

It might seem that among today's advocates of multiculturalism, a left has emerged that recognizes the problems I have been raising. Certainly, parallels to earlier discussions of national identity and culture can be found in the debates on multiculturalism. Yet I fear that too many votaries of multiculturalism have become unreflective celebrants of particularism, now that the working class has not fulfilled its universalizing mission. Missing is adequate meditation on the grounds of cultural diversity within a democratic society. Too often, the word "difference" is intoned indignantly without consideration of the "trans" of trans-nationality, of the intersection of the hyphens Bourne—rightly—celebrated.

Bourne spoke of a cloth of many threads, but he still spoke of a cloth. If one asserts differences without conceptualizing the territory of multicultural exchange, one may reinvent just those particularist perils dreaded in nationalism by the historical left. In a world of resurgent nationalisms, and in an America debating multiculturalism, what is needed is the fashioning of a dialectical concept of rooted cosmopolitanism, which accepts a multiplicity of roots and branches and which rests on the legitimacy of plural loyalties, of standing in many circles, but with common ground.

20. Ethnicity, Migration, and the Validity of the Nation-State

Eric Hobsbawm

Bush's new world order is a new world disorder, and for the time being, no restoration of stability is visible or even conceivable. It is against this background that we see the present rise of ethnic or nationalist or separatist phenomena in various, but by no means in all parts of the world. But on the other side of the coin is supranationalism or transnationalism, that is, the development of an increasingly integrated world economy or, more generally, a world whose problems cannot effectively be tackled let alone solved within the borders of nation states.

The paradox of the situation is that some of these agitations are recreating nation-states of the ethnic/linguistic type, often on a much smaller scale than before, at a time when this makes no rational sense and, indeed, is particularly dangerous. This is not a universal tendency. Today, ethnic or similar movements do not necessarily or even typically find a nation-state of their own relevant to their problems. The United States demonstrates this in general and the black population of the United States demonstrates this in particular. In short, we must not equate ethnicity and nationalism or ethnicity and other interests aiming to set up territorial states. However, very often they are confused.

I want to draw your attention to three aspects of this new instability: First, the specific and explosive situation between the frontiers of Germany, Austria, and Italy in the west and those of Japan in the east, including the Middle East and central Asia; second, the phenomenon of ghettoization within states; and third, the actual or potential consequences of living through a period of global mass migration comparable to and potentially much bigger than the European mass migration of 1880 to 1920.

What we are seeing today is not a proof of the irresistible force of national or ethnic identity, but it is the result of the outcome of the First World War in a situation analogous to that in 1917-1920, namely the breakdown of old pluri-ethnic empires. The collapse of the Hapsburg and Ottoman empires and the temporary collapse of Czarist Russia produced two equally impracticable forms of postwar settlement. On the ruins of the European empires, it produced the Wilsonian plan of a Europe of, in theory, homogeneous ethnic linguistic nation-states. In the Middle East, it produced the imposition of British and French formal or informal empire over nominally independent territories with little or no historic political presence, plus a half-hearted Wilsonian formula for the Jews in Palestine.

The European settlement broke down before the Middle Eastern one. It became clear that the distribution of ethnic groups and languages is such that homogeneous national territories could only be achieved by forcible assimilation, by mass population transfer, and/or by genocide. The Turks initiated this in a modest way, by forcible assimilation of the Kurds, mass transfer of the Greeks, and genocide of the Armenians. But in the 1940s, the whole matter was taken up again on a much larger scale with the genocide of the Jews and others, and the mass expulsion of the Germans from Central and Eastern Europe.

In short, in spite of this, the basic situation in large parts of Europe remained as before. Homogenous national territorial states can still only be imposed at the same cost. And meanwhile international migration has created—or recreated—ethnic diversity even in states which previously, through the barbarism of the 1940s, had eliminated it. The former Yugoslavia demonstrates this. Concretely, the explosive issues today in Europe are issues that were created by World War I and not before. Yugoslavia, the Croats and the Serbs in the same state, the Czechs and the Slovaks in the same state, and so on. This applies also in the explosive Soviet national problems which were of no significance before 1914. Neither the Caucasian nor the Baltic problem was in any important sense an historic problem of nationalism. Conversely, the historic problems of nationalism that were explosive or present before 1914 have been relatively quiescent today. The most obvious example is the Macedonian question in the Balkans, which only became explosive when—for reasons that had nothing to do with Macedonia—Yugoslavia fell apart; and also the Ukrainian question in the former Soviet Union, which similarly came to the fore only as the Soviet Union collapsed. In 1917 there was strong Ukrainian nationalism, though it was not separatist. There was no Baltic nationalism worth mentioning.

A brief note. Replaying 1918 not only creates instability and solves no problem—although actually in a transnational economy it becomes possible to think of an economically viable Slovakia and Serbia, as it was not between the wars—but it is actually dangerous to democracy. It is dangerous to culture. It is dangerous to freedom because the small nations, unlike the big nations, in establishing homogeneity insist on dominating their minorities.

The problem in Quebec is not directed against the English; it is directed against the Italians, the Greeks, the Inuit, the Native Americans who are to be forced to be culturally assimilated to French culture in Quebec. And the same is true in Slovakia, in Croatia, in Serbia and anywhere else.

A brief word about the second point: ghettoization. The modern pattern of migration produces, at least initially, a diaspora of ghettos, mostly urban. Democracy produces a machine for minority groups to fight effectively for a share of central or national resources, which is why the classic nationalist program is so totally irrelevant to groups in this situation.Ghettoization is politically effective, which is why it develops so rapidly in countries like the United States. In recent New York elections, redistricting was specifically designed to produce minority representation, not only of ethnic minorities. For instance, in the West Village and Chelsea, it was designed to produce a specific territory of gay representation, and the candidate who won advertised himself as being not only gay, but HIV positive.

Mass migration also produces group friction. In extreme cases, it creates areas barricading themselves against hostile or unacceptable outsiders. This is worse than living side by side, as was possible in the past, within limits. But it is better than mutual massacre or the racist transformation of national politics, which we see in many European countries. In this respect, events in the United States are more acceptable than what is happening elsewhere. Racism in the United States tends to be less dangerous and less pervasive than in other countries because it is much more limited to a grassroots struggle, as opposed to countries like France or even countries with apparently no racist tradition, such as Sweden or Italy. Even when ghettoization turns into civil war at the grassroots, as in Northern Ireland, it has so far proved containable. It is one of the saddest paradoxes that in actual fact, in most sociological terms, Northern Ireland is a more peaceful, more stable, and a more sane society than most of the rest of Britain, in spite of the fact that a certain number of people are being killed on the borders of these two ghettos.

The obvious negative side is that no common national ground may remain in the end by the division of the population of a state into self-contained sub-units. And, in fact, the ability which once provided the Democratic Party with its unity, namely the skill to forge a single unit out of ethnic diversity and, if you like, class unity, ceases to be valid. What we find today is the complete absence of the kind of concern with Americanization which one found in the United States in the 1880 to 1922 period. And this is a real problem. Possibly only in Australia, among the countries with mass immigration, does one find a basic concern for integrating and creating a sort of national unity.

We are today in an era of global and not only of European mass migration. It is potentially far bigger than we realize. The percentage of the demographic excess of the European population that migrated between 1880 and 1914 was enormous. Whereas today, even in Latin America, which has the largest mass emigration, it is tiny, relatively speaking, compared to what the Italian or Norwegian or Swedish emigration was in the earlier era. The potential is far greater. The United States, Canada, and Australia are quite exceptional so far in permitting, with very little hindrance, free immigration of this kind. Everywhere else, even since the Gulf War, the response has been to close doors and barricade national gates, though this has not prevented the appearance of permanent and growing Third World minorities in most developed countries. The developed world is becoming a steadily tinier percentage of the globe. Between 1750 and 1900, it grew, demographically, absolutely, and relatively from about 15 percent of the world population to about a third of the world population. Since 1900, or more exactly since 1950, it has fallen. It is now back to 15 to 20 percent, if one takes OECD countries as a percentage of global population. This is the rich world, the land of milk and honey and gold, toward which the poor of the world are naturally drawn, particularly in an international capitalist society theoretically encouraging free movement of the factors of production. What is more, they are being lured by the fact that the developed world, including the ex-socialist countries, do not reproduce themselves and therefore have a problem of labor shortage.

One possible solution to this situation is, of course, to refuse the strangers, to barricade ourselves. I think this is no longer actually possible. The second is an apartheid solution—to admit or accept these new immigrants, but to turn them into a permanent under-class. Whether this is possible any longer now that it has proved impossible even in South Africa is a matter for debate.

The third is to allow it and to face a long-term, quite fundamental transformation—such as is happening in the United States, of course, where already in the big cities the majority of the population are of non-European and nonwhite origins. I do not think that this necessarily means the end of a basic culture, particularly a culture of the kind established in the United States. Essentially, the Roman Empire followed this particular strategy or was forced to follow this political strategy. But in the end, the area of the Roman Empire remains, to this day, culturally marked by the Romans, the Latin culture, whether in the religious or in the civilian form.

Finally, I draw your attention to simply one further possibility. Namely, that modern transportation and the modern globalization of the world make possible simultaneous, binational or multinational existence, such as, of course, many members of the upper middle class, especially academics, are already engaged in. There are people who habitually spend part of the year in one country, part of the year in another, without necessarily losing their roots. This may be happening not only at the upper level. There are already many people from Israel who habitually, while either remaining Israelis or permanent Israeli immigrants, spend many months each year in New York making a living and then return to Israel. I have myself come across a case of an Ecuadorian from Guayaquil who comes for six months to New York, earns dollars driving a cab, and then goes back home, where his wife is looking after their business in Guayaquil.

Where does this leave exclusive ethnicity, exclusive nationalism, the exclusive division of the world? I raise these questions not to answer them, because there is no answer. I raise them because they are problems that the left and the right must face today.

21. Neither Politics Nor Economics

Alan Wolfe

Americans are increasingly oblivious to politics but exceptionally sensitive to culture. What constitutes for other countries the meat and potatoes of political conflict—the distribution of income among classes, regulation of industry, protectionism versus free trade, sectional antagonism—here captures only the attention of the interests immediately affected. Politics in the classic sense of who gets what, when, and how is carried out by a tiny elite watched over by a somewhat larger, but still infinitesimally small, audience of news followers. The attitude of the great majority of Americans to such traditional political subjects is an unstable combination of boredom, resentment, and sporadic attention.

Culture, on the other hand, grabs everyone's attention all the time. What for other countries are peripheral if not downright trivial issues—prayer in schools, condoms for teenagers, drinking, Armageddon, the theory of evolution, date rape, and the pledge of allegiance—in this country constitute moments of intense, almost furious, concern. Acquiescent when their natural resources are turned over to private development, unfazed when close advisors to their president create secret and unaccountable governmental action, willing to tolerate fantastic abuses of the public trust in the name of deregulation, Americans will nonetheless call radio talk shows and write letters to the editor when they feel their cultural values are threatened. The smart politician is the one who mouths cultural platitudes for general consumption while supporting the self-interest of those immediately concerned with specific public policies.

Americans have reversed the usual understanding of public and private. The great political and economic forces that are usually understood to shape public policy are viewed as clashes between private interests. At the same time matters of religious belief, taste, and cultural preference—once thought of as private and individualistic—become center-stage in the large public dramas enacted in the media. We shine light on the shadowy regions of the soul even as we darken the stage on which our common destiny is enacted.

Because they practice politics in cultural terms, Americans cannot be understood with the tool kits developed by political scientists. Their attitudes do not fit the convenient ideological categories of right and left. Their behavior is not predictable on the basis of class, family background, or gender. They do not do what theories of democracy suggest they ought to do to make democracy work. (And yet, contrary to another set of theories about democracy, it seems to work anyway). They are ashamed by the very things that less democratic societies lack, freedom of the press for example, while taking pride in matters, such as their insistence that politicians not give themselves raises, that other democracies find vulgar. It is not because Americans are politically sophisticated that they constantly frustrate those who would understand them but because they are politically innocent. Unable to abolish war, they have abolished politics instead, simply by declaring the subject no longer interesting. The state has not withered away, but the amount of attention paid to its affairs, for all intents and purposes, has.

It takes a sociologist to understand the priority Americans give to culture, one like James Davison Hunter. Rather than starting with a theory about democracy, Hunter talks to the culturally engaged: religious fundamentalists of all faiths and liberal modernists concerned with individual and group rights. He finds that "America is in the midst of a culture war that has and will continue to have reverberations not only within public policy but within the lives of ordinary Americans everywhere."[1] Culture in America is war by other means, except that wars are usually concluded through negotiations, an option not generally available to those struggling over the nature of the Holy.

---

1. James Davison Hunter, *Culture Wars: The Struggle to Define America*, (New York: 1991).

Hunter is concerned with the lack of "conceptual categories or analytic tools for understanding cultural conflict," and in his own modest way, he is trying to develop some of them.[2] The most important of his insights is that life was easier when we merely fought over ecclesiastical differences. No matter how bitter the struggles between Protestant and Catholic, pluralistic assumptions enabled both of them to maintain their identity within their specific religious communities. Thinking they had settled their historic differences over religion through Supreme court interpretations of the first amendment's establishment clause, Americans stopped killing each other over theological disagreements. But in so doing, they merely prepared the ground for cultural struggles even harder to resolve.

Religious pluralism and first amendment tolerations are the answers to theological conflict favored by "high" churches and their leaders. No matter what their doctrinal background, liberal Protestants, Catholics, and Jews all agree that we can compartmentalize religion and politics: six days a week we devote to political economy and one day, if we choose, to God. But it is just this liberal solution to religious difference that defines the gap between what Hunter calls the progressive and the orthodox outlook on the world. For the orthodox—whether rabbis in Brooklyn, Catholic anti-abortion activists, or Protestant fundamentalists—share a refusal to participate in a spiritual division of labor. They have more in common with each other than they do with more modern adherents to their own theological tenets.

Hunter argues that this shift from conflict between religions to those within them constitutes a cosmological, not a theological, split. At war are two fundamentally different visions of man in the world. Modernists, inspired by life rather than the word, begin with the everyday and tailor their creed to adjust to its pressures. Fundamentalists, who reverse the priority, begin with an ethic and are determined to shape modern life to fit its requirements. Authority is external to the individual for the orthodox, internal to the individual for the progressive. Both perspectives have among their adherents people with a wide variety of psychological dispositions, but certainty and conviction are more apt to characterize the fun-

---

2. Ibid.

damentalist, while guilt and insecurity seem inevitably associated with the modernist. It often appears that the two groups live in different worlds, even on different planets. Americans who adhere to one of these poles literally have nothing to say to those who adhere to the other.

Expressed this way, cosmological conflicts are far more serious than theological ones. "The conflict is much deeper now," Hunter writes, "for it centers on what we believe, what we celebrate, how we live together, and who we are as a community and as a nation."[3] Historians are likely to be surprised by this assertion, given the amount of blood spilled between religious groups in the past; as furious as current debates have been, they remain essentially verbal and symbolic. Still, Hunter has a point, if not necessarily a historically accurate one. There is a *Kulturkampf* taking place in the United States. It has displaced politics for most Americans, it shows no sign of being resolved, and it is most assuredly "a conflict over how we are to order our lives together."[4]

Hunter follows the culture war through five different fields of battle: the family, education, the media, law, and electoral politics. For the orthodox, families are characterized by duty, hierarchy, obedience—but above all else by two biological parents who marry for the sake of having children.

Public policy that touches on issues of family life arouses passions on both sides. The battle over whether schools in New York City should provide condoms with or without parental consent to students, a battle fought after Hunter finished his book, illustrates perfectly how the war over the family is conducted. For cultural conservatives, parental responsibility over children is sacred. Gay activists and the coalition against AIDS, at least in their public advertising campaign, appeal over the heads of parents to the teenagers themselves. For the one group, the family is what makes life possible. For the other the preservation of life must take priority over traditional family values.

---

3. Ibid.

4. Ibid.

That the battle of the condom was fought within the schools only illustrates how difficult it is to draw the line between one field of combat in our cultural wars and the others. No other area of American life has seen a more complete victory for the triumph of the liberal modernist vision than education; the 1960s generation, thoroughly defeated at the level of presidential politics, won the battle for the public schools. Teachers' unions became powerful forces, not only in educational policy, but in politics in general. Hypermodernist demands for multicultural education received a warm welcome from liberal school administrators. Entire fields of educational inquiry are dominated by the progressive vision; Hunter points out that more than 25 percent of the resolutions passed by the American Psychological Association since the 1960s take positions in the culture war, nearly all of them on the modernist side. But the result of this victory did not still the culture war over the schools. Instead fundamentalists created their own schools, more and more students left public schools for private ones, and an eventual backlash against liberal values in the schools erupted. This is a battle that is by no means over.

Conservatives argue that the media and the arts are the institutions in American society most thoroughly dominated by the liberal outlook. There clearly is some truth in this charge, since not too many fundamentalists experiment with new literary techniques or avant-garde choreography. Yet although progressives feel best about themselves when they can protest censorship, and fundamentalists give them plenty of reason to feel good, this battle is far from one-sided. A stand against censorship, in the context of television, places liberals together in an uneasy alliance with corporate advertisers. It is not completely clear why those who support the use of public funds to exhibit Robert Mapplethorpe's photographs should also support unlimited reruns of commercials for Egoiste. When rock music turns sexist, movies glorify violence, television sells junk to children, and pornographic comic books appeal to teenagers, liberals ought not be too certain that they hold the moral high ground. Hunter is right to argue that too many people have lost the distinction between censuring and censoring; fundamentalists prefer to censor rather than censure, but liberal modernists, caught up in their own relativism, have lost the art of censure completely. Without it, they are increasingly irrelevant to larger numbers of Americans.

What makes the legal system such an important field of contention in the battle for America's soul is that it is both undemocratic as well as the field of choice for American liberals. Key modernist positions, including most of those dealing with the legal status of church and state, would not win popular referenda; they can only remain the law of the land if ensconced in Supreme Court decisions. As in the case with education and the media, liberal elites are comfortable with legal institutions and legal arguments; fundamentalists usually have more to occupy them than writing articles for law reviews. But it is in the area of law where the conservative backlash against liberal hegemony has been strongest. Liberals have no appropriate arguments to challenge the Reagan-Bush effort to pack courts, since they packed a few of them themselves. Moreover, many liberal legal opinions rest on shaky ground; why is it permissible for public schools to loan books to parochial schools but not maps? The new Supreme Court that may overturn *Roe v. Wade* could also have fun with *Everson v. Board of Education,* which established the basic principles of liberal pluralism with respect to church and state.

The culture war, finally, has invaded the turf upon which electoral campaigns are conducted. Hunter argues that the culture war creates the language of politics, and all those who would seek office must respond. As Michael Dukakis and Walter Mondale learned, there is much truth in this argument. Yet it is also the case that politicians themselves are part of the culture war. Liberal modernists tend to dominate local politics, even in conservative states, because they believe in government and are willing to accept low pay. Meanwhile the ability of fundamentalists to shape what national Republicans say and do remains striking, epitomized by the low moment when George Bush's Department of Justice gave support to illegal anti-abortion actions in Wichita. Politicians of both parties cannot insulate themselves from the culture war; increasingly they are among its most active participants.

It is tempting to want to take sides in this culture war. As a sociologist, Hunter is driven by the logic of his profession to do so, since sociology—cosmopolitan, urban, and the product of a secularized "high church" worldview—is, from a fundamentalist view-point, indistinguishable from socialism. It is therefore greatly to Hunter's credit that he remains neutral. He never stoops to make easy points against easy targets. He does his best to move inside the minds of his subjects and present the world as they understand it. He asks us to at least consider the proposition that, for many people, blasphemy does exist. And although he argues throughout the book that the two worldviews he describes are not reconcilable, he does attempt to lay out positions in between them that can strengthen the commitment to a common life that both sides, in his view, tend to reject.

Hunter's evenhandedness is a rare treat in a book dealing with such contentious topics. But it is finally not convincing. Carried away by parallelisms, Hunter asks us to accept that both sides in the culture war mirror each other. Each paints the opposition in extremist terms. Both are intolerant. Seeking a monopoly over legitimation, each seeks to rally national symbols—the Constitution, the Bill of Rights—on behalf of its partisan vision. Both use similar direct mail and advertising techniques. "The rhetoric infused into public discourse by each side is so similar," Hunter concludes, "that without identifying the object of derision and aversion, it is nearly impossible to distinguish which of the two coalitions is speaking."[5]

While Hunter is correct to point out the occasional arrogance and intolerance of the liberal modernists, they do speak a different language than the fundamentalists. There are liberals who care about procedure and not just about whose ox is gored—more, I would venture to say, than there are honest conservatives who repudiate opportunism for the sake of principle. The terms by which most liberal modernists propose to understand the world include room for dissenting opinions, which is not true of the terms by which most fundamentalists operate. From a liberal perspective, a woman can choose whether or not to have an abortion; from a fundamentalist perspective, she cannot. (Only those free to choose can make a moral choice not to have an abortion, should they so decide). Randall Terry (of Operation Rescue) is not the moral

---

5. Ibid.

equivalent of Fay Wattleton (of Planned Parenthood). Liberals discovered tolerance for a reason; fundamentalists have yet to learn what it is.

Nowhere is the difference between these worldviews clearer than in the fundamentalist assumption, quoted numerous times throughout Hunter's book, that we are a Christian nation. At the risk of seeming intolerant to those who hold this position, we are not. There are Jews, Moslems, and, by now, any number of other non-Christians who live here and claim citizenship rights. Fundamentalist language does not include them; liberal modernist language does. Hunter's evenhandedness finally fails because one side in the culture war can live with the other, while the other cannot reciprocate the favor.

If there is any similarity between these two sides, it is because the fundamentalists are far more modernist than the modernists are fundamentalist. Hunter admits as much. "Virtually everyone, nowadays, is influenced by the profound philosophical reorientation of the Enlightenment," he writes. "Even the most Bible-believing Evangelical, the most Rome-bound Catholic, and the most observant orthodox Jew has been influenced in subtle even if unacknowledged ways."[6] Perhaps the proof of this point is the fact that fundamentalist Jews, Catholics, and Protestants formed an alliance in the first place, despite their theological differences. That alliance was not, as Hunter argues, "pragmatically necessary"; it was instead a result of the fact that even reactionaries are, in Max Weber's term, "this-worldly." They accept the state, however secular, as the turf on which to fight, and they fight.

Who will win the fight? True to his sense of fairness and balance, Hunter provides no answer but considers the strengths and weaknesses of each side. Moreover, despite his claims at the beginning of the book that the two sides are engaged in an irreconcilable struggle in which compromise is not possible, he concludes by laying out some principles that might make the debate at least somewhat more rational. But one wonders if the war is not already over. The Moral Majority is no longer, there is an air of ridicule surrounding television evangelists, the evil empire wants to join the

6. Ibid.

International Monetary Fund, and the teaching of creationism as a science will hardly help us compete with the Japanese. Modernity is corrosive, giving modernists an incontestable advantage. The proof is Ronald Reagan—a product of the movies, our only divorced President, a man who lived a fully modern life even while appealing for fundamentalist votes.

Hunter knows that, finally, the modernists have the upper hand. Although they speak out for the poor and the minorities, modernists have significant class advantages: they tend to be wealthier than the fundamentalists, better positioned to exercise influence, and more comfortable with the tools of persuasion. Moreover the orthodox communities, if they are to be politically effective, can only do so on terms established by the modernists. In the process they may, in Hunter's words, "become so assimilated to a progressive political (and linguistic) culture that they will not be capable of offering any effective opposition to the worldview that currently plagues them."[7]

Like many other sociologists, Hunter worries that too thorough a modernist victory may turn religious belief into a matter of personal taste. At times Hunter's book reads like a lament for a lost world of faith, as if he were returning back to the world of Protestant theology out of which sociology originally emerged. But in a nation composed of people with diverse religious beliefs, no single religion can provide the moral framework for a public vocabulary. Faith in private and toleration in public is the best we can do. If that is a modernist and progressive solution, so be it. We have no choice but to find a way to live together, and the only way available exists on modernist, not fundamentalist, terms.

---

7. Ibid.

22. The Left in the Process of Democratization in Central and Eastern European Countries

Milos Hajek

Other than the time between the two World Wars, democracy has been a remarkable success after World War II. From 1918 through 1939, after the progression of democratic tendencies in the beginning of the 1920s, most countries in Europe gradually returned to autocratic, even fascist regimes. Today it is a fact that democracy is deeply rooted in Western European countries and all communist regimes in the eastern half of Europe have failed. Some countries, in that region, though, are on their way to democracy, and in other countries democratic governments are trying their first steps, which turn out to be hopeful, yet difficult. I deliberately call it the eastern half of Europe—not Eastern Europe—because very often Central European countries are called Eastern European. Czechs, Slovaks, Poles, and Hungarians, however, consider themselves Central European, not Eastern European.

The developments in Eastern and Central Europe over the past six years have shown that the democratic potential of these peoples has been much stronger than the West had expected. The fast collapse of the conservative coup attempt in the Soviet Union in August 1991 proved that six years of Gorbachev's perestroika policy had brought a strong democratic consciousness to a people that had never experienced a longer period of democracy. Today, more than ever, we can hope for the irreversibility of the democratic processes in the former Soviet Union.

Despite the joy and the high hopes, one has to recognize the enormous difficulties the young and victorious Russian democracy is facing. The Soviet society is completely unprepared for deep economic and governmental reforms. The stabilization of democracy within the former Soviet republics, for which the functioning of the economies is a precondition, is a task for the entire democratic free world, just as environmental problems or the suffering in the Third World countries are.

Most of the Eastern and Central European countries have experienced two dictatorships—one from the Right and a communist one. For this reason, there is a very strong aversion to dictatorship. This is especially true for conservative communists. This is a very important positive factor. There are still a lot of negative elements, though, so that we cannot talk about a secured democracy yet. The main reason for the weakness of the new democratic governments lies in the political experience of the societies. About the former Czechoslovakia (but not exclusively) one might say that most people have opposed the dictatorship. However, their previous attitudes used to be more negative. They accepted the idea of democracy, but only a small percentage of the society had a concrete idea about what democracy is—not to mention the fact that most people pictured a consumer's, not a democratic society. Even the political elite, who had been relatively well informed about the functioning of a democratic state, didn't have personal experience.

People under the age of sixty never had the chance to experience a democratic system, except for the year 1968 in Czechoslovakia. This resulted in a low level of political culture, a low level of political behavior and participation. Sessions of the Czechoslovakian parliament were often chaotic and its authority was weak. A low election turnout in Hungary and relatively strong autocratic tendencies in Poland—all this proves that the new democracies have considerable weaknesses. In the other countries of the Eastern half of Europe we find even more serious threats to democratic developments.

A further roadblock on the way to a democratic system is posed by stronger nationalist feelings. Democratic progress requires strong international cooperation as well as integration. Today, however, we witness the disintegration of the former nation-states. The former Soviet Union has become the Commonwealth of Independent States, Czechoslovakia has been split into the Czech Republic and the Slovak Republic, and Yugoslavia has fallen apart.

I now turn to the main issue at hand: the situation of the Left. The main task of the Left, just as of all democratic tendencies in the Eastern half of Europe, is developing and securing democracy.

Social democratic parties have resumed their activities in all post—communist countries. They all belong to the Socialist International, and it was expected that they would emerge as centers for the new democratic Left. Unfortunately, this didn't happen. They remained weak, sometimes extremely weak, with the exception of East Germany, where specific conditions existed. This also occurred in Poland, Hungary, and Czechoslovakia, where these parties failed to succeed in gaining parliamentary representation. In other words: building a strong, democratic Left doesn't only mean strengthening today's social democratic parties.

I think it is necessary in this connection to mention the problem of the communist parties or their succeeding parties in the three countries. I think there are two ways to approach this issue. On the one hand people become members, who had been party members throughout the entire Brezhnev era and who either actively participated or opportunistically stood by. On the other hand, we should note Willy Brandt's statement: the new social democratic parties in Eastern and Central Europe will be recruited from some groups among which we will also find former reform communists. I want to add that I find it interesting that Willy Brandt made this statement in Prague and no Czechoslovakian newspaper printed it.

To solve this problem in reality, we will have to define the border between reform communists and former communists, who either converted to become democratic socialists or remained communists. This problem has presented itself very differently in each country. Unfortunately I cannot go into further detail. I just want to point out two facts: In the first parliamentary elections in Hungary, the socialist party, which under the leadership of Nyers, Nemeth, and Horn broke with the semi-conservative Gros-trends, gained 10 percent of the vote, whereas the Social Democratic Party only gained 3.5 percent. This is not only about percentages, though. I want to refer to three Hungarian political scientists—Heiszler, Markus, and Hülvely. All three are independent democratic socialists and expressed their opinion at a Friedrich Ebert Foundation seminar in Freudenberg, Germany. They believe that in Hungary we find more future Social Democrats among the former reform communists than there are in the Social Democratic Party.

Is there a danger for democracy in the three Central European countries? I believe there is no immediate threat. However, the problem has been the most serious in the former Czechoslovakia. There the Communist party was purged after 1968 from its reform wing. This totally re-Stalinized party excluded the old leadership after the revolution, elected a new one and adopted a democratic platform. However, the old neo-Stalinist functionaries stayed on and are now waiting for their turn.

While the Slovak part of the party became the "Party of the Democratic Left," thus initiating a reconstruction by eliminating many conservative elements, the Czech party leadership refused to do so. The neo-Stalinist danger, however, was limited: the Communist Party gained just 13 percent of the vote. Furthermore, their voters were on average relatively old.

Therefore, there was no real danger on that side. However, if economic reforms were to cause social unrest, communist conservatism might gain importance. In that case, democracy is more threatened from the Right. The separatist Slovak National Party kept the cult of the executed war criminal Jozef Tiro alive. The nostalgia about the clero-fascist Slovak state during the war is not only alive among supporters of that party. In the Czech Republic we find a Republican Party, similar to the German Republicans. They compare in beliefs and in strength.

I return to the core problem: Why is the democratic Left, more specifically the social democratic parties, so weak in the post-communist countries?

After forty or even more years of dictatorship, the "left" democratic parties were restructured. This happened under totally different conditions than in the nineteenth century, when Social Democratic Parties were founded. These circumstances were even different from the time, when these parties were dissolved by the communist regimes. Social democratic parties emerged during the last century at a time when there already existed a strong and spontaneous labor movement, especially of union character. The political socialist movement came into being—according to Horst Heimann—through an alliance of the ad hoc labor movement with the socialist intellectuals; this is the fundamental element of European Social Democracy. In the Eastern and Central European countries the old, state-ruled labor unions have collapsed and the succeeding unions are still too weak. The only notable exception is "Solidarnosc" in Poland, but they are not "left"-oriented.

The groups that renewed and refounded the social democratic parties did not thoroughly analyze the situation. They renewed them on the basis of the old parties' tradition. In reality, developments have proven that these traditions do not work any more.

A further explanation for the weakness of the democratic Left lies in the lack of a precedent for the situation and the challenge. Never before in history has a society had to undergo the transformation from a centralist to a market economy. The same is true for the transformation into a mixed economy with a superior private sector.

The failure of communism discredited not only the word "communist." The communist regime called itself "socialist" and this Stalinist understanding of socialism was accepted by the majority of the Czechoslovakian people. And this was not only the case in Czechoslovakia. Throughout the social democratic press the word "socialist" can only be found in reference to the Socialist International or to a foreign socialist party. Even the word "left" has been discredited. I will talk about that later.

These challenges require strong intellectual resources. And I have to note that the intellectual resources of the democratic Left are not able to deal with the historic challenges in Czechoslovakia and other countries. The Czechoslovakian reform movement of the 1960s proved to have a high level of intellectual potential. During the twenty years of the so-called Normalization of the Rusak-Jakes Regime, the intellectual powers of the Prague Spring have dissolved, just like Czechoslovakian reform communism, which provided the main activists, though not the only ones of the Prague Spring. After 1968 the Communist Party got rid of them. While the reformers in Poland, Hungary, and the Soviet Union remained part of the party, the communist activists of the Prague Spring were excluded. They played an important role in the dissent, and among the signers of the Charter '77 they were in the majority. Reform communism, however, was just a stage in their political development. None of them rejoined the Communist Party, but only a fraction of them openly declared their belief in socialism. All former politically active communists participated in founding the Citizen's Forum. This was the broad coalition, ranging from conservative to Trotskyists, that became the main body of the November revolution. Some of the politically active former communists were in important government positions: Dienstbier, Rychetsky, and Vales became Deputy Minister Presidents, Dubcek became Chairman of the Federalist Union, Jiciansky his first deputy, Pitthart became Prime Minister, Dobrovsky became Defense Secretary and many others held offices.

When the Citizen's Forum split up in late 1990, we found Dienstbier, Rychetsky, Pitthart, Jiciansky, and Dobrovsky among the founders of a movement that characterized itself as the Liberal Center. Some of the former reform communists turned even further right.

Within the Citizen's Forum, only one group can be noted for representing the Left and Democratic Socialism. It is the Club Obroda, meaning renewal or reincarnation. This Club, mainly recruited from 1968 people, has already been integrated into Social Democracy. During the disintegration of the Citizen's Forum, three more parliamentarians joined the social democratic movement, several of whom played an important role in the post-revolutionary Citizen's Forum.

This is the difference between the developments of the Czechoslovakian social democracy and the Hungarian and Polish PPS. In the Hungarian and Polish parties, quite a few splinter groups formed, whereas only one group separated itself from the

Czechoslovakian party, while simultaneously new groups were being integrated. Thus Czechoslovakian social democracy was strengthened, in contrast to the Hungarian and Polish party.

To sum this up, I want to point out that the spheres of influence among left social liberals and former reform communists are the two directions in which the basis of social democracy should expand.

I have already mentioned the political collapse of the intellectual powers of the Prague Spring. These have turned old by now, too. Today younger socialist intellectuals can mainly be found among the former or current members of the communist parties. The most capable economists, best informed about current world literature, are leaning toward the "right." And even students, who played such a major role throughout the entire revolution, are really depoliticized today.

We should not foster hopes that the process of uniting and strengthening the democratic Left will be a short one. The situation of the Left is not entirely negative, though. Basic values of democratic socialism existed during the communist rule, particularly that of social justice. Milton Friedman concluded, after discussing with Polish anti-communist intellectuals, that their principles could be characterized as socialist. I believe that the same might be true for Czechoslovakia. Opinion polls referring to the state's obligations concerning education, health care, or social welfare show that peoples' opinions are much closer to social democratic values than to conservative or liberal ideas.

The weakness of the Left has to be examined within the framework of a not yet fully developed spectrum. Today's Right is not stronger because of a more thoroughly developed political concept, but because of a wave of anti-communism. This term doesn't describe the rejection of Leninism—which goes without saying for democratic socialists—but a vulgar campaign, which heavily relies on a concept of the enemy.

We know that the Western European Left considers the fate of the Left in the Eastern part of Europe their own and has been trying to help. I want to mention two forms of international support, that I consider most promising. First, there is the support of all tendencies toward an integration into the democratic Left. And second, there is the training of social democratic functionaries. The German SPD and the Austrian SPÖ supported Czechoslovakian social democracy by providing seminars for mayors and members of municipal bodies. The SPÖ, for example, offers training for government positions and other state offices.

Perhaps I have been too pessimistic. The fast transition from dictatorship to democracy disillusioned many people. I am convinced though, that the problems I mentioned here—from a more global perspective—are not the most pressing problems in our contradictory world. *Sub specie* this view, and not *sub specie aeternitatis,* but for the next ten to twenty years—if our planet still exists—I am not a pessimist.

Part V

EUROPEAN SOCIALISM AND AMERICAN SOCIAL REFORM

23. After the Disappointment of the Epoch: American Social Tradition between Past and Future

Norman Birnbaum

There are indeed liberal and productive forms of capitalism. Invariably, these bear the indelible imprint of Western socialism or of solidaristic social Christianity. The collapse of the Communist regimes by no means entails the imminent triumph of an enlightened capitalism across large areas of the earth's surface. An appreciably more savage version of capitalism is dominant in many societies (in Latin America, for instance). As they consider the economic and social costs of their integration into the world market, the peoples of the former Soviet Union and Eastern Europe have good reason to be apprehensive. In our own nation, meanwhile, the loud, triumphant rejoicing of 1989 has given way to more sober reflection on our own condition. We struggle, after all, with cultural confusion, economic stagnation, and social conflict in equal measure—while our citizenry is increasingly ambivalent about the remnants of our public life. This essay asks if we in the United States have the intellectual and spiritual resources to think anew about the relationships of individual liberty and social obligation, market function and public sovereignty, public good and private interest. The metahistorical flatness of our imaginative horizon, the increasing fragmentation of our social existence, have so affected our cultural institutions that the sphere of public argument is constricted and deformed. We confront, instead, a situation rather like that depicted in Breughel's painting of the tower of Babel. Work on the edifice of our common life has all but ceased, as architects and artisans contend with one another in strange tongues. Political and social philosophy have become domains for yet another set of academic specialists, who hardly address a public. Those pursuing inquiry into history and society often suppose that they can dispense with questions of direction, purpose, and value—and so philosophize uncritically. The larger issues that underlie our problems, then, are often relegated to a background dimly perceived and even more dimly depicted.

Was there an American consensus, in the nineteenth century, that our nation's foundations were a capitalist economy, a liberal politics, and a Protestant religion? Perhaps—but everything that has happened since then requires us to think of our history in much more complex ways. The North Atlantic remains a philosophical as well as a geopolitical ocean, and our own society and that of Western Europe have taken increasingly divergent paths. That is a sufficient reason to see how the Europeans interpreted have recently their own traditions in the realms that connect society and the state, the economy and the polity.

That singular European, the Pope, is heir to several traditions. Ever since the end of Polish Stalinism in 1956, the Church has functioned not only as a surrogate for the nation, but as custodian of an idea of solidarity rather different from the rigidities of administered and obligatory social justice. Coming from a Poland definitely post-Stalinist, but still fully incorporated in the Soviet bloc, John Paul II was certainly not narrowly limited by the Eastern European experience. He had been, after all, President of the European Bishops' Conference. As Pope, he had to deal with a Church still caught between its universalist claims and its Eurocentric habits: the Pope's frequent travels are intended, clearly, to insist on the dimension of universality.

The Pope's 1991 encyclical, *Centesimus Annus,* issued to commemorate the anniversary of Leo Thirteenth's *Rerum Novarum,* is an effort to synthesize the sometimes conflicting and frequently disparate elements of a contemporary social Catholicism. On any reading of the document, the Pope is a Social Democrat. He acknowledges the efficiency of the market, but holds that equity and social justice are more important than criteria of efficacy. He favors the political function of private property, pluralism in the control of society's resources. He thinks well, too, of private property's motivating capacity. He insists, however, that excessive concentrations of property can become as oppressive in private hands as in those of the state. The Pope, then, does not think of the market in absolute terms. Society as a whole, either through the state or the institutions of civil society, bears the responsibility of ensuring an adequate standard of living for all. The mixed economy and the welfare state, and economic planning, are for the Pope positive components of a moral society.

Where the Pope is certainly not a contemporary Social Democrat, he comes closest to Marx. The socialist and social democratic parties of Western Europe are like their liberal or, frequently, Social Christian counterparts in one major aspect: they conceive of the ends of economic and social policy in individualized terms. These are not to be prescribed by politics but left to a large area of private, ostensibly apolitical decision. Alternatively, they do concede to communities and families the rights to organize their own life worlds, as long as they let others do the same. The Pope's own criticism of Marxist "materialism" is embarrassingly inaccurate. He does appropriate as his own and gives a Catholic gloss to the spiritual legacy of early Marxism, the theory of alienation. Humans who exist only as creatures of the market, who seek only the indefinite increase of their material wealth, are moral cripples, alienated from the true ends of human existence. These are set by God, and specified in the soteriology of the Catholic Church. His Holiness, however, concentrates on an intermediate realm of human potential and social value, in which we find fulfillment not as individuals but as members of society. It is in this realm, indeed, that the Pope seeks allies from among those who are neither Catholics, nor Christians, nor believers of any sort. No one, he declares, who understands the aesthetic and moral dimensions of human life can accept either the social inequalities that disfigure world society or the specific form of alienation inherent in consumerism. The Pope is not alone in taking liberalism's attachment to individualism rather more seriously than many liberals. Precisely because human individuals are so precious in his eyes, they cannot be left to the impersonal and implacable laws (if such there are) of the market.

The Pope's view of our common life, then, goes beyond the responsibility of state and society for the material well being of their citizens and members. A pedagogic responsibility is incumbent upon these institutions as well: the realization of an authentic human potential. That, in its turn, requires that some social institutions assume the responsibility of deciding what is and is not authentic. Put another way, the Pope advocates a politics of culture, a politics of value.

Is a politics of this sort possible? In what historical context could it be grounded, and on what historical groups could it rely? Who among our elites and publics would pursue it? Does it not carry explicit and implicit authoritarian implications?

Let us begin by examining the history of social reform in Western Europe, extend the analysis (however schematically) to world society, and then return to our American problems.

Western socialism, to a large degree, has succeeded. The nations in which there are strong socialist and social democratic parties have effective welfare states which are the result of over a century of ceaseless effort by these parties. The extension of citizenship, the legitimation of the unions and in some cases their role as major partners in enduring social contracts, the provision of health care and income during incapacity and old age (and unemployment), the regulation of the workplace, investment in social infrastructure generally, are indeed triumphs of the socialist movement. Other forces were also at work. The European states could draw upon a precapitalist tradition of regulation of the market. Well before *Rerum Novarum* in 1891, the Catholic Church promulgated ideas of solidarity that inspired a politics of welfare. Moreover, enlightened elites saw that it was senseless to ignore the material and moral deprivations that called socialism into life. Recall Disraeli and Tory Socialism. A striking ideological paradox was also at work. Liberalism was in large measure of capitalism a derivative. The very doctrines of individualism and free association indispensable to capitalist jurisprudence also provided space for the socialist movement. The liberal idea of citizenship legitimated a social movement that sought to free large segments of society from economic limits on the practice of citizenship.

Suppose, however, that the welfare state was equally the consequence of an inner imperative of capitalism. The Webbs argued for its introduction in Britain on grounds of imperial competition with Germany; national solidarity was necessary in a situation of international conflict. Capitalism expanded through the fabrication of new needs. If the working class was to acquire these, it would have to rise above its original misery, and become healthier and richer. Moreover, capital had a clear interest in socializing the cost of infrastructure —whether roads or schools. A large measure of what resembles socialism is indispensable to the functioning of capitalism. I have used the term "resembles socialism" purposely. Socialism can be reduced neither to equality nor efficiency and contains an inexpungable element of solidarity. Appeals to solidarity based on its utility are of a different quality.

Ideas and sentiments of solidarity, whether derived from the secular progressivism of socialism or from Christian social doctrines (or from the kind of reflective liberalism we had in Smith's "moral sentiments") were fundaments of the welfare state. Those ideas are now attenuated; why? The welfare state does take an increasing share of the social product. Those who argue that this has curbed productive investment and discouraged entrepreneurial motivation have not made their case. The health and welfare of the citizenry are also productive investments and if economic elites are slothful, they do seem still to care about making money. The bureaucratization and centralization of the welfare states frequently impede their attainment of their ends. Impersonal standardization and remoteness from the citizenry constitute problems for which no solutions are simple. The problem may lie elsewhere, in the very inequalities generated by the welfare state.

These states rest on social contracts, periodically renewed. With an increasing standard of living, the agreed provision of universal social benefits has been supplemented by gains negotiated by one or another group. Sometimes exploiting critical positions on the labor market, sometimes exploiting their electoral strength, occupational, social and regional groups have altered the welfare state in the direction of corporatism. The idea of strengthening the social body as a whole has given way, in practice if not in theory, to the struggle for sectorial advantage. If the power of the unrestricted economic market has diminished, that of a political market has increased. The recrudescence of Social Darwinism in Europe, Thatcher's Britain excepted, cannot be compared with the morality of the Reagan-Bush years in our own society. The exhaustion of the welfare state has less to do with the revival of old ideas of the struggle for existence than it is a consequence of the ways in which that state—in the absence of a generalized idea of solidarity—allowed partial conflicts within it to expand and proliferate.

The very successes of the welfare state have led to its present difficulties. Once groups with much to win, many segments of modern society have been transformed into enclaves of those with something to lose. The socialist and social democratic parties bear a good deal of the responsibility for the moral and political consequences of this situation. They have largely renounced an explicit pedagogic project. In a compromise with a version of liberalism, they have assumed that given sufficient material goods, people would proceed to develop more ample lives —especially by more civic participation. The assumption having been proven incorrect, they have been left with a doctrine of the pluralism of ends. We could term it a randomness of ends, were it not for the highly visible existence of a cultural industry, producing cultural goods for a market it has constructed and organized for its own purposes. The socialist and social democratic parties in office have not been very vigorous about pursuing a politics of culture. It is true that Jack Lang, as Minister of Culture in France, has sought a wide diffusion of high culture —but Malraux did the same as de Gaulle's Minister of Culture. The Lutheran Church elder, Helmut Schmidt, was derided for a perfectly serious proposal that Germany have one day a week free of television, so that the public could spend its time less passively. He made the proposal even before private television systems in Germany forced down the general level of that nation's television programs. Of course, the socialist and social democratic parties have done much to equalize educational opportunity—generally leaving it to the educational system to define opportunity in very conventional terms.

The failure of the democratic left to make cultural policy a major element in its program can be described as a concession to liberalism. On this account of things, autonomous citizens or civil society as a whole assumes responsibility for culture; the state's paternalism is neither needed nor wanted. That is convincing, until we ask ourselves whether consumer sovereignty in culture (and even more, in values) is real. Do the media giants with their oligopolistic cultural powers actually represent civil society? We can attribute the socialist renunciation of a cultural project either to the influence of liberalism or a recognition of the supposed pluralism of our societies. We may suspect that the initial socialist project of a transformation of culture proved too difficult. A half-hearted liberalism, postponing to the unspecified future an effort at transformation, was and is the path of least resistance. The Pope, not only in his critique of consumerism but in his effort to deal with what he describes as alienation, seems rather more Marxist than most of the Socialist International.

There is a major set of ambiguities in the liberal tradition. Is it a doctrine of the sovereignty of persons, who contract to enter society only if they retain large powers over their choices? If so, liberalism in many of its variants is rather silent, or at best tentative, about the sorts of persons its presupposes. There is another current in liberalism, which does not insist on the complete randomness of human ends. Smith and Mill thought of liberalism as a precondition of human education. There are liberal institutions, and not just persons, and the institutions are necessary to the development of persons, since they enable persons to enter into dialogue with one another on equal terms. The Pope implies that this sort of liberalism is compatible with the view that there are higher and lower elements in culture. He conceives of liberal institutions as educational. This element in the encyclical, along with his appeal for a broad coalition to transform our social existence, sets the supposedly integralist Pope in the tradition of Vatican II. The problem is compounded when we consider economic liberalism. It is something other than the view that free markets being the most efficient ones, they contribute more to the sum of human happiness —an arithmetic judgment reminiscent of Bentham. It is, rather, the assertion that free markets are an absolute precondition of a free politics. The assertion has an unstated premise that is false—

that there is nothing apart from the antithesis of a state economy and a private one. There are institutions other than highly centralized national governments that are capable of exercising sovereignty over the market. Municipal and regional enterprise, public corporations, firms controlled and owned by consumers and workers, private firms with public and worker representation on their boards—the possibilities are many. There are, equally, many possibilities for connecting these enterprises to political institutions—consensual and consultative relationships as well as more direct forms of public control. The problems of economic coordination remain. The market cannot be counted upon to increase the general welfare. The usual liberal answer is that planning is more inefficient and, in addition, a step toward tyranny. Surely, planning after open debate on alternatives by different and opposed groups is not tyrannical. It is interesting that behind a facade of liberalism, no small number of advocates of the market insist on the necessity of unchallenged authority and hierarchy within economic units.

In any event, the fact of the market (and, as we shall see, increasingly of the market in its global form) as well as the residual force of liberal economic ideas—the one reinforcing the other—have combined to limit the projects of Western socialism.

The Western socialists and social democrats have appropriated the best of liberalism; its doctrine of individual freedom and its aversion to authoritarian constraint. In some cases, indeed (Germany and Italy, most notably) the socialists and social democrats were often truer to liberal political ideas than many who were formally liberal. The Western socialists, however, have compromised with the worst of liberalism, the identification of the market as an entirely liberal and morally positive political institution.

Not all socialists have been so pliant, and perhaps the parties of the Socialist International will take courage from the serenity with which the Pope separates the question of human integrity and liberty from the question of the market. The Pope insists that there are enduring circumstances in which the market cannot guarantee either integrity (in the sense of the capacity to develop morally) or liberty. The Pope's position is not quite equivalent to his accepting liberal conceptions of personality and combining these with a critical attitude toward a rigidified economic liberalism, fixated on the market. His persons are not the solitary individuals of vulgar liberalism but the soldiery beings of a social vision of human existence.

We come to the Catholic doctrine of subsidiarity—more precisely, to its connections with what was once termed gild socialism, or the workers council movement. The human beings depicted in this aspect of Catholic doctrine are embedded in institutions in which they deepen their humanity. The idea of subsidiarity is not just a doctrine of the intricate subdivision of the social whole. Society on this view can govern itself, not by taking some grand Tennis Court Oath, but by coming to awareness of its own potential for generating autonomy. An entire range of institutions may be thought of as subsidiary—from families and communities to work groups. In their own spheres of activity, these groups can exercise the widest possible autonomy. Profound problems of coordination and legitimation remain, but subsidiarity is another and rather more complex way of addressing problems sometimes treated under the terms of civil society or community. (Just as a vulgar liberalism reifies individuals, a vulgar communitarianism does the same with community. It also has to be said that in their undifferentiated enthusiasm for civil society, some of our contemporaries display the uncritical tendencies they once exhibited with reference to entities like "history" or "the working class.") In the idea of subsidiarity, human groups assume concrete and living forms, and are viewed as potential islands of existential freedom, in which self-determination can be learned. Movements of Catholic inspiration like Solidarity in Poland and the student-worker alliances of the Italian movements of 1969 ("Autumno Caldo") suggests that the idea is by no means limited to theological texts.

Of particular interest in an American context is the fact that the idea does not exempt economic activity and structures from scrutiny. Conventional American liberalism stops, or at best hesitates uncertainly, at the door of the economic enterprise—and is quietly ambivalent or resigned before the market. Catholic ideas of subsidiarity do not exempt economic institutions from the moral scrutiny applicable to all institutions.

In fact, Catholic politics has often ignored the dimension of potentiality in the idea of subsidiarity. The Church and its allies have reified society's institutions, to be defended against a host of dangers—the levelling uniformity of the modern world, the central power of the state at the service of abstract notions of equity and justice, the belief that social nature could be changed. The philosophy of Catholic Integralism was hardly monolithic, but it did hypothesize an intact world to be preserved, and reviled the notion that a better one could be made. By a curious process of inversion, Catholic thinkers and movements most repulsed by the consequences of modern capitalism allied themselves with capital in defense of a putative social order against the disorder of experiment and revolution. With his appeal to others who seek a more just society and a higher level of existence for humanity to join Catholics in the struggle, the Pope has, rhetorically, chosen another path. His declaration that the encyclical intends no one social model is not to be read as a concession or capitulation to that utter randomness of human ends that characterizes a schematic liberalism. It may be read as a project of inquiry and social experiment.

This is the place to remark that the Pope's vision of the Marxism of Marx is utterly inaccurate—and ignores the careful scholarship of Catholic thinkers like Jean-Yves Calvez. Marx sought to replace a realm of necessity with one of freedom. He insisted that humans could eventually overcome the economic determinism that ruled their existence under capitalism—precisely because of their spiritual potential. He was not a crude materialist nor even an economic determinist. The residual pedagogic pathos, the ritualized progressivism, of the language of Stalinism and its leaden successor movements and states is a tribute paid to the virtues of original Marxism by those whose vice it was to have so degraded the doctrine. The Pope attacks a degraded Marxism, whereas in fact his affinities are with what we may term authentic Marxism. Have not Catholic theologians, indeed, criticized Marxist humanism as a transmuted religious belief—a tribute to its spirituality?

The energies expended by many to demonstrate that Marx was, *ab initio*, wrong seem to draw upon an inexhaustible source; one wonders what would happen if a substantial number of these persons were to turn their attention to less repetitive intellectual tasks. There is one thing, however, they have overlooked—an important respect in which he was right. The unification of the world market is proceeding apace. Indeed, the integration of the

Communist bloc in that market was probably a major contributing factor in its collapse. The process of unification has been dealt with in rather different ways. Much of the literature on modernization deals with it (and is an attempt to do so without resorting to such uncomfortable terms as the destruction of cultures, domination, exploitation, or pauperization). For our immediate purpose, a consideration of the possibility of moral and institutional paths to more justice and solidarity in our own society, two questions arise. One is factual: To what extent are we affected by the world market? The second is moral: To what extent are we morally obliged to take action to correct the more flagrant global inequalities (and to what extent are we obliged to consider long-term projects to reduce global inequalities on a permanent basis?) Looking back on the period 1945-70, we can say that the steady rise in the West European living standard was due to favorable global economic conditions. These enabled the economies of nations like France and Germany to grow so much that they could afford to expand their welfare state arrangements. Such redistribution as occurred came from increments to growth, and so evoked less political resistance that it would have done in a period of slower growth or stagnation. Now the world market has imposed harsher conditions upon these societies: the increased competitiveness of the Asian and newly industrializing nations, decreases in demand in both the Third World and the industrial heartlands of the Northern hemisphere, higher prices for raw materials, especially oil.

Some of the effects on the Western socialist project have been obvious. Consider the very early postwar blockages in British Labour's program, as Labour governments sought desperately to strengthen the pound. Much later, economic stagnation was a major factor in inducing the German Social Democrats' liberal coalition partners to cast them back into opposition: the liberal electoral clientele did not wish to pay for economic justice in a period of economic constriction. Mitterrand in 1983 was obliged to change course completely and to abandon the project of constructing socialism in a France whose foreign creditors were not prepared to join the enterprise. The Spanish socialist government and the unions have been at odds over economic policies that favor capital import, that is, which keep wages and social costs low. In each and every case, the self-designated realists in the socialist parties have insisted that the structure of the international economy left them little or no choice.

The European socialist and social democratic parties are now strenuous proponents of the European Community. Their version of the Community, however, is strikingly opposed to that of significant segments of European capital. Europe's major banks and firms, increasingly multinational, think of the Community as an opportunity to expand into areas of cheap labor costs and undeveloped markets (the Southern European countries) as well as a field for the economies of scale. The socialists support the Community's departing President, a Catholic and a socialist, Jacques Delors, in his plan for a European Social Charter that would eventually raise the level of social legislation throughout the Community. The European unions have as yet been unable to develop effective means of action within the Community. Europe's most powerful industrial union, the German metal Workers' Union, has allowed Volkswagen to produce in Spain, where labor costs are half as much as in Germany. We must prepare markets for the future, explained the union, by helping to expand purchasing power in Spain. The union also said that it had an obligation toward international solidarity. All no doubt true, but the union had to take account of capital's mobility—even in a firm that is partly public and on whose board it is represented. The European Community is a relatively homogenous area, culturally and economically, and political solutions to these problems are conceivable. What can be said about the rest of the world?

A rampant Social Darwinism is the one discernible organizing principle of the world economy. Rich nations against poor nations, raw materials producers against producers of finished goods, capital and labor opposed within nations, and segments of capital and labor aligned in each nation to struggle against similar coalitions— the terms "interdependence" hardly describes these interconnected conflicts. The nation counts for less in this system, the rise of new nationalist sentiments to the contrary. International capital constantly integrates national elites into its camp. Consider, in Mexico, the opposition of Cardenas, insistent on autonomously-engendered growth and distributive justice, and Salinas, the Harvard educated technocrat with his eyes fixed to the North.

The strong, no doubt, have an interest in preventing the weak from becoming too weak. Still, sentiments of human solidarity are difficult to maintain across large cultural barriers and geopolitical distances. If there is a world system, power is exercised in it almost entirely in one direction. The multiplicity of international institutions dealing with the world economy are effectively under the control of the rich: consider how little American military power weighs in the balance when the rich (the United States) contend with the richer (Germany and Japan) on economic issues. The national governments, regional alliances, international agencies, and social movements that speak for the poor must negotiate in international forums on very unequal terms.

In the northern hemisphere, some societies have combined decent minimum of institutionalized solidarity with productivity. These societies, despite the efforts of opinion-forming institutions like the churches, have not developed a sustaining network of sentiments that would extend the idea of solidarity in a systematic fashion well beyond national borders. That would provide the moral energies for the difficult economic and political tasks of fashioning new institutions of solidarity across national and hemispheric boundaries. Meanwhile, the minimums of solidarity within these nations have become more fragile, as the ruthless mechanisms of competition threaten to reproduce within their borders the moral anarchy that prevails internationally.

The internationalization of the economy, then, is most definitely not a precondition of the global diffusion of an enlightened capitalism. Those who, with savage delight, remind us of the economic failures of state socialism might tell us, one day, what they think of societies ravaged by current capitalist modes of accumulation—like Brazil. In the long run, we are assured in an unintended parody of Stalinist thinking, Brazil will be the richer for its current distress. Perhaps—but the Brazilians do not live in the economist's hypothetical long run. Capital's demand for cheap labor does not invariably improve the latter's lot: cheap labor is eventually reduced to unemployment by cheaper labor, or rendered cheaper still. The incorporation of large areas of the world in the capitalist economy is also accompanied by the weakening or disappearance of the social support systems devised earlier to make irregular and low levels of income more bearable. The very opportunities for the emergence of forms of subsidiarity as modes of resistance to deprivation and encroachment are increasingly lacking. In its turn, this deficiency may well be a source of that fundamentalism that so bewilders and disturbs the Western world. The false utopia of state socialism has collapsed, democratic socialism and the western European welfare state are at an impasse, the developing nations struggle vainly against exploitation and poverty. Everywhere, the capitalist world market imposes the lowest common denominator of morality, reducing or destroying property, tradition, and solidarity as it spreads. It is commonplace to point to Japan and a few of the Asian nations as happy instances of material progress, but a close look at their societies justifies no such judgment—and, in any event, few will be prepared to make the Japanese Finance Ministry the primary arbiter of our fate.

Where, in this unhappy sequence, stands the United States? Are we to continue to play a hegemonic world rule by using our military power—even as our economic dominance recedes? Alternatively, are we to turn to the tasks of domestic reconstruction— and, if so, with what projects? Are we to favor investment by encouraging the already prosperous, treating present and future inequalities as a cost of an eventual general prosperity? Are we to develop our own version of industrial policy, the better to compete on the world market? Are we to pursue redistribution of wealth, both for the sake of equity and to rescue for productive existence a part of our population that might otherwise sink into utter deprivation and pathology? Meanwhile, the claims of the vast American middle class are increasingly strident, as millions become aware that their own living standards have been lowered, perhaps for the indefinite future.

The discussion of these matters in the public forum is made exceedingly difficult by an interconnected set of barriers. A part of our elite, avaricious, cynical, and unremitting in the defense of its class interests, portrays discussions of alternatives to the regnant Social Darwinism as either utopian or un-American. In the guise of neutrality, the mass media connive at setting limits to public discussion. Think of the obsessional iteration of the phrase, "mainstream." The articulation of interests by the disadvantaged in the

United States has been made much more difficult by the systematic erasure of historical memory: the grandchildren of the New Deal have little or no idea of what was done and said in our country but two generations ago. The residual power of possessive individualism in the American psyche owes much to want of opposition. Millions of Americans, objectively dependent upon economic circumstances they can hardly analyze, much less control, repeat—with varying degrees of conviction—leaden clichés about personal autonomy and sovereignty. Racial conflict, too, has its effects—diverting attention from the common tasks of the nation, and diverting anger from the very rich to the very poor, as groups at the margin of decent minimums of existence contend for employment and public benefits, while others above the minimums are beset by anxiety at the possibility of losing income and status. That much said, a new debate on the market and its limits, on citizenship and the duties of solidarity, on the American class system itself, is likely to erupt. Lowered expectations for many, deprivation and hardship for many others, must raise questions about the efficacy and justice of our society. The privatization that has been the dominant American mode recently has not been without components of anger and frustration. One way in which these could be worked through might be a renewed public effort to find meaning in a public sphere.

What are the chances, then, for a revival of American social reform—and on what models can it draw? The American model of the postwar years, an expanding capitalist economy with a minimal welfare state, has lost its power to convince—within as well as outside our borders. In the ensuing ideological vacuum, we experience a cacophony of voices, surges of fear, eruptions of hatred—along with the metahistorical flatness of resignation and the sullenness of the renunciation of hope.

The question of the economy can hardly be separated from the idea and the practice of American nationhood. The search for opportunity is indelibly imprinted upon the American self conception, and it has real roots. The Europeans came to seek larger horizons, the black struggle after Emancipation was one for a just share in the nation. The very phrase, however, has connotations that transcend the market. White immigrants and the offspring of slaves were pursuing not wealth alone, but a different sort of existence. We have recently experienced a separation of community and economy—not, if we recall the Gilded Age, for the first time. Social vision has failed; the public capacity to think has been degraded. The wide spectrum of academics and quasi-academics whose primary article of faith is that the market cannot be interfered with are, perhaps, engaged in a gigantic if unintended parody of liberalism. They can hardly be absolved of blame for their failure of intellectual leadership. Where can we now find resources for a recuperation of other elements in American tradition, which could activate new social movements and cultivate a political consciousness that would end the idolatry of the market?

It may be objected that it is odd to be insisting on the imminent end of one American model of society when liberal capitalism is so obviously triumphant in Eastern Europe. That remains to be seen. The Kennedy School is indeed advising the former Soviet Union on the transition to capitalism, but the school's contribution to our own domestic welfare is not immediately apparent. In any event, the citizens of the former state socialist regimes are entirely right to be ambivalent about the introduction of the market economy—the more so, as the phrase has a multiplicity of meanings. Sometimes it stands for investment by foreign capital, sometimes it represents the dismantling of rigid bureaucratic structures, but it can also mean the introduction of a Western version of Social Darwinism to replace neo-Stalinism's organization of the struggle of each against all. The East European's neighbors, the West Europeans, for their part remain attached to their welfare states and mixed economies, whatever their present difficulties.

In any event, the compulsive optimism of the past decade in the United States has dissipated. Anxiety and doubt about the future now seize large parts of the public. Often enough these take economic form, the conviction that neither present nor future generations will be as prosperous as past ones. Political abstentionism, and distrust of the *bona fides* of our political elites, is another sort of expression of doubt. The public temper resembles less an articulated critique of our society than a diffuse disappointment. Little or nothing in the public sphere engages those higher aspects of the person which Aristotle thought cultivated by public life—and to which the Pope refers in his criticism of the egoism of capitalist culture. Privatization in the United States sometimes seems to be the one public good we share. Of course, it is immensely encouraged by the ideology of possessive individualism, which we could rename combative individualism.

It is increasingly difficult, in our society, to distinguish between the institutionalization of privatization and symptoms of social disintegration. The recent heightening of cultural and racial conflict is clearly connected to the consolidation of economic inequality. The churches and the reduced reformist party in American politics apart, increasing inequality has not led to a renewal of a larger demand for social solidarity. The reformist party has consoled itself by supposing that Americans are capitalist and individualist in ideology but rather more attached to our welfare state in our political behavior. Our present coalition government (which does not quite dare avow its name) is offered as evidence for the bifurcation of the public mind. Perhaps, however, we confront an American version of corporatism, the fragmentation of the electorate into interest groups seeking to maximize their benefits from government. Corporatism of this sort is antithetical to the practice of solidarity. The debate in the Democratic Party, between those who wish to pay more attention to the suburban middle class and those with electoral clientele among the disadvantaged, is hardly about a new approach to the common good.

The ways in which Americans deal with fundamental economic and social questions is a consequence both of their worldviews and of levels of knowledge highly stratified by social class. We are far from that nation of educated citizens envisaged by the founders of the republic. Even in our universities, a technocratic cast of thought often blocks deeper debate. The claim that the advocates of a "political correctness" of the left rule our universities is untenable. The fundamental "political correctness," reigning in the universities is the affirmation, fervid or not, of the permanency of the current structure of society by a majority of those who work on modern historical and social problems. Even in disciplines ostensibly remote from the flux of events (in which scholars do not habitually anticipate governmental appointments) the imagination of social possibility is often very limited. The present condition of the nation suggests that the fear of Left indoctrination of the ascendant generation in our universities is grotesquely exaggerated. Most university teachers, of whatever political persuasion, have to struggle against the obdurate resistance of their students to any sort of idea.

In their immobile unreflectiveness, our students are surely preparing themselves for ordinary life. The gap between even the most routinized of thought in the academy and everyday conceptions is large. Conventional language sometimes voices awareness of and resentment at avarice and privilege, but uses crude notions of social possibility, and vulgar attributions of cause and motive. American popular thought may be described either as pre-political or primitive. Some prefer the imprecise term, populist. Our cultural institutions, above all the media, function to an equivalent of Gresham's Law, by which unauthentic intellectual currency drives out the authentic kind.

The American tradition of thought, and our historical experience as a whole, have encompassed attacks aplenty on the market—and an entire assortment of visions of solidarity. Is there any way in which the moral constriction of our public language can be overcome? Perhaps we can begin by reexamining an American liberalism that has become deformed. Its individualistic component has been converted to a depiction of abstract individuals wrenched out of their social contexts. A narrow calculation of self-interest is the predominant motive ascribed to these abstract entities. The resultant view of what we may find (or seek) in society is empty. Yet this contentless individualism has been incorporated in a view of politics in which private actions have been preferred to common efforts (save for the singular exception of external or internal threats to the nation, deemed to legitimate American versions of tribalism). The early legal fiction that economic corporations were persons with a person's rights no doubt was an innovation that contributed to the nation's economic growth. It also contributed, however, to that fetishization of property (particularly large-scale property with its political power) that has often turned American liberalism, in its effects, into the very opposite of the practice of moral sovereignty by autonomous persons. With the emergence of a highly organized corporate society in the second half of the nineteenth century, liberalism gradually ceded to an American version of corporatism. Conflictual bargaining among powerful groups became the dominant technique of American politics, even if a rhetoric of popular sovereignty still prevailed. One understands the rage of the Populists.

This sort of pseudo-liberal pluralism left little or no room for the Catholic doctrines of subsidiarity entering the United States with the Catholic immigration. Subsidiarity rested on an idea of the social whole, and it was just this that a deformed American liberalism denied. An American Protestantism that took its own traditions (of congregationalism in a wide sense and of the moral integrity of individuals) seriously also had profound reasons to feel alien in what had been its country.

The true heirs of American liberalism may well be the nation's radicals with their insistence on the primacy of the individual's rights against all concentrations of power. They saw no reason to suppose that a democratic state was more of a threat to American liberty than a gigantic corporation. Of course, they presupposed a citizenry, a community of argument and dialogue in public space. It is true that radicalism had its own difficulties. It could and did develop at times into the doctrine and practice of an imperial self—the limitless demands of a social monad floating in antinomian space. What could be more contributory to the imperialism of the self than the cultivation of limitless wants by a capitalism that assigned the market primacy over community? Some of the recent work on these fused cultural and psychic ills of the end of the last century do attach some importance to the connection between these ills and the consolidation of a very different set of institutions of consumption and production than had prevailed in the earlier phases of American history. At any rate, American radicalism did not stop at the factory gate (or, for that matter, at the threshold of the patriarchal home.)

Is there an American conservatism that can be likened to the European kind—an idea of a community of deference rooted in tradition? The slaveholding South apart (distinctly non-European, come to think of it), American conservatism has been very different. Liberalism in America has become conservative by the absolutization of the individual, by the primacy given to property rights, and by an interpretation of national history that declared it to be the incarnation of progress. The idea of progress may well be a secularized eschatology, in its modern American version an uneasy and unstable joining of Darwinism to an earlier, Providential view of the origins of the Republic. Let us understand the common elements of the idea of progress to be: the extension of human mastery over nature, the pacification of human society by the construction of a structure of reasoned solidarity, and the attainment by humans of a rising plateau of intelligence and morality. The party of progress has been split, one part insisting on progress already achieved, the other segment locating the nation's destiny in the near or remote future. The party of a sublime present is the party of American conservatism.

Catholic and Protestant strains in American culture have contested, sometimes, these ideas of progress. Abraham Lincoln is in this respect, surely, a spiritual descendent of Jonathan Edwards. We can hardly place those bothered by human sinfulness and those who believe in a secular idea of progress on a political continuum. Those skeptical of the notion that the nation incarnated progress were, often enough, quite able and willing to use their very considerable moral energies to contest injustice, as they saw it, in slavery or finance capitalism. American votaries of the idea of progress have often regarded the Catholic Church as a medieval remnant cast up on our shores. They have been surprised (when they bothered to look) by its economic and social positions. The black American Protestant churches, meanwhile, are frequently on the Evangelical side of Protestantism, but are by no means politically conservative. Had William Jennings Bryan been more sophisticated, he might have tempered his attacks on capitalism—but in 1896, any number of university professors were voicing, if in other tonalities, the same criticisms of American society. In short, the sources of an idea of solidarity, of systematic refusal to accept the omnipotence of the market, are various in American history.

Can we reach back into our history and find ideas and models of solidarity of use to us in our vastly different setting? Perhaps, since no direct extrapolation will serve, retrospection will prove to have other uses. Jeffersonian solidarity rested on the idea of a community of freeholders, free especially of the corruptions of commerce. Americanists like Leo Marx have seen in the Jeffersonian distaste for commerce and the cities the beginnings of American pastoralism—a rejection of the modern age. They also, however, have reminded us that even nostalgia has its uses, if it provides moral energies for a society otherwise cut off from its own past and a possible future. Early Republicanism, with its ideas of free soil and free labor, looked back to Jeffersonian ideas of a republic rooted in local communities. Later, American trade unionism was motivated by familial and local solidarities that had little direct connection with the generic emancipation of the human race. Nonetheless, Marx himself praised the American working class and American protest movements generally for their emphasis on practical goals, their refusal of theoretic obsession. The Populists did battle to defend their rural communities, menaced by impersonal capital. Their view of solidarity was hardly entirely benign, since it also involved anti-Catholicism, anti-Semitism, and xenophobia. American Social Catholicism was the result of a mixture of theological interpretations of society (of the sort that eventually found their way into *Rerum Novarum*) and the immediate imperatives of immigrant communities in a very hostile environment. American socialism was itself a very complex formation. It included imported ideas (like the secularized messianism of the Jewish immigration) but was marked by a very American sense of loss, a longing for the promise and the practice of the early republic. We can conclude that solidarity is not a fixed set of values—little changed over time—but a specific derivative of a process of common learning in new situations. We can now rephrase our question: how, in the past, have Americans learned to exercise solidarity?

Let us begin with the Populists, despite the fact that the movement exhibited crabbed provincialism—and worse. Its idea of solidarity was restricted. Its Protestant character made an alliance with an ethnically diverse and increasingly Catholic urban working class impossible—quite apart from a view of social virtue that was exclusively agrarian. It lacked an effectively true account of the social world. The farmers who profited from incorporation in the world market naively supposed that they could easily be protected from its effects. The very failures of the Populists are, however, instructive. In an ethnically diverse nation, no one group can attain major general changes on its own; coalitions are needed. That is equally true of economic groups in a very complex society. The Populists' anticapitalism was specifically agrarian, and alliance with urban protest was precluded. Finally, the Populists' rootedness in local churches suggests the limits of church and religiously engendered social movements that speak only in one idiom. The translation of particular ecclesiastical and theological ideas of community, economy, society into a general language shared with others of different traditions can act as a moral multiplying device, focusing while retaining energies—and pooling these in the public arena.

Historians of the Progressive movement have been ironic about its moralizing, its genteel repugnance for what America had become. Men and women of the word (lawyers, pastors, professors, social workers, writers), the Progressives indeed resented their displacement as an American elite by those whose only virtue was their wealth. The pathos of the Progressives merits our respect. They espoused civic responsibility and did not intend to leave the nation to those who had bullied, bribed, and clawed their way to the top. When the American Economic Association was formed in the Progressive epoch, intending members were required to abjure the free market and endorse a socially controlled economy. The Progressives made a serious effort to reconcile the technical imperatives of governance in a complex society with civic liberalism. In the end, they failed to convince the masses they sought both to lead and uplift. They succeeded in opening the way for their successors: an academically qualified elite in business, government and cultural and public life generally. Beginning by advocating older civic values, they ended as agents of the transformation of American society into a new giganticism—with its own and entirely impersonal inertia.

The New Deal, especially in its heroic period (1934-1937), for a while succeeded where both Populists and Progressives failed. It combined popular impulsion and technocratic experiment. It joined Social Catholicism, Jewish messianism, liberal Protestantism, and several varieties of secular reform. These extended from Progressive and Populist remnants to American socialism—including the American Communist Party. Franklin Roosevelt, of course, had immense political skills and a patrician capacity to speak not only to but for the socially mute. During the New Deal, they were hardly mute. It was a period of angry skepticism of the competence and good faith of the business elite, matched by a positive appreciation of collective action and the practice of institutionalized solidarity. It was also a period in which the new technocratic elite made common cause with the disenfranchised. The lessons to be learned from the New Deal are several. It is important to unite, however unsteadily, diverse motives and traditions. Concentration on a few major ideological themes made political mobilization on behalf of social reform possible. The New Deal was, no less importantly, an alliance across class lines, linking the economically exploited with the reformist elements of finance and business. Its project invoked deep reservoirs of national democratic tradition to revivify citizenship. When the sit-down strikes in the automobile industry ended with a victory for the union, the workers streamed from the factories carrying American flags.

It was not, however, the New Deal but war production that brought full employment to the nation in the forties. Roosevelt presided over a social partnership (business and the unions) that endured into the Nixon-Ford Administrations. A consensus on expanded purchasing power for the labor force, social expenditure, and a large military-political apparatus to deal with the rest of the world was the political fundament of a state that could afford both warfare and welfare. (When Paul Nitze drafted the charter document of our Cold War role, NSC 68, he was assisted by a Truman economist from the unions, Leon Keyserling.) The postwar American model entailed political negotiation over allocation of the national product—on the assumption that national income would rise continually. Capitalist expansion did provide rising living standards for a majority, while the minority remained invisible in what Harrington termed "the other America."

Lyndon Johnson made his early career in the New Deal, but his program for a Great Society lacked the New Deal's scope, its moral appeal and its interclass basis. Roosevelt in 1936 spoke of one third of a nation in poverty. By the time the spread of black protest from South to the North (and the conscience of a part of the nation) impelled Johnson to begin his campaign for programs to assist the deprived, these numbered but a fifth of the nation. Johnson's appeals mixed moral rhetoric and utilitarian argument. An instructive footnote was provided by Messrs. Merrill, Lynch, who in a brochure entitle "The New American Horizon" informed clients that there were splendid investment opportunities in education, health, and urban renewal as a result of Great Society legislation.

Global economic and political changes (exemplified by the defeat in Vietnam and the devaluation of the dollar) slowed and eventually stopped the Great Society program. As the nation's living standard (for most citizens) ceased to rise, the postwar consensus gradually gave way to what was to become the unashamed Social Darwinism of the eighties. It would be a mistake to attribute the change solely to the ideological effects of objective shifts in our position on the world market. The national ideology of the postwar years had as its major elements two themes. One privileged group was bargaining for economic advantage. The other held that these advantages best took the form of increased familial buying power—not cultural and public expenditure.

The Great Society program was explained as a way to allow the poor (including the black population) to enter the process. The arguments that a successful program of social rehabilitation would enrich the nation as a whole or somehow improve its world standing were of as little use as the arguments of moral solidarity. Those who felt that they had the most to lose considered that they were being asked to pay, disproportionately, for the venture. The corporatist criteria that accounted for the postwar consensus effectively blocked the effort to extend it. When we add racism to the situation (even if a majority of the poor were in fact white) we see why reform in American society has been blocked for the past two decades.

The disintegration of the postwar consensus released the very unequal forces that have set the agenda for much of recent American debate—which appeared to pass over the heads of beleaguered liberals of the New Deal sort and of many of their erstwhile antagonists among Eisenhower Republicans. The New Left has affirmed community and solidarity, but lacks the old left's (and the union movement's) dogged attention to organization and persuasion. The New Left's original critique of bureaucracy and consumerism reflected the spirituality of middle class protest. Its own cultural politics was—not all that far from the limitless self of the imperial self—almost a parody of the old American religion of the heart. A new conservatism has been more successful—possibly because it appeals to the most contradictory groups and positions, without too much concern for intellectual or moral consistency. Disciples of Hayek and cultural authoritarians, Protestant Fundamentalists and former Trotskyites, many who still claim to be liberal Democrats and unrepentant antagonists of even the minimal American welfare state, have entered into a series of strategic and tactical bargains. They do agree, after all, on keeping the rest of us from exerting influence in culture or power in politics.

The demonic image each alliance has of the other is often undisturbed by the complexities of reality. The New Left thinks of our cultural institutions as agencies of oppression, the new right supposes that they are sites of subversion. The New Left's antinomianism, its rejection of the nation's institutions, is matched by the new right's trembling anxiety at a hint of doubt that the United States as it now is represents the unsurpassable summit of the entire human experience. The vocal communitarianism of the New Left is ostensibly opposed by the rigid individualism of the new right. The right evokes individualism, but defends highly centralized and hierarchical institutions. The New Left bespeaks solidarity but legitimated highly self-indulgent expressions of impulses. The New Left has now come apart. Its multiculturalism verges on a denial of the possibility of national citizenship and solidarity. Its adherence to our traditions of grass roots democracy is curiously helpless before the national and international reach of capital. The new right's individualism, meanwhile, is silent before the standardization of the capitalist cultural industry, whose wares it assures us it abhors. Meanwhile, the middle of our common life is occupied by the ordinary lobbying, parasitism, and profiteering of much of American business. In a period of deregulation, the independent mechanisms of the market take on a virulent life of their own. No wonder that so much discussion of public policy is conducted in the shallow and unreflective language of what purports to be economic accounting—but which is in fact an intellectual capitulation to a world without empathy, love, or judgment of value.

Is a political economy of care and hope, of provision for the future, possible? If not, our moral aspirations will continue to be nullified by brute facts. A political economy of care would substitute a different sort of benefit and cost accounting for the presently prevailing one. The present mode of reckoning eternalizes (or deifies) our present social arrangements in their most visible form. It takes little or no account of very tangible costs born by the collectivity (and unequally distributed) over a longer term—for instance, the cost of not attending to environmental degradation or educational deficit. A legal scholar, Edith Brown Weiss, has likened our responsibility to the earth to that of those trustees of an intergenerational trust, and the likeness tells. Meanwhile, on the eastern and southern borders of Western Europe, and along our southern border, we are beginning to experience a very initial impression of the long-term cost of attempting to maintain our societies as islands of prosperity in an ocean of poverty. Our wealth, in other terms, has costs actual and potential greater than the price of external and internal police actions. The moral message of many of the Churches, that solidarity with the rest of humankind demands different sorts of assistance policies from us than repeated eulogies to the market is far more realistic, in every sense, than much of what the World Bank has had to tell us.

Reflective economists will acknowledge that it does not suffice to deal with major phenomena not immediately quantifiable by ignoring them, or by employing the anodyne phrase "externalities." They, and not they alone, will hesitate, however, at the inclusion of value judgments in economic reasoning. Does this not render us less and not more able to make enlightened decisions, by blurring the distinction between reality and our preferences? One answer is that entire systems of social preference are usually built into the assumptions and methods of the social sciences—despite their claims to the objectivity of the natural sciences. An open acknowledgment, and open argument, about the ideological components of our views of the world is intellectually and morally wiser than allowing these to function covertly. A far more serious difficulty is the question of what values to include in the economic reasoning of public decision. At the moment, the market (which is to say, those who are strongest in their market positions) preempt much public decision. Opening the question of values is another way of saying that we ought to return to politics.

Again, it is absurd to suppose that our choice is between a monolithic and indeed tyrannical state and a free market on which individuals are sovereign in the expression of their wants. Wants are no less socially engendered than anything else and American wants, in particular, are a product of the interposition of constructed and indeed manipulated social values between the ultimate demands of human nature and their expression in consumption. The very unequal division of power is now an inextricable aspect of the market—whether in the form of authority structures in the workplace or the command of resources by those who own and manage wealth. We think of public office, in the best case, as stewardship— a notion Calvinist in its original American reception but with sufficient roots in other traditions to be common spiritual property. How can stewardship in the administration of property be strengthened? A glance at our own situation suggests that the term, strengthened, may by overly complacent and perhaps we should say, reintroduced? For the moment, the practice of stewardship in large firms is limited to the professions of it written by their public relations departments. For those with smaller firms, pervasive anxiety about their existence takes precedence over other criteria of behavior. One way to enlarge the space of stewardship in large firms is to place public representatives on their boards, just as one way to reduce the dysfunctions of hierarchy in the workplace is to give workers a role in management. An entire range of possibilities would allow us to experiment with a variety of institutional forms for public participation in the control of property.

Much of our own debate, recently, has been about the important but limited issue of regulation. Our grotesquely poor record in protecting our people, whether as citizens, consumers or workers (or annuitants or depositors) is an argument for renewed stringency in regulation. The democratic control of the market, however, is not a matter of regulation alone, but of bridging and eventually fusing what we now think of as separate public and private spheres. We now conduct a rather fragmented and obscured debate on economic goals and policy, but more often than not essential decisions are taken in arcane ways by those whose only legitimacy is their strong position in the market.

A new economic reasoning as an indispensable element of a new political economy presupposes a citizenry educated both generally and, specifically, able to make judgments about complex economic matters. Presently, our citizenry in its majority does not vote.

How can it be expected to advance to a level of performance that would combine (idealized) reminiscences of the Athenian Polis or the Swiss Canton with conceptual powers not invariably salient in our universities? One answer is that our present mode of doing public business is very unsatisfactory; it is right to begin experimenting with alternatives. Another is that nothing can be expected to change at once, but that a beginning has to be made, somehow. A citizenry can educate itself only by the practice of citizenship, and a public interest in acquiring the institutional and personal resources for that practice can hardly be generated in the absence of opportunities to use these. The creeping monopolization of the public mind by full-time ideologues and their natural children, technocratic experts, has not been accompanied by a notable improvement in the quality of our republic's politics.

The sorts of institutional arrangements we can theoretically envisage presuppose not only educated citizens but solid majorities attached to an idea of solidarity that has become increasingly attenuated in our nation. Can we seriously anticipate the resurgence of an idea of solidarity when circumstances seem to encourage, if anything, its opposite?

The problem of a politics of personhood (what I have termed a cultural politics) returns. A new politics would care for the moral integrity of persons. I would define morally integral persons as those able to reflect critically on the choices before them and able, too, if necessary to seek to enlarge their possibilities for choice. A politics of personhood would also assume that some personal traits are more valuable than others: autonomy, the capacity for care and responsibility, empathy and (another way of describing empathy) the ability to take some distance from one's own immediate groups and traditions. Persons, then, are not receptacles or bearers of infinitely variable needs and wants. How can persons of this sort be educated? Education, of course, is larger than a formal system of schooling and includes the spheres of culture and the family—as well as the moral instruction, or its opposite, afforded by the behavior of a society's elites.

As general as these terms of personhood may be, it can be objected that in a modern and multicultural society, the very terms represent a form of ethnocentrism and even implicit oppression. A modern and multicultural society, however, requires a common set of moral expectations and moral language if it is to remain a society—and not a haphazard association or even assemblage of groups and persons ready to do cultural and economic battle with one another at the least inducement. The fact that we are a multicultural nation does give us specific opportunities and responsibilities. The present global extension of the market creates new differentiations and hierarchies and angry peoples have turned to the opium of absolutized cultural differences. Were our nation to succeed at synthesizing multiculturalism and moral and political citizenship, its attractiveness might again resemble that of the young republic of the nineteenth century. That, however, is a matter beyond the competence of the present National Security Council.

The question of needs and wants is essential. I have criticized liberal or, rather, vulgar liberal ideas of the indefinite amplification of wants. Criticism is possible from any number of perspectives, and an ecological one is not the least telling: if industrial society keeps on expanding as it has, the environment is likely to be terminated. If we remain, for the moment, with moral and political choices, there are other grounds for criticizing the contemporary organization of needs and wants (what the Pope has termed —making common cause with the cultural left or some of it—consumerism). If needs and wants cannot increase indefinitely, what compensatory or substitute gratifications can the advanced societies offer? They might try to become morally advanced, by placing a positive value on the practice of citizenship, the instinct of workmanship, on just the sorts of contributions to society a market-based scale of values does not reward. One is struck by the reservoir of civic and social responsibility that lies beneath the surface of American life. Think of the persons who take early retirement from business to do community work, making their own exegesis of a text many will not have read, Aristotle on politics. Still others, in pursuing aesthetic, craft, intellectual, and sporting interests, illuminate yet another unread text, Marx on the difference between a realm of necessity and one of freedom.

Our problem, indeed, is to rethink our views of necessity. Our society can afford a decent minimum of existence for all of its members. Its present structure of inequality (which is deepening) is not reproduced in many other industrial nations. There, a narrower range of differentials in income and wealth (and heavier tax burdens on the prosperous and on the middle levels, too) do not seem to make them unhappier, more divided, and more liable to suffer social pathologies than ourselves. The differences seem to lie not only in a heightened general sense of solidarity, but in the solidary institutions of the welfare state. There are, however, other contributory causes: the material and psychic rewards for ordinary work are higher elsewhere than for those who in the United States are made to feel somehow not very valued. There are, it appears, uses to a differentiated notion of equality that minimize the dreaded effects of levelling. In any event, the view that humans were created either by God or nature to play preordained roles in our present economic and social system is unconvincing. Human nature itself is deeper and richer, and social possibility is larger.

There are indeed sorts of income that cannot be described in cash terms. One of the advantages of some sorts of work is that it is "interesting"—a term that covers autonomy, challenge, responsibility, and other kinds of psychic rewards. The delights of friendship and neighborliness, the (admittedly mixed) blessings of family life can hardly be reduced to derivatives of material prosperity. A society that honored public service and economic stewardship, which indeed treated these as close or identical, would rechannel and redefine what is now the expenditure of energy in selfish ways. The golden west of the imagination of the poorer nations, of course, is a good deal less golden for those who live in it. Suppose that there is a connection between the stress-induced diseases of civilization and the structure of the economy. Reverting briefly to cost-benefit analysis: we would pay a good deal less for medical care if, psychically, we lived in a healthier fashion.

Can Americans be persuaded to alter their attitudes, beliefs, expectations, and habits so profoundly as to participate in a major institutional reform—one that would tax all of our moral resources? Many citizens do express a sense of disappointment, emptiness, and loss. For the moment, these feelings of discontent remain semiprivate, indulgences in nostalgia or personalized and ineffectual utopias. A renewed appeal to common purpose, to public engagement, might mobilize more readiness to experiment than we can now imagine.

A society of this kind would be a learning society, one able to respond to new exigencies because the persons who constitute it are capable of replacing, after critical reflection together, acquired and accustomed ideas and habits with new ones. It would be a society in which presently intangible achievements in humane skills are made more tangible, in which leadership would be exemplary and pedagogic rather than narcissistic and solitary. The beginning point, of course, would be a reconsideration of our treatment of children, a broad attempt to think of family and school in ways begun by John Dewey, as places where the generations meet to teach each other things each alone cannot know. We would also have to look at the entire spectrum of our cultural industry. Here, too, the issue is not the replacement of the present market system by an omniscient ministry of culture. There is a strong case, however, for the development of self-governing cultural institutions (publishing houses managed by their editors, newspapers published by journalists, television stations owned by viewers) that might possibly cultivate views and sensibilities different and new, bewildering and disturbing, and on these accounts instructive even if not profitable. (Here speaks an author whose most recent publisher was ejected by a once-distinguished New York house whose present director refers to books as "units.")

Experiments in new economic and social institutions, attention to the dimensions of care in society, a large reintroduction of moral argument in public debate—to what extent are these notions illusory in the face of the sheer institutional inertia of our present society? Even those who are not so well served by society are rendered anxious, after all, at the possibility of change—as if the fear of losing what they now possess made them spiritually immobile.

Does American culture and tradition have resources that would make new emphasis possible? Could the public be persuaded to see in a new New Deal, for instance, a true instance of national continuity—as opposed to the contentless nationalism now advanced by manipulative politicians and media managers anxious to please them? Another way to ask the question is, perhaps, blunter: are the

292 • *Norman Birnbaum*

American people potentially better than those who now assert that they are only responding to their preferences and values?

The term grassroots democracy calls up images of Populism, of movements like Abolitionism, of Shays' Rebellion and, more recently, of the rise of phenomena as diverse as the Farmer Labor Party and the community organization programs of the Great Society project. Even the Republican Party has seen fit to pay tribute to the concept, with its rather cloudy notion of "empowerment" (which claims, to be sure, to be something else than a plan to dismantle Federal social programs). Some critics of excessive enthusiasm for grassroots democracy warn us of its ambiguities. It can encompass angry resentment and utterly unworldly proposals, the Ku Klux Klan and the Townsend Plan, as well as the more noble sorts of protest. Perhaps, but the tradition of grassroots democracy is not limited to systematic negativism or resentment but advocates an active idea of citizenship.

American Federalism, meanwhile, and much of the sovereignty exercised by state and local government, rests on notions of the sufficiency of local rule, on the idea that larger and smaller settings of citizenship are not mutually exclusive but complimentary. With that, it goes a long way to meeting the imperatives of the Catholic idea of Subsidiarity, the view that autonomous and real units of society should govern themselves. The national and international market, however, now threatens to erase these boundaries and with them, the autonomy of communities. That is all the more reason for a new version of the grassroots democratic idea with a pronouncedly modern economic component. Global interdependence seems to make nineteenth-century American democratic ideas quaint. The extension of the world market, however, requires that somewhere, somehow, ideas of citizenship assume forms adequate to the newer forms of economic domination. As a nodal point of global capitalism, the United States can reclaim its model democratic function only if it can offer the world something other than the spectacle of a nation subsumed by a market. Those American politicians who now decry the consequences of foreign investment, loss of control over the economy by the American people, ignore the frequent partnership of foreign banks and firms with American counterparts. They might also ask to what extent American ownership has been compatible with a deepening and extension of our democracy.

The development of citizenship in a multicultural nation would have the value associated with its general and universal character. It would not be compatible with recent attempts to propagate an American tribalism ("we are number one"). Those attempts, apart from their aesthetic and moral repugnancy, are very likely on account of their ultimate vacuity to increase the present national malaise. The surcease from our national conflicts and problems they offer is very ephemeral, and the resultant shock of a return to reality is all the more painful.

Some years ago, the Bishop of Denver wrote of a "Catholic moment." The extreme individualism of the Protestant tradition, he said, had exhausted its usefulness for the nation as it entered an epoch in which cooperation and solidarity were far more essential values. The Bishop may have underestimated the social component in Protestantism, as well as the cooperative elements of a secular American radicalism. He is surely correct, however, in locating the space that a Catholic contribution to the American future can now occupy. Original liberalism broke with a constraining society, one of tradition and not consent. A modernized liberalism, despite its alertness to the dangers of bureaucratic tyranny, (which is by no means always the tyranny of the state) will have to ask how communities and solidarities can be purposefully constructed, or renewed, by citizens who recognize that a large degree of mutual dependence is in the nature of things. An episode in which American denial of this truth was especially evident, despite the fact that much of American history is a struggle for liberty and mutuality in equal measure, is now coming to an end. The regressive and rigid ideas of community offered as solutions by some will not serve any more than the schematic individualism propagated by others. The development of a new birth of liberty in social complexity is the conceptual and the political task that lies before us.

24. Pluralism and the Left Identity

Chantal Mouffe

If the project of the Left is to survive the discredit that the collapse of "actually existing socialism" has thrown over the very idea of socialism, it requires a new formulation. Even social democracy is presently suffering from the impact of the events in the East and the proclaimed triumph of liberal capitalism. Claims for social justice, economic democracy and struggles against inequalities are increasingly dismissed as relics of a foregone age dominated by the rhetoric of class struggle.

The recognition of the virtues of pluralist democracy is indeed an important achievement, but it would be a serious setback for democracy if we were to accept "actually existing liberal capitalist democracies" as the "end of history." There are still numerous social relations where the process of democratization is needed and the task for the Left is to envisage how this can be done in a way that is compatible with the existence of a liberal democratic regime.

To be sure, such a project has been on the agenda for some time and from many quarters proposals have been made for different forms of what we could call "liberal socialism," but today this question has taken a dramatic urgency. I think that it is important to show not only how socialist goals can be reinscribed within the framework of liberal democracy but also how the Left project can be redefined as the extension of democracy to a wide range of social relations so as to include the demands of the new movements. This is the meaning of the "project of radical and plural democracy" that we have put forward in *Hegemony and Socialist Strategy.*[1]

What I propose to do here is the following: (1) to affirm that pluralism is the central characteristic of modern democracy, i.e., of the liberal democratic regime whose principles of legitimacy are the assertion of liberty and equality for all; and (2) To show that the Left project can be visualized as the deepening of that pluralism and that socialist goals can be an important step towards such a development of pluralism.

In other words, I am arguing in favor of a complete reversal of the Left identity. So far it has been generally identified with a view of society that put homogeneity, equality, and harmony as its central values. Pluralism, difference, and heterogeneity were seen as the ills of capitalist society to be overcome because of signs of inequality. It is such a view of society which has to be discarded. The left should cease to see individual freedom in negative terms and begin to take liberty as seriously as equality in order to examine how they can be both enhanced.

This requires that we envisage democracy in a different way. First it is necessary to recognize the specificity of modern democracy that consists in the articulation between liberalism and democracy and accept that the logic of popular sovereignty, on its own, is not enough to guarantee individual freedom and the respect of rights of minorities. Here we must admit, following Bobbio, that only a liberal state can guarantee the basic rights without which the democratic game cannot take place. We should also agree with Bobbio that the struggle for democracy is the struggle against autocratic power in all its forms. What is at stake is not the creation of a completely new form of democracy but the struggle against hierarchic and bureaucratic forms of organization in an increasing number of social relations and institutions: the family, schools, the economy, public administration, etc.[2]

---

1. Ernesto Laclau and Chantal Mouffe, *Hegemony and Socialist Strategy: Towards a Radical Democratic Politics*, London, 1985.

2. See: Norberto Bobbio, *The Future of Democracy*, 1987 and *Liberalism and Democracy*, London, 1990.

Nevertheless, contrary to Bobbio, I believe that this cannot be done without breaking with the framework of individualism. I am not postulating a return to an organicistic and holistic conception of society, which is clearly premodern and does not make room for pluralism. It is rather that I think the individualistic conception predominant in liberal theory is not the only alternative to such a view. The problem is to theorize the individual not as a monad, an "unencumbered" self, existing previously and independent of society, but as constituted as an ensemble of "subject positions," members of many communities and participants in a plurality of collective forms of identifications.

In that line, the question of "representation of interests" as well as the question of "rights" have to be posed in a completely different way. The idea of social rights, for instance, needs to be envisaged in terms of "collective rights" that are ascribed to specific communities. It is through its inscription in specific social relations that a social agent is granted rights, not as an individual outside society. Some of these rights can of course have a universalistic character and correspond to all members of the political community; but some others will only correspond to specific social inscriptions. It is not a question of rejecting universalism in favor of particularism, but of acknowledging the need for a new type of articulation between the universal and the particular. There is indeed a way in which the abstract universalism of human rights can be used to negate specific identities and to repress some forms of collective identities corresponding to specific communities.

Once we have accepted that the crucial question of modern democracy is pluralism and the struggle against autocratic power, it is important to show how the capitalist system in its present stage of big corporations constitutes a fetter to the development of pluralism and the enhancement of individual freedom. Here I think that we can find an important source of inspiration in the attempt by Paul Hirst in several articles[3] to retrieve the tradition of associational socialism that flourished during the nineteenth century and the early 1920s both in France and Britain. It is generally consid-

---

3. Paul Hirst, "Associational Socialism in a Pluralist State," in *Journal of Law and Society*, Vol. 15, No. 1, Spring 1988; "From Statism to Pluralism" in *The Alternative*, ed., B. Pimlott and others, 1990.

ered as utopian and obsolete but Hirst argues that the end of the Cold War and some recent changes in the West have created conditions in which those ideas could become applicable. His main thesis is that the current move toward flexible specialization in several countries has increased the importance of regional economic regulation and small- to medium-scale firms. Associational socialism, says Hirst, could be relevant in the struggle for democratization of the economy and decentralization because its central idea is that economic units should be cooperatively self-governing associations. If we want to redefine socialism as a dimension of the struggle to deepen liberal democratic values and against all forms of autocratic power, associational socialism can provide us insights into how to establish the democratic governance of private corporations and the democratization of state administration. More specifically, because of its emphasis on the plurality and autonomy of enterprises and collective bodies as decision-making agencies, it can show us the way to enhance the tradition of Western pluralism and liberalism. Because associational pluralism encourages the organization of social life in associations and challenges forms of hierarchy and administrative centralization, it can give us important models for the democratization of corporations and public bodies. For instance, education, health, welfare, and community services could be provided by cooperatively or socially owned and democratically managed bodies that set their own objectives. Hirst shows how associational socialism is compatible with a pluralistic society in which there are distinct sorts of values or organized interests. He indicates that it could tolerate and indeed welcome the Catholic church and the gay community, which provide health and welfare services for their members.

I find Hirst's analyses very convincing and I think that in that tradition of socialism we can find important insights on how to overcome the obstacles to democracy constituted—as Bobbio has pointed out—by the two main forms of autocratic power: large corporations and centralized big governments. In that way we would be able to enhance the pluralism of modern societies. But this requires a break with the universalist and the individualistic modes of thought that have been dominant in the liberal tradition. Today to think of democracy exclusively in terms of control of power by individuals considered separately is completely unrealistic and democracy's future rests less on the choices of individual voters than on the effective representation of organizations representing major social interests. The central issue of democratization today is how antagonistic interests can be controlled so that no concentration of interests can be allowed to exercise a monopoly on economic or political power and dominate the process of decision-making. Western societies are democratic because of the pluralism of interests that they have been able to effectively secure and the competition that exists among them. A multiplicity of associations with real capacity for decision and a plurality of centers of power are needed to resist effectively the trends towards autocracy represented by the growth of bureaucracy and technocracy. In that defense and deepening of pluralism and democracy, the Left could find a new identity and appear as the only consequent heir to the ideals of liberal democracy and as the only force able to resist the increasing dangers facing the democratic process today.

25. What's Left After Socialism

Didier Motchane

As the Berlin wall and the Gulf War underscored, the European Left is out of step with history. As long as Europe remains little more than an alibi for surrendering or converting to liberalism, it will continue to be a non entity.

The basic foundation for a European renaissance is to understand that the reemergence of Europe and the left are one and the same.

The collapse of communism is not a victory for capitalism, but the sign of the failings of Social Democracy. Democracy cannot be restricted to political institutions, but must spread throughout society, internationalism, as well as global and local solidarity. Human rights, citizen rights, and humanitarian intervention rights are inseparable and indivisible.

According to F. Furet, the end of communism—the counter-Bolshevik revolution occurring in the former Soviet Union—shows that the propelling force of the French Revolution in Europe has worn itself out. Such a statement, from one who has spent his life putting an end to the Revolution, comes as no surprise. What is more startling is that this point of view is the dominant one in Europe—not only on the right, but among a good many of those on the left as well.

There are those, however, who feel that the French Revolution is an infinite process, and will be at the center of future events more than ever before. For others who are taking part in this vital debate, one must first take inventory of what already exists, both in the realm of social representation and the consciousness , and within the movement of social forces and the functioning of institutions.

Contrary to the thinking that many international socialist parties are trying to uphold, the collapse of communism is neither a victory for Social Democracy nor proof that it has been right. Rather, it is a sign of a double failure. First, the inability, followed by the renunciation of European Socialists to safeguard in the European consciousness an historical domain which is their own. Second, the failure to devise a practical process that would trace their perspectives in the social consciousness. This is what has enclosed the Soviet system in a desperate dilemma, and condemned Gorbachev's attempts to retrace, in the opposite direction, the path of the Western European societies. The latter had to some extent revised the welfare state after World War II to include human rights and citizenry, almost as though they were once again taking up the movement that the French Revolution had intended to accomplish.

Gorbachev had intended to introduce freedom in a post-Stalinist Etat-Providence. However, once the Socialists rallied around or converted to liberalism—call it social liberalism—it became impossible for Soviet society to challenge the totalitarian system, flanked by its appointed party and army, without challenging the Etat-Providence as well.

Second, we were not always sufficiently aware of the ambivalent way in which the scission of the workers' movement and the historical conflict between Communism and Socialism acted on the evolution of the relationship between political and social forces in Western Europe. For, if the example—the counter-example of which can be termed real socialism—hampered the political progression of the Left in the industrialized capitalist countries, at the same time, Social Democracy made very effective use of it to wrench concessions from capitalism and convince it to regard the welfare state as an unavoidable insurance policy.

Since the early 1970s, with computerization and automatization of production, the second Industrial Revolution, which is still underway, has raised some profound questions about Social Democracy as a form of society. The latter has not managed to find a second wind or renewed inspiration. This current absence of reflection will condemn the left to an exorable withering away. In order to find a path to revival, Socialists will have to refrain from committing as many sins against the mind as there are problems. One could describe the logic of their folly by a successive series of non sequiturs, whose origin can assuredly be found in economicism as the savior of this period in history; a non sequitur to the unification of the world and to the nature and conditions necessary to put democracy into practice; a non sequitur as well to the relationship between man and nature, and perhaps a non sequitur to the very concept of nature itself.

In short, the perfection of the world market as a replacement for the internationalization of the political consciousness of peoples constitutes the global village as the meditation of the unconscious—"Democratism" and human rights as the ideology of the loss of political consciousness; the decline of public civicism as ecologism. This perversion of ecology is in the process of becoming the ideology of the disappearance of social linkage and the all-purpose ersatz of religion. These are issues that are the most critical for the end of our century and the beginning of the next one. Economicism is the virus that has been devastating Social Democracy and Communism. Its impact is all the more destructive in that it has finally disarmed itself before the beast that, I would venture to say, has not only been merely its chosen ground, but its very raison d'être: liberalism, the European name for capitalism.

Is Social Democracy doomed to vanish into the ocean of historical capitalism? It can commit itself to rediscover humanity, society, democracy, and to make the will of nations prevail upon the hegemony of empires.

The marriage of democracy and the nation has been characterized by turmoil, its history a list of collective events often painful and unfortunate. In France, the nation, as the daughter of the French Revolution, was a creation of the left. Of course, I refer to the "nation" in its modern sense—the nation of the Republic, the political nation, the nation of the citizens. The nation was born on the left and it soon became—approximately ten years later—the hostage of the right. It was confiscated, distorted, and perverted, and has not managed to survive unscathed from this long separation. Maurras ended up in Vichy, but so did many left-wing political figures as well.

Opposing the "ancien régime," the French Revolution invented the republican nation. The entire history of the working class movement is that of a fight to achieve the republic, the "republique jusqu-au bout," the social republic, the pinnacle of the republic that Jaurès also called socialism. However, the "bourgeoisie" has frozen the Republic into a free-trade abstraction. By reducing the republican democracy to the democracy of the bourgeoisie (which is not the middle class), and in particular by disuniting the working class from the nation over the course of a century, the bourgeoisie began to pervert the nation. And, because this misrepresented nation was no longer acknowledgeable, the left ignored it. It is the divorce between the left and the nation which is the origin of the divorce between the people and democracy, and from which derives war and fascism.

We know how many unspeakable deeds, how many crimes were organized, committed, or else forgiven by the successive governments of France, or with their silent approval, in the name of the nation. An we can therefore understand where this idea—that the nation is an emblem of the right—originates in the tradition of the left.

But the republic and democracy cannot be cultures without a basis. When the nation is not, except in words, the nation of the people, when the nation is not—as used to be said some time ago, particularly in another part of Europe—the state of the whole people, but is working in the interest of the privileged, the rich, and within the framework of a historical perversion of the nation and the state, democracy is dying out.

When, as a result of weaknesses and the lost battles of the left, democracy is sold out to long-established interests, to institutionalized lies and powers, when the impotent, ignorant, or idle left allows the right to hail the nation, it (the left) gives away the nation to nationalists, and democracy suffers.

This mistake was, in my opinion, the worst and the most permanent mistake of the left in history. There were exceptions: Jaurès, and slightly further down the line, the Austro-Marxists. The mistake lies in not seeing that those who fail to keep together cohesively the three dimensions of democracy—society, nation, and universality—do not maintain anything at all. If the unity of these principles is not maintained because their relationship is not understood, the republic cannot remain stable.

I leave aside what happens when, as during a crisis, national and social viewpoints are circumspect; it was exactly the elimination of a universal perspective that brought about Nazism in the past. I leave aside the oblivion of the social aspect—and if only the national aspect remains, the result is the ascendency of the right.

However, the present situation does not represent a post-World War I period, but a time when world-wide capitalism has existed and operated successfully for twenty or thirty years. Today, when the left—the institutionalized left—refers to internationalism of the people, we know that its aim is to conceal that the left embraces world-wide markets. To associate the internationalism of the people with world-wide markets is the trick by which the socialists have allowed the Europe of commerce to take over in the name of a Europe of the people. This has resulted in a France of unemployment and a collapse of its industry, all in the name of a monetary Europe and of freedom of trade. Through the proclamation of the death of nations—of nations' obsolescence—the freedom of the people is sold out to the freedom of finance, the ubiquity of which eliminates those who cannot keep pace.

When these socialists turned into masked liberals—more and more obviously—they eventually forgot that their party had, once upon a time, embraced the slogan: live, work, and (many used to add) decide. Everywhere, "au pays," it is democracy and the nation together that they abjured, betrayed, and abandoned. To separate democracy and the nation is a threat to both; it causes them to decay. Instead of making Europe the creation of those nations which have to accomplish themselves as they surpass themselves, one pretends to build Europe on their ruins, on their vanishing, their integration, their dissolution into the empire in which "Money is King" of financial markets. Instead of building up a community of European public policies, they are dissolved everywhere into the acid of deregulation, threatening both democracy and nation.

Thus, what is the Maastricht Treaty really? What would Maastricht have been and what does the spirit of Maastricht still mean? Maastricht's choices are against democracy and against the nation because Maastricht is a deal sealed between federalists and liberals. In other words, the deal is between those who believe that political life can do without the nation and those who want the market to do without the political life because they do not see an alternative policy to the market-oriented economy. Obviously the federalists will be the losers in this game.

Let us not be intimidated by allegations that we are chauvinists, nationalists, cowards, or full of archaisms, all the more because those accusations have been echoing in our minds for a very long time with the belief in this long-standing mistake, this long separation between democracy and the nation, which has led the left to abandon the distorted values of the nation to its opponents. What a blessing for our political opponents if they had managed to convince the majority of the citizens that between themselves, however strong they might be, between the party of money and the extreme right, between the party of money and neo-fascism, there was nothing but a wasteland.

26. Some Reflections on the New World Order and Disorder

Julian Santamaria Ossorio

The breakdown of the Berlin wall and more generally, the failure of communism in the (now former) Soviet Union and eastern Europe has suddenly put an end to half a century of cold war. The division of the world in two opposing blocs is over. The nuclear danger looks much less imposing and real. The existential enemy has vanished and the political, ideological, and military threats that the enemy was supposed to embody have faded within a short period of time. Democracy has become the only legitimate principle of political organization accepted almost worldwide, while the market economy and the autonomy of civil society have simultaneously become universal paradigms.

Thus, the process initiated in the autumn of 1989 generated a wave of worldwide optimism, as the outcome of the cold war was indeed perceived everywhere, particularly in the West, as a most positive and promising development. However, this optimistic mood dissipated almost immediately. The tremendous hopes and expectations spurred on by the 1989 revolutions have been replaced by subsequent conflicting appraisals and increasingly gloomy views. The frame of reference that for the last fifty years structured world conflicts and tensions along the East-West divide is obsolete. In a perverse way, the East-West divide was a central contributing factor to political cohesion and predictability during the cold war, and its absence opens very complex questions about peace and security policies and strategies.

At the same time, democratization and the introduction of market mechanisms face enormous difficulties in the territories of the former Soviet Union and in eastern Europe. The rise of nationalistic sentiments is the source of growing instability in these regions, while the inability of the Twelve to cope with the phenomenon causes skepticism about European integration and the role of the EU in managing security affairs at its own borders. In the field of futuristic theories, Samuel Huntington's notion of the "clash" of civilizations with its pessimistic outlook has replaced Fukuyama's naive anticipation of the end of history.

The overall importance of this phenomenon is enhanced by its chronological coincidence with other important developments that crystallized at the turn of the last decade. I refer here to the globalization of the economy and the technological revolution, on the one hand, and the economic recession sweeping the industrialized world, on the other. But I also call attention to the tremendous amount of social and political change that has accumulated around the world over the last ten to fifteen years, affecting working conditions and the quality of life, reshaping value systems, and feeding the impression that the current era nears its end.

As a consequence of the accumulation of substantial and accelerated change, a general mood of uncertainty about the future is indeed spreading. The nature and profile of the international system, the limits of both the nation-state and the welfare-state, and the workings of democracy itself are being reexamined. As a matter of fact, it is their critical review that is at the center of the political debate about the end of the century. Within this frame of reference I would like to make a few remarks.

First of all, orphans of *the* enemy, we are left without a frame of reference that for the last fifty years or so helped us to understand international conflicts. So far we have been offered no substitute. It is not even clear how to define the threats we now face and how to discover their origin. It is a matter for discussion whether we will move from a bipolar to a multipolar or (although temporarily) even a unipolar universe. The need for a new international order is broadly shared, but there is no agreement about the criteria that should inspire it. The pursuit of the national interest, the exportation of democracy, the creation of a global partnership with Russia, or any combination thereof has been considered in the US.

The proposal of a *new world order* as advanced in 1989 by President Bush seems provisional and extremely general. Replacing confrontation by cooperation in order to fight against international terrorism, to protect the environment and to promote joint space research are broad aims that may find ever-widening acceptance. The concept of a *new world order* has the merit of identifying a number of relatively non-controversial areas where cooperation is indeed mandatory. It does not include, however, any reference to more divisive areas where cooperation may prove indeed indispensable for a balanced evolution of the relations between the developed and the developing world.

Secondly, the globalization of the economy has brought about an ever-growing consciousness of the interdependence among nation-states and their relative obsolescence as central political structures in the world. Decisions affecting millions of people are made far from the territorial borders of their respective nation-states, leaving the national authorities without appropriate resources to control them. Yet, competition now occurs at a worldwide level, which has created tremendous strains on different sectors of the national economies seeking to modernize and adapt to the new challenges without much help from their respective state.

This, together with the technological revolution of the past decade and the fiscal crisis of the state, has given shape to the current structural economic crisis in which the shortage of jobs is a main feature. The number of unemployed has increased astronomically throughout Europe and the US, and there are indications that the lack of jobs is permanent, even after the recession ends. Keynesian economics seem no longer applicable in the framework of a global economy, and there are doubts about the ability of the old welfare state to provide the assistance and social services that are its landmark. Yet, more than a decade of Thatcherism and Reaganism did not provide support to neo-liberal doctrines that ultimately led the British and American economies to the verge of an abyss. However, these neo-liberal doctrines strongly influenced economic policies all around the world, tempting even some social democratic parties, contaminating the discourse of many of its leaders, and generating great confusion among voters of the left.

Thirdly, by the time democratic principles attained universal recognition, democratic praxis was under fire everywhere. Empirical as opposed to normative theories of democracy were prompted by European experiences of the 1920s and 30s. It is no coincidence that Schumpeter's classical work *Socialism, Capitalism and Democracy* appeared in 1941. Empirical definitions of democracy have made possible a better and deeper understanding of contemporary government. At the same time, by neglecting any of their normative dimensions, such empirical definitions helped to legitimize existing democracies as the true and only possible embodiment of democracy, as put so bluntly by Lipset in his widely acclaimed *Political Man.*

Empirical definitions of democracy suited very well the ideological and political requirements of the cold war. It was clear after WWII that democracy, as imperfect as it might have manifested itself, is still to be preferred to its authoritarian or totalitarian alternatives. The very existence of the latter allowed for, by comparison, democratic inefficiencies and deficiencies. But when these alternatives vanish, existing democracies are confronted solely with themselves. To be more precise, empirical democracies have been compared with prevailing models and ideals of democracy. Concerns with the viability and consolidation compete with new concerns about the performance and quality of democracy. As the evaluative standards rose, a vague but ascertainable atmosphere of democratic malaise began to spread. In the US this goes back to the days of the Vietnam War and Watergate. Political dealignment and declining rates of political participation may be construed as two signs of that climate. In Europe opinion polls show clearly that in 1991, for the first time in twenty-five years, Europeans evaluating the performance of democracy in their own countries in negative terms outnumbered those with a positive assessment of it.

Without going into a more extensive analysis of these points, it is quite evident that they open a number of questions about the future. The national and international political systems as well as the economic system that shaped the world over the past fifty years are now clearly inadequate and have either broken down or are becoming ever more obsolete. And there does not seem to be either a theoretical or a practical substitute for them. The criteria for structuring the world order, the social and territorial boundaries of the nation-state, the goals and resources of the welfare state, and the nature and workings of old and new democracies are at stake. In a word, the old world may be passing away before a new one clearly evolves. Needless to say, such a situation provides the optimal grounds for ideological disputes about its nature and its likely outlook.

Conservatives have tried to present the argument in terms of a natural return, following an historical pause, to a unipolar world order based on a single economic model of unfettered market sovereignty and a neo-liberal non-interventionist kind of state. For them the failure of communism proves the superiority of capitalism over any kind of socialism including social democracy whose current difficulties in some industrialized countries they directly link to that historical debacle. Conservatives would also like for others to believe that theirs is the only reasonable view of the ongoing process of change. Unfortunately, social democrats have frequently divided as they tried to reaffirm their own identity in a world where some of their old ideological references were fading away. However, Norman Birnbaum is right when he claims that the difficulties of social democracy in Europe have much to do with its won success or more precisely iwht the success of the Welfare State and are not a consequence of the failure of the so-called *real* solicalism.

The question, however, remains open about what is the meaning of the left, what is really meant when one identifies oneself as belonging to the left. As this is no longer self-evident, social democrats must come up with some answers to the uncertainty connected to, I repeat, the need to reconstruct a safe, balanced and secure world, the need to compensate for the distributive inability of the market place and the need to promote the cultural and economic conditions that might permit a significant improvement of the quality and performance of existing democracies.

Needless to say, this is a very hard task that I do not dare to undertake to develop here. But I would like to pinpoint some of the criteria that might inspire such a reflection.

First of all, the changes that have taken place in the recent past and that continue to unfold today are not natural but rather social, economic, and political changes that are the product of human action and can therefore be channeled and regulated in different ways. The engineering of political transitions from authoritarianism to democracy in southern Europe, Latin America, and now eastern Europe points in this direction. These situations prove the extent to which politics and policies matter. Reductions of inequality combined with economic growth, as observed in different European countries under social democratic governments until very recently, confirm the impact of political action.

Secondly, the remaking of an international order requires some discussion about the set of goals that should be given priority and the most effective means to implement them. I will not go into detail about what is ultimately a broad debate. It may prove extremely difficult until such questions as the future of the former Soviet Union, especially Russia, are clarified. Meanwhile, conditions are right to explore which may be the appropriate instruments to stimulate cooperation in order to promote peace, democracy, and development around the world. These are sufficiently encompassing aims as to include the defense of human rights and the struggle against famine, illness, tyranny, or discrimination. Policies of disarmament, however, should free resources in the industrialized countries to a sufficient degree as to make possible and encourage cooperation in order to advance these goals.

Thirdly, the welfare state is an historical creature related to social democracy, and although it has been fully incorporated into the political culture in most European countries, discussions about the future of the welfare state get frequently mixed up with discussions about the future of social democracy. Some people speak indifferently of the "crisis" involving the two, although rarely is it spelled out what kind of crisis is meant. In any case, the debate carried out both inside and outside socialist parties has centered in recent years around the following topics: Does the end of communism imply the end of any form of socialism?; how does the former affect the latter?; does it make any difference the implementation of reformist policies as those usually promoted by social democratic parties?; even if they matter, do contemporary states have the resources to maintain the social services they have so far been providing?; and finally, can the state compete in any meaningful way with the market?

I do not intend to address all these questions but simply introduce them here for discussion purposes. Certainly, some of these questions are of a rhetorical nature but are brought to the fore once and again. For example, the inefficiencies of the market to assign certain resources have been so firmly established that there should not be any argument about it. Nor should there be arguments about the proposition that the provision of those goods can only be guaranteed by the state. Therefore, to continue opposing in the abstract the market to the state makes very little sense. Similarly, a number of studies have shown that reformist strategies and policies have been extremely successful in Europe in reducing inequalities over the last five or six decades without hindering economic growth. Finally, the identification between *real* and *democratic* socialism, the notion that the end of communism brings with it or is a sign of social democracy's demise, also shows an unmistakable ideological perspective that ignores past history and refusing to understand the differences between totalitarianism and democracy.

Other questions may be more pertinent. For example, will there be the fiscal resources to maintain the number and quality of the services provided by the state? Second, how will the Europeans be able to compete with the US or Japan if they bear the burden of much higher social costs? These are difficult and complex issues that hardly allow for simple responses. The issues address the political culture of each country, its fiscal habits and the different patterns of social and political arrangements. At any rate, the welfare state should not be reified in its present form. There may be a diversity of ways to combine market and state operations in order to obtain an appropriate combination. Public management may be stripped of some fat. Inefficient management and corruption are not the hallmark of public intervention; nevertheless, this kind of practice should be drastically eradicated. Some former public services may be discontinued, as others may yet be initiated. But two things remain clear: First, equality is a historical force and a condition for social development that any modern polity should support; second, equality is *the* key democratic value. There is no working democracy without some degree of equality, and therefore one of the most important roles for public authorities is precisely that of removing the obstacles hindering it.

The last point I wish to address concerns some of the issues surrounding what I have called democratic malaise. Democratic malaise has its roots in the divorce between democratic theory and practice but also in the elevation of ethical and public standards of judgment over the unequal distribution of political resources, the quality of representation, and the material performance of democracies. In other words, the unease affects the entry, the interior, and the exit of the system. Again, there is no room here to deal with all the details. Therefore, I will refrain and make only a few general remarks.

Let me say first of all that some of the new arguments are not really new. For example, the most critical one refers once again to the representative nature of modern democracies, and the alternatives proposed remain participatory democracy or direct democracy. The former is supported on the basis that it is the only form that considers men as political beings. Unfortunately, it lacks a clear definition of its workings. The material impossibility of running a large territory through direct participation has been a pretext but also a reason to historically discard direct democracy as a form of government and to accept a representative assembly instead. This argument remains a powerful one, and supporters of direct democracy have not been able to decide whether their proposal intends to substitute one type of political system with an entirely different one, or simply to complement representative democracy with a broader use of the popular vote.

Secondly, some of the proposed reforms concerning the electoral system are introduced without having convincingly established the existence of a causal relationship between existing arrangements and the problem at stake, without any consideration that the state may be taking for granted that the remedy perfectly suits its purposes, and of course that there are no counter indications to be explored. Blaming the electoral system not only for the unequal distribution of political resources, but also for any defective institutional workings or poor performance is common practice among opinion leaders and politicians. As a result, electoral engineering is frequently contemplated as a universal panacea. Electoral reform may indeed be a powerful instrument but one that has to be managed very carefully and one that cannot simultaneously satisfy conflicting or even contradictory purposes.

A third point concerns political parties. There is no democracy without parties. Together with elections they are the basis of democratic government. They are huge organizations that need great amounts of money to finance elections and to survive and grow between elections. Private funding of parties and candidates is not only a source of inequality but often a source of corruption. Public funding can alleviate but hardly remedy this because it will always be considered insufficient by some. This presents us with a difficult dilemma. People in charge of managing or controlling the management of public funds may be constantly under suspicion and hardly trusted in the framework of a political system that is supposed to be based on trust. Thus, parties are at the same time a necessary component of democracy and a latent danger.

Furthermore, if there is no democracy without parties, there is no quality democracy without a high level of competitiveness. It is precisely the existence of several parties with the possibility of moving in and out of power that makes governments responsive and opposition responsible. Now, as parties become ideologically closer and try to fish in all electoral waters, the stakes go up, and the competition gets tougher. As a consequence, in order to compete in the electoral market, parties are forced to strengthen their organizations, to insure very strict patterns of discipline and a highly hierarchical bureaucracy just as industrial concerns do in the commodities market. The lack of party-internal democracy has already been pointed out by people like Ostrogorsky and Michels in the early years of this century, but it did not arouse the unfriendly sentiments toward parties that today appear almost everywhere.

To improve the quality of democracy requires getting rid of both corrupt and authoritarian practices. The two of them have become structural predicaments for the reproduction of democratic legitimacy. There are no easy remedies to be found in legislation. Legislation may help to alleviate the situation but not to solve these two problems that must be of special concern for social democratic parties. What is needed is the political will to fight and defeat them. A large consensus among all relevant parties and a blunt commitment of their leaders to put an end to these perverse practices are the necessary prerequisites. These may not be sufficient, but without them, nothing significant can be achieved.

Notes on Contributors

Elmar Altvater is Professor of Political Economy at the Institute for Economic and Social Analyses of Political Systems in the Department of Political Science, Free University of Berlin. He is the author of publications on state theory, crisis theory, the world market and global ecological problems. He is also co-editor of the Social Science Quarterly *Prokla.* His most recent publication is *The Future of the Market—On the Regulation of Money and Nature after the Collapse of "Real Socialism."*

Norman Birnbaum is University Professor at the Georgetown University Law Center. Educated as a sociologist (Ph.D. 1958), he has taught widely in Europe and the United States, at Nuffield College at Oxford University and the New School for Social Research, among others. A founding editor of *New Left Review* and editorial board member of *The Nation,* Professor Birnbaum has contributed actively to research in the areas of sociology, philosophy, culture, and education. He was one of the founders of Democratic Socialists of America, has served as a consultant to numerous international trade unions, several governors, legislators, and U.S. presidential candidates as well as the Socialist International. Professor Birnbaum's most recent book is entitled *The Radical Renewal: The Politics of Ideas in Modern America* (1988).

Jean L. Cohen is Associate Professor of Political Science at Columbia University. Professor Cohen focuses on contemporary political theory and is the author of *Class and Civil Society: The Limits of Marxian Critical Theory* (1982) and co-author with Andrew Arato of *Civil Society and Political Theory* (1991). She is Associate Editor of *Constellations, European Journal of Politics and Political Theory, Dissent, Thesis 11, Philosophy and Social Criticism,* and *Praxis International.*

Mitchell Cohen is co-editor of *Dissent* magazine and Associate Professor of Political Science at the Graduate School and Baruch College of the City University of New York (CUNY). He is author of *The Wager of Lucien Goldmann, Zion and State,* and editor of *Rebels and Reactionaries: An Anthology of Great Political Stories.*

Dieter Dettke has been Executive Director of the Friedrich Ebert Foundation Washington, D.C. Office since 1985. He holds a Ph.D. in political science from the Free University of Berlin, and studied from 1962 to 1967 at the University of Bonn, the Free University of Berlin and at the University of Strasbourg (France). In 1967/68, he was a Fulbright scholar at the University of Washington in Seattle. Prior to his tenure in Washington, D.C., he served as political counselor of the SPD Parliamentary Group of the German Bundestag from 1974 to 1984, and as Staff Director at the Office of the State Minister of the German Foreign Ministry from October to May 1982. Dr. Dettke is a foreign policy and security policy specialist and started his career at the Research Institute of the German Society for Foreign Affairs in 1969. His publications include *Allianz im Wandel* (Frankfurt, 1974), and various articles and papers on security issues, East-West relations and U.S. foreign and domestic policy.

Jean Bethke Elshtain is the Centennial Professor of Political Science and Professor of Philosophy at Vanderbilt University. Her books include: *Public Man, Private Woman: Meditations on Modern Political Thought; Women and War;* and *Democracy on Trial.* She is the author of over 100 essays in scholarly and popular journals. Professor Elshtain has been a Fellow at the Institute for Advanced Study, Princeton, a scholar-in-residence at the Bellagio Conference and Study Center, Italy, and a Guggenheim Fellow.

Amitai Etzioni is the first University Professor of the George Washington University. For 20 years (1958-1978), he served as Professor of Sociology and at times as chairman of the department at Columbia University. He founded the Society for the Advancement of Socio-Economics and the Center for Policy Research. He is the author of *The Spirit of Community,* founder of *The Communitarian Network,* editor of *The Responsive Community* as well as the author of 14 books including *The Moral Dimension: Toward a New Economics* (1988). He is currently president of the American Sociological Association.

Jeff Faux is President of the Economic Policy Institute (EPI) in Washington, D.C. Mr. Faux previously was a co-director of the

National Center for Economic Alternatives and an economist with several U.S. government agencies. In 1978 he received a Presidential appointment to the National Advisory Council on Economic Opportunity. Mr. Faux is the co-author (with Gar Alperovitz) of *Rebuilding America* (1984), the author of *New Hope of the Inner City* and the co-author of *The Star-Spangled Hustle* .

Günter Frankenberg is Professor of Public Law at the J.W. Goethe-Universität/Frankfurt and is Senior Research Fellow at the Institute for Social Research in Frankfurt. Professor Frankenberg has published extensively in the areas of legal and constitutional theory, constitutional and administrative law. He is the author of *Die Demokratische Frage*, with U. Roedel and H. Dubiel (1989), *AIDS-Bekämpfung im Rechtsstaat* (1988), and *Von der Volkssouveränität zum Minderheitsschutz—Die Freiheit politischer Kommunikation im Verfassungsstaat*, with U. Roedel (1981).

William Galston is Professor at the School of Public Affairs, University of Maryland at College Park, and Senior Research Fellow at the Institute for Philosophy and Public Policy. During 1991/1992, he was a Fellow at the Woodrow Wilson International Center for Scholars in Washington, D.C. Professor Galston (Ph.D. 1973, University of Chicago) is the author of five books and numerous articles on political theory, public policy, and American politics. He served as Chief Speechwriter in John Anderson's independent campaign for president, 1980; as Issues Director during Walter Mondale's presidential campaign, 1982-1984; and as a Senior Advisor for Albert Gore's campaign for the presidential nomination, 1988. Professor Galston is currently on leave serving as Deputy Assistant to the President for Domestic Policy.

Peter Glotz is a member of the German Bundestag for the Social Democratic Party of Germany (SPD) and a member of the SPD National Executive Committee. He is the SPD Executive Committee's spokesperson for media policy. Dr. Glotz was National Executive Secretary of the SPD from 1981 to 1987. He has served in various government positions in the areas of education, science, and research. Dr. Glotz was Vice President of the University of Munich and has been editor-in-chief of the journal *Neue Gesellschaft/Frankfurter Hefte* since 1983. Holding a doctorate in journalism and German, Peter Glotz has written widely on political, social, and economic policy. He is Professor for Communications Research at the University of Munich.

Ottokar Hahn has been Principal Advisor of the Commission of the European Communities since March 1990. From 1985-1990, Dr. Hahn was Minister for Federal Affairs and Special Tasks, Charge for European Affairs and Representative of the State of Saarland to the Federal Government in Bonn. He previously served in numerous financial administrative and advisory capacities in Germany and in the Commission of the European Communities in Brussels and Luxembourg. He is Visiting Professor in St. Gallen in Switzerland and in Amiens, France. Dr. Hahn's publications focus on economic, monetary, and taxation matters as well as European and Development policies.

Milos Hajek is a historian focusing on the Third International. He was one of the first members of the Czech human rights group "Charter 77" and became its spokesman in 1988. In early 1989, Dr. Hajek founded the political organization "Obroda" (Renewal) which joined the Social Democratic Party of Czechoslovakia in 1991. Dr. Hajek entered the (at the time) illegal Communist party in 1941. He was arrested by the Gestapo and sentenced to death and regained his freedom during the Prague uprising in May 1945. He served in the Foreign Ministry during the 1960s. Dr. Hajek is the author of *The History of the Communist International 1921-1935* (publ. in Italian, Rome 1969) and co-author of a history of Marxism and Einaudi (1980) as well as numerous historical works in Czech.

Eric Hobsbawm is University Professor of Politics and Society Emeritus at the New School for Social Research and Professor Emeritus of Economics and Social History at the University of London. Since the 1950s, Eric Hobsbawm has been setting the pace for economic and social history with studies of revolution, working-class struggle, peasant rebellion, culture, and ideology. His *Age of Revolution* (1962) initiated a classic series of syntheses that now includes the *Age of Capital, Industry and Empire, The Age of Empire,* and *Nationalism* among others. After a distinguished career at the University of London, Professor Hobsbawm helped initiate the New School's interdisciplinary programs in Historical Studies.

Otto Kallscheuer, Ph.D. (Goethe Universität/Frankfurt) born in 1950, has been a lecturer, visiting professor, and researcher in the field of political theory at the Free University of Berlin, the Istituto Universitario Orientale of Naples and the Institute for Advanced Study, Princeton, N.J. Currently, he is Visiting Fellow at the Institute for Human Sciences, Vienna. Dr. Kallscheuer, a frequent contributor to German and Italian newspapers, has been editor of the theoretical series *Rationen* (Rotbuch Verlag), and is now editor of the European review, *Transit*. His books include volumes on Marxism, on religion and politics, most recently *Gottes Wort und Volkes Stimme* ("The Word of God and People's Voice", Frankfurt a. Main: Fischer Verlag 1994).

Didier Motchane currently serves at the French Cour des Comptes (National Accounting Office). He has been a Member of the European Parliament for 10 years. As a long-time member of the Parti Socialiste, Didier Motchane has held numerous positions in the executive committee and secretariat of the party. Author of numerous books and articles, he is now national secretary of the *Mouvement des Citoyens*, a new party of the left.

Chantal Mouffe, a political philosopher, currently directs the Program on Citizenship and Modern Democracy at the College Internationale de Philosophie in France. Born in Belgium and educated in Louvain, Paris, Essex, and London, she has lectured at the National University of Colombia in Bogota and at the City University of London (Westfield College). Dr. Mouffe has published numerous articles on new social movements, political and feminist theory. She is editor of and contributed to *Gramsci and Marxist Theory* (London, 1979) and co-authored, with Ernesto LeClau, *Hegemony and Socialist Theory: Toward a Radical Democracy:*(London, 1985). She also is editor and contributor to *Dimensions of Radical Democracy; Pluralism, Citizenship and Community* (1992).

Terry Nardin is Professor of Political Science at the University of Wisconsin-Milwaukee. He has been a Rockefeller Foundation Humanities Fellow and a Visitor in the School of Social Science at the Institute for Advanced Study, Princeton. Professor Nardin is the author of *Law, Morality and the Relations of States* (1983) and editor, with David R. Mapel, of *Traditions of International Ethics* (1992).

Kai Nielsen is Professor Emeritus of the Department of Philosophy at the University of Calgary. He is a member of the Royal Society of Canada and is a past president of the Canadian Philosophical Association. Professor Nielsen has taught at Amherst College, New York University and the University of Ottawa. He is an editor of the *Canadian Journal of Philosophy*. His more recent publications include: *Marxism and the Moral Point of View, Equality and Liberty: In Defense of Radical Egalitarianism; After the Demise of Tradition: Rorty, Critical Theory and the Fate of Philosophy;* and *God, Skepticism and Modernity*. He is editor, with Robert Ware, of *Analyzing Marxism: New Essays on Analytical Marxism*.

Terry Paul Pinkard is Professor in the Department of Philosophy at Georgetown University, where he has taught since 1975. Professor Pinkard previously taught at Vanderbilt University and State University of New York-Stony Brook. The recipient of a number of research and teaching awards in the U.S. and Germany, Professor Pinkard is the author or co-author of four books including *Ethics and Public Policy* (1983) and *Democratic Liberalism and Social Union* (1987) as well as numerous works on social and moral philosophy, Hegelian Dialectic, justice, and ethics.

Julian Santamaria Ossorio is Professor of Political Science at the Universidad Complutense de Madrid. He was a Visiting Fellow at Yale University and has also been a Professor of Constitutional Law at the University of Santiago de Compostela (1981-1983). Professor Santamaria has served as an advisor to various parliamentary groups and joined the PSOE in February 1981. He was General Director of the CIS, the Center for Sociological Research (1983-1987). From March 1987 to April 1990, Professor Santamaria was Ambassador of Spain in Washington, D.C. He has published internationally on questions of political transitions, parties, elections and political culture.

Philip Selznick is Professor Emeritus of Law and Sociology at the University of California, Berkeley. He was the founding Chairman of the Center for the Study of Law and Society and of the Jurisprudence and Social Policy Program in the School of Law at UC Berkeley. Professor Selznick has held numerous visiting fellowships in Europe and the U.S. and is a Fellow of the American Academy of Arts and Sciences. The author of numerous classic works in sociology, law, and organizational theory, Professor Selznick took early retirement in 1984 to write a comprehensive study of moral and social theory, *The Moral Commonwealth*, whose unifying theme is the moral relevance of social inquiry and the contribution of sociology to "communitarian liberalism."

Johano Strasser has been a freelance writer of philosophical and political thought, poetry, fiction (short stories and novels), and plays. Dr. habil. Strasser holds degrees in philosophy and political science. Among his most recent books are *Der Klang der Fanfare* (1987), *Die Heimsuchung. Erzählung* (1989), *Leben ohne Utopie? Essay* (1990) and *Die Wende ist Machbar. Realpolitik an den Grenzen des Wachstums* (1994).

Tracy Strong is presently professor of Political Science and the editor of *Political Theory.:An International Journal of Political Philosophy*.

Among his books are *Friedrich Nietzsche and the Politics of Transfiguration; Right in Her Soul: The Life of Anna Louise Strong; The Idea of Political Theory: Reflections on the Self in Political Time and Space;* and *Rousseau and the Politics of the Ordinary.*

William Sullivan is Professor of Philosophy at LaSalle University, Pennsylvania. He is co-author with Robert Bellah, et al. of *Habits of the Heart,* (1985) and *The Good Society* (1991). He is author of *Reconstructing Public Philosophy* (1982). Professor Sullivan's research focuses on political philosophy, theory of culture, and philosophy in the social sciences. He is currently completing a study of the professions and professionalism as factors within civil society.

Michael Walzer has been a permanent faculty member at the School of Social Science, Institute for Advanced Study in Princeton since 1980. He previously taught at Princeton University and Harvard University, where he also holds a doctoral degree. Professor Walzer teaches and has written extensively on political philosophy and theory, citizenship, and civil society. He is an editor of *Dissent* and a contributing editor of *The New Republic,* and has published among numerous works *The Company of Critics* (1988) and *Interpretation and Social Criticism* (1987).

Alan Wolfe is University Professor and Professor of Sociology at Boston University. Professor Wolfe is the author of numerous books including *The Limits of Legitimacy* and *Whose Keeper?,* which won the C. Wright Mills award of the Society for the Study of Social Problems. His most recent books are *The Human Difference* (1992) and *America at Century's End* (1991). He is also a frequent contributor to magazines and newspapers, especially the *New Republic* and the *Washington Post.*

Index